Published by Startup Mixtape Media

182 Howard St. #118
San Francisco
94105

themixtape.co

First Edition 2017

10 9 8 7 6 5 4 3 2

Printed in **PRC**
Book design by **Russ Atkinson**
Cover design by **Luiz Aro**
Logo design by **Jude Goergen**

ISBN-13: 978-0-692-87839-2

KICKSTARTER BACKERS

The Startup Mixtape met a fundraising goal of $5,000 on the first day of its Kickstarter campaign. We're very grateful to all of the backers who helped fund the project past 350% of the goal.

STRETCH GOAL PARTNERS

These organizations work with underrepresented groups in startups and technology, and were partners in the Kickstarter campaign to help reach two stretch goals. We applaud their work and are excited to send them copies of the book for their constituents.

AVATECH *TEHRAN* / HUBDHAKA *BANGLADESH*
UK LEBANON TECH HUB *LONDON/BEIRUT* / DIVINC *AUSTIN*
DRIVEN *TORONTO* / CODE 2040 *SAN FRANCISCO*
CODE FOR PROGRESS *WASHINGTON, DC* / STARTUP52 *NEW YORK CITY*

ADAM RAWOT / ADAM SADOWSKI / ADAM WATTERS / AHMAD FAIRIZ / AJ KIM / ALEX HERTZ / ALEX HILLIS / ALEX RYAN / ALEXANDER BOON / ALFRED MOYA / ALICE FINCH / ALWYN RUSLI / AMBAR AMLEH / AMBER BRANDNER / AMIT BISWAS / AMOGH KANADE / ANDERS ANDERSEN / ANDERSON LIM / ANDRE KRAUSE / ANDREAS THORSTENSSON / ANDRES ESPINOSA / ANDREW KONSTANTARAS / ANDREW RYAN / ANDY KEIL / ANGELA KYLE / ANNA YAP / ANTHONY STEWART / APRIL SHUNN WILLIAMS / ARNOLD JOHN ANTHONY ALMEIDA / ARUL ISAI IMRAN / ARVE PAALSRUD / ASAF ATIYA / ASHOK KAMAL / ASI KAUFMAN / ATHENA KARP / AUREOLIEN VECCHIATO / AVA PIPHER / AXEL ERIKSSON / AYMAN AWARTANI / AZMIR SALIEFENDIC / BASTIAAN VAN ROODEN / BEEKEY CHEUNG / BERNHARD FRALING / BILL DYBAS / BIRGER LIE / BONNIE THACKER / BOWEN FENG / BRENDAN IHMIG / BRIAN HARIHARAN / BRITTANY SICKLER / BRUCE A. LEVINE / BRUCE BARRINGER / BRYAN ADAMS / BRYAN MOONEY / CADE PETERSON / CAREY FAN / CARLA PEREZ VERA / CESAR FIGUEREDO / CHAD D. F. MARCUM / CHARLIE WILLIAMS-BROWN / CHARLOTTE ZOLLER / CHETT MATCHETT / CHRIS LAWSON / CHRIS MCLEOD / CHRIS SCHULTZ / CHUANG-MING LIU / CLAIRE MCHUGH / CLAY SOELBERG / CLEMENT LEE / COLIN CHEN / COLIN MATHEWS / COLTON KENNELLY / CRASH WAVE GAMES / CRYSTAL COLLINS / DAISY PISTEY-LYHNE / DAN MACKIE / DANA FALSETTI / DANIEL OPATICH / DANIELLE WEN / DANNY / DANRIC JAIME / DAVE MARVIN / DAVID DEHGHAN / DAVID HERRERA / DAVID HY / DAVID SWENSON / DEBI KLEIMAN / DEEPAK C. SEKAR / DENNIS BONILLA / DENNIS ZELL / DERRICK CORNELL / DHIMANT DALAL / DORTHEA HALDRUP / DRAKE TURNER / DUANE WILSON / DUSTIN MCDONALD / ELI RABEK / ELIZABETH FERGUSON / ELIZABETH NIELSEN / ELLIOT NAM / EMAN IGBINOSA / EMANUEL TRINDADE / EMILY KAN / ETHAN LEVY / ETIENNE MERINEAU / EUGENE MALEEV / FAZLE FYZER / FEDERICO FACCHINELLI / FELIPE QUINZIO / FELIPE VALDES / FERMIN MATA / FERNANDO JASSO / FIDY RAKOTOMANGA / FLOR SERNA / FOLI AYIVOH / FRAN ACASUSO / FRANCOIS GROS / FRANCOIS POIRIER / FRANK VINCENT BOMBACI / FRIEDRICH ARNOLD / FRODE JENSEN / GABRIEL LINTON / GARRETT GEE / GAVIN NICHOLL / GENCER ERDEM / GENE MURPHY / GENEVIEVE APHRODITE / GEOFF DAILY / GEORGE LAMBRIANIDES / GEORGE SARANTOPOULOS / GEORGIA MCBRIDE / GIUSEPPE LIPARI / GYULA TELEKI / H. COLE WILEY / HAITHAM SALEH / HAN MENG TEO / HARVIE BRANSCOMB / HEATH JONES / HENRY VAN RODEN / HERNAN LOPEZ / HUBERT NIJMEIJER / IAN ULLRICH / IDAROSE SYLVESTER / IGOR GOZHENKO / ILAN KIRSCHENBAUM / ILIA BAKHOV / ISHMAEL KHALID / JACQUELINE CABLE / JALEH AFSHAR / JAMES TYLER / JAMES YANG / JAMIE CHVOTKIN / JAN HEIN HOOGSTAD / JARED LOFTUS / JASON CARPENTIER / JASON KAPLAN / JASON LAMANQUE / JAVIER L. VELASQUEZ / JEAN-LO MICHAUX / JEAN-LUC LELEU / JEFF HUNT / JEFF SCHIEBE / JENIFER DANIELS / JENNIFER KLECKER / JERMAINE JOHNSON / JERRY FARMER / JESSICA SEMAAN / JILL BOURQUE / JILL CORCORAN / JILL URBANEK / JIM CALL / JOB VAN HARDEVELD / JOE MCHUGH / JOHN HAMLIN / JOHN HEIKS PAUL IV / JOHN JUSTICE / JOHN KERBER / JOHN L COLLINS / JOHN LAMAR / JOHN PAUL MACDONELL / JOSEPH BOWEN / JOSH BENJAMIN / JOSHUA FLEIG / JUDE GOERGEN / JUN SUZUKI / JUSTIN FONG / KAI HSING / KAITLIN MEEK / KAREL BOURGOIS / KARLIS BERZINS / KATJA VOGER / KE JING GOH / KEITH MUTCH / KEN ADAMS / KENNETH MAK / KENNETH SKODJE / KEVIN ELLIOTT / K ING HEIPLE / KOTA GERSON / KYLE LEAKWAY / LARS BOEHNKE / LAURA DAVIDSON / LE QUOC VIET / LEILA IRANMANESH / LENNART BADER / LEONIDAS VRACHNIS / LEV ANDELMAN / LEWIS KING / LIN SEBASTIAN KAYSER / LLOYED LOBO / LOLA SCOBEY / LUIS GOMEZ-GUILLAMON PEREZ / LUISA ORTU / LUKA CRNKOVIC-FRIIS / LYNN HOANG / M. PHANI SASANK / MAC MCMAHILL / MAHYUDDIN MUHAMMAD / MALCOLM DOWLEY / MARC DE LAUNAY / MARCO PASQUA / MARK ALAN EFFINGER / MARKUS KLINTON / MARSHALL BUXTON / MASHA ADAMIAN / MATT ALCOCK / MATTHEW ROGAN / MATTHIAS LUDWIG / MATTI ERMOLD / MAY SUN / MAYUR SANGHVI / MEGHAN AULD / MICHAEL FALOTICO / MICHAEL KUNTZ / MICHAEL REICH / MICHAEL TSAI / MIKE JARRELL / MIKI UCHIDA / MILESH KUMAR / MING-TANG YANG / MONICA SACK / MY TOURS / NAOMI MATTHEWS / NATHALIE ARBEL / NIC MASON / NICHOLAS HODDEVIK / NICHOLAS ZHANG / NICK AZINAS / NICK PATTERSON / NICOLE WITTY / NIELS NUYTTENS / NIKLAS LENKEL / NILS SCHAGE / NOAM BEN-ZVI / OBED / OIVIND RUUD KRINGSTAD / OLIVIER KAESER / OMER BARAK / ONY MALLE / PABLO AUMENTE GALLEGO / PAM LANKFORD / PATRICK LEITGEB / PAUL ANGUIANO / PAUL HARRIS / PAUL KATZ / PAUL TIMPSON / PAULINE WILLEFORD / PAVAN KUMAR / PETER MORCINEK / PETER SHIMSHOCK / PHILIP HAGGAR / PHILLIP LEAR / PRISCILLA MARIE GONZALEZ / RAFAEL FRACALOSSI SANCHES / RANDY LAU / RAUL PEREZ / RICK TUROCZY / RISHI SHAH / RO OLUFUNWA / ROB SMITH / ROBBIE JACK / ROBBIE KLEIN / ROBERT NGUYEN / ROCHELLE KOPP / ROMAN LION / ROSS JASON / ROSS WILLIAMS / RYAN BRIGHT / RYAN CROSS / SAMANTHA MARKHAM / SAMMY SCHUCKERT / SAMUEL SJOSTROM / SANAZ SUNNY SATTARI / SANDIP PANDEY / SARA USINGER / SARAH NICOLE SALADINO / SEAN LITTLE / SEBASTIAN / SEBASTIAN KELLNER / SEBASTIAN WEILANDT / SEBASTIAN Z / SERGEI TIMASHEVSKII / SHAFILE RASHID / SHARIF HELMI / SHASHI JAIN / SHAWN ALTMAN / SHERRI MCCONNELL / SORAYOT PHANAYANGGOOR / SOYEB SHAIKH / STANLEY PANG / STEVEN GANZ / TEDDY KIM / TEODOR BJERRANG / THEIS BINGER / THOMAS BACKLUND / THOMAS HANSEN / THOMAS JOHNSON / THOMAS QUERTON / TOAN MAIQUOCSONG / TOMASZ SIKORA / TOMAZ PRAZNIK / TOMER HAZAN / TRAVIS CANNON / UMESH TIWARI / VALENTIN MARIN / VALERY KOMISSAROVA / VANESSA MORGAN / VASILI SVIRIDOV / VU VAN / WALI AKANDE / WARREN CHUNG / WHITNEY NASH / WITAWAS METAPAKWATPAN / XAVIER SEGUIN / XIAOPING LI / YARIV SADE / YEE GIN PAK / YING HAO MA / YOSEF JAVED / YOUSSEF ADEL YOUSSEF / ZANDER FUTERNICK / ZANE SHANNON

INTERVIEWEES

CHRISTINE TSAI **500 STARTUPS** *FOUNDING PARTNER* SAN FRANCISCO

MARVIN LIAO **500 STARTUPS** *PARTNER* SAN FRANCISCO

MATHEW JOHNSON **500 STARTUPS** *PARTNER* SAN FRANCISCO

JAKOB GAJŠEK **ABC ACCELERATOR** *CO-FOUNDER & HEAD OF VENTURE RELATIONS* SLOVENIA

PARKER THOMPSON **ANGELLIST PARTNER** SAN FRANCISCO

DANIEL SAKS **APPDIRECT** *PRESIDENT & CO-CEO* SAN FRANCISCO

CHRISTINA KOUNTOURIOT **ATHENS STARTUP BUSINESS INCUBATOR** *MANAGER* GREECE

MATT MULLENWEG **AUTOMATTIC INC.** *FOUNDER & CEO* HOUSTON

SARA USINGER **AVATECH** *PROGRAM MANAGER* IRAN

RICARDO LOENEN **B. AMSTERDAM** *CO-FOUNDER* AMSTERDAM

DAVID HEINEMEIER HANSSON **BASECAMP** *FOUNDER & CTO* CHICAGO

LUKAS WAGNER **BERLIN PARTNER** *PROJECT MANAGER INFORMATION AND COMMUNICATION TECHNOLOGIES* BERLIN

UMAIR AKEEL **BESSEMER VENTURE PARTNERS** *OPERATING PARTNER* SAN FRANCISCO

RICARDO MARVÃO **BETA-I** *CO-FOUNDER* LISBON

CHAD KAUL **BLACKBOX** *SENIOR DIRECTOR* SAN FRANCISCO

FADI BISHARA **BLACKBOX** *FOUNDER & CEO* SAN FRANCISCO

ANDREW HYDE **BOULDER STARTUP WEEK** *FOUNDER* BOULDER

MARIAN GOODELL **BURNING MAN** *FOUNDING BOARD MEMBER & CEO* SAN FRANCISCO

ALEKSANDER TYSZKA **BUSINESS FRANCE** *HEAD OF TECHNOLOGY DIVISION - NORTH AMERICA* SAN FRANCISCO

DORTHEA HALDRUP NIELSEN **CANOPYLAB** *ADVISORY BOARD MEMBER* COPENHAGEN

KRISH SUBRAMANIAN **CHARGEBEE** *CO-FOUNDER & CEO* CHENNAI, INDIA

DEEPAK SEKAR **CHOWBOTICS** *FOUNDER & CEO* SAN FRANCISCO

JONATHAN REICHENTAL **CITY OF PALO ALTO** *CHIEF INFORMATION OFFICER* PALO ALTO

VINEEL REDDY PINDI **COLLAB HOUSE** *FOUNDER & CEO* HYDERABAD, INDIA

ANDREA BARRICA **DEEP CONNECTION TECHNOLOGIES** *FOUNDER* SAN FRANCISCO

CRAIG WALKER **DIALPAD** *FOUNDER & CEO* SAN FRANCISCO

FABRICE GOULD **DIGGEN** *FOUNDER & CEO* SAN DIEGO

EMMA CHESHIRE **DOTFORGE** *CO-FOUNDER & CEO* LEEDS, UNITED KINGDOM

ZACH ONISKO **DRIBBBLE** *GENERAL MANAGER* SAN FRANCISCO

CINDY COHN **ELECTRONIC FRONTIER FOUNDATION** *EXECUTIVE DIRECTOR* SAN FRANCISCO

VU VAN **ELSA** *CO-FOUNDER & CEO* SAN FRANCISCO

ALLEN TAYLOR **ENDEAVOR** *MANAGING DIRECTOR* SAN FRANCISCO

LINDA KOZLOWSKI **ETSY** *COO* NEW YORK CITY

MAREN LESCHE **ETVENTURE STARTUP HUB** *ECOSYSTEM & COMMUNICATIONS MANAGER* BERLIN

DANIEL DANKER **FACEBOOK** *PRODUCT DIRECTOR* SAN FRANCISCO

BILL REICHERT **GARAGE TECHNOLOGY VENTURES** *MANAGING DIRECTOR* SAN FRANCISCO

DON DODGE **GOOGLE** *DEVELOPER ADVOCATE* BOSTON

TARA RAUCH **GOOGLE** *INTERNATIONAL EDUCATION* NEW YORK CITY

JON STROSS **GREENHOUSE** *CO-FOUNDER* NEW YORK

MAK GUTIERREZ **HACKERS / FOUNDERS** *DIRECTOR, MEXICO* GUADALAJARA, MEXICO

OISIN HANRAHAN **HANDY** *CEO* NEW YORK

NIR EYAL **HOOKED** *AUTHOR* SAN FRANCISCO

SAJID ISLAM **HUBDHAKA** *FOUNDER* BANGLADESH

KAUSTAV MITRA **INFOSYS** *VICE PRESIDENT, INNOVATION ECOSYSTEMS* PALO ALTO

CHAD NITSCHKE **INSURE.VC** *CO-FOUNDER & CEO* SAN FRANCISCO

DES TRAYNOR **INTERCOM** *CO-FOUNDER, CHIEF STRATEGY OFFICER, VP OF MARKETING* IRELAND

JUSTIN MARES **KETTLE & FIRE** *FOUNDER* SAN FRANCISCO

CHRIS SCHULTZ **LAUNCH PAD** *CO-FOUNDER & CEO* NEW ORLEANS

LOIC MEUR **LEADE.RS** *FOUNDER & CEO* SAN FRANCISCO

BRIEN BUCKMAN **MAGIC LEAP** *PRODUCT MANAGEMENT* MIAMI

MICHAEL JOHNSTON **MOATBOAT** *CO-FOUNDER & CEO* SAN FRANCISCO

JULIE FOULON **MOLENGEEK** *CO-FOUNDER* BRUSSELS

MEAGEN EISENBERG **MONGODB** *CHIEF MARKETING OFFICER* SAN FRANCISCO

THUNDER WANG **NEXPCB** *FOUNDER* NINGBO, CHINA

SAMIR SABERI **NODE1** *STARTUPS AND INNOVATION EXPERT* THE HAGUE, NETHERLANDS

PARIS THOMAS **OPEN BOX COMMUNICATION** *DIRECTOR, CO-FOUNDER* CYPRUS

ROB SMITH **PECABU** *CO-FOUNDER & CEO* SAN FRANCISCO

GREG GOTTESMAN **PIONEER SQUARE LABS** *MANAGING DIRECTOR* SEATTLE

HOLLY CARDEW **PIXC** *FOUNDER* SAN FRANCISCO

DANIEL GWERZMAN **POW THINK BAND** *TECHNOLOGICAL STRATEGY ADVISOR* ISRAEL

PETER ARVAI **PREZI** *CO-FOUNDER & CEO* SAN FRANCISCO

PATRICK CAMPBELL **PRICE INTELLIGENTLY** *CO-FOUNDER & CEO* BOSTON

SARAH KUNST **PRODAY.CO** *FOUNDER & CEO* SAN FRANCISCO

RYAN HOOVER **PRODUCT HUNT** *FOUNDER* SAN FRANCISCO

TRAVIS CANNON **RADAR, INC** *DIRECTOR OF PRODUCT MANAGEMENT* PORTLAND

JENS WIECHERS **RETROBRAIN R&D** *CTO* BERLIN

SUPACHAI PARCHARIYANON **RISE ACCELERATOR** *SERIAL ENTREPRENEUR AND INVESTOR* BANGKOK, THAILAND

DON RITZEN **ROCKSTART** *CO FOUNDER* AMSTERDAM

CORINNE CLINCH **RORUS** *CO-FOUNDER & CEO* PITTSBURGH

LUDOVIC ULRICH **SALESFORCE** *SR DIRECTOR, STARTUP & APPEXCHANGE MARKETING* SAN FRANCISCO

ELAY COHEN **SALESHOOD** *CO-FOUNDER & CEO* SAN FRANCISCO

THOMAS AREND **SAVVY** *CO-FOUNDER & CEO* SAN FRANCISCO

SOFIJA SPIROVSKA **SEAVUS INCUBATOR** *MANAGER* MACEDONIA

CARLOS EDUARDO ESPINAL **SEEDCAMP** *SEED INVESTOR & PARTNER* LONDON
CARLOS SILVA **SEEDRS** *CO-FOUNDER, PRESIDENT & HEAD* LISBON
GEORGE ARISON **SHIFT TECHNOLOGIES INC** *FOUNDER & CEO* SAN FRANCISCO
FORREST DOMBROW **SOLVE SALES** *FOUNDER* DENVER
PAUL TOMITA **STANIFORD TOMITA LLP** *CO-FOUNDER* SAN FRANCISCO
AARON BIRKBY **STARTUP CATALYST** *CEO* BRISBANE, AUSTRALIA
ADITYA PATRO **STARTUP DIGEST** *CURATOR* HYDERABAD, INDIA
ADAM JERMANN **STREAMBRIGHT DATA** *CEO* BUDAPEST
RAHUL VOHRA **SUPERHUMAN LABS INC** *FOUNDER & CEO* SAN FRANCISCO
ARTURO CALLE **SURUNA** *CEO* PERU
OLIVER WALZER **SWISS STARTUP FACTORY** *FOUNDER & CTO* CHAM, SWITZERLAND
CATHRYN POSEY **TECH BY SUPERWOMEN** *FOUNDER* SAN FRANCISCO
ASHOK KAMAL **TECH COAST ANGELS** *EXECUTIVE DIRECTOR* CARDIFF BY THE SEA
MARTIN BRYANT **TECH NORTH** *COMMUNITY EDITOR* MANCHESTER, UNITED KINGDOM
JENNY FIELDING **TECHSTARS** *MANAGING DIRECTOR* SAN FRANCISCO
SEMYON DUKACH **TECHSTARS** *MANAGING DIRECTOR* BOSTON
MARC NAGER **TELLURIDE VENTURE ACCELERATOR** *MANAGING DIRECTOR* TELLURIDE, COLORADO
SARA HILL **THE MILL ACCELERATOR** *CO-FOUNDER & MANAGING PARTNER* SAN FRANCISCO
ALICE ARMITAGE **THE STARTUP LEGAL GARAGE** *ASSOCIATE PROFESSOR & DIRECTOR* SAN FRANCISCO
ABHISHEK GUPTA **TLABS** *COO* NOIDA, INDIA
ALESSIO BORTONE **UK LEBANON TECH HUB** *ACCELERATOR MANAGER* LONDON
FRED DAVIS **UPLOADVR** *MENTOR* SAN FRANCISCO
SHOTA TAKASE **WINCAM** *CEO & FOUNDER* JAPAN
FABIO TORLINI **WP ENGINE** *MANAGING DIRECTOR EMEA* LONDON
QASAR YOUNIS **Y COMBINATOR** *PARTNER & COO* SAN FRANCISCO
BRIANNE KIMMEL **ZENDESK** *GROWTH MARKETING* SAN FRANCISCO
SEPIDEH NASIRI *STARTUP ADVISER* SAN FRANCISCO

PLAYLIST

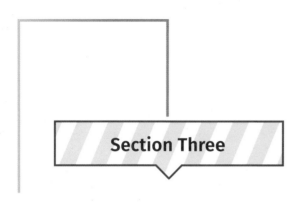

PREFACE

> **"An entrepreneur is someone who will jump off a cliff and assemble an airplane on the way down."**
> *Reid Hoffman, Co-founder of LinkedIn*

Entrepreneurship has never been more popular. And many people don't want to start just any business; they want to build a tech startup. High-growth tech startups have simultaneously created incredible wealth and broken rules of business to build more enlightened and customer-centric brands that people can't get enough of.

Perhaps this is also your dream, but the the odds are unfortunately against you, no matter how smart, talented, and accomplished you are.

Most startups fail. And sometimes this happens because the market boots them out due to factors outside an entrepreneur's control. But even if conditions are perfect, there are plenty of opportunities for new founders to slip up and many misconceptions that can lead them astray.

Let's begin with the word itself: in this book, "startup" is shorthand for a high-growth technology company. Not just a company that has tech as part of its business operations, not just a new company with hip branding, and not just any app. It can also be referred to here as a "tech startup," "high-growth startup," or some variation thereof; the point is that it's not a small business (as we'll see in *Chapter 1 (Are You a Startup or a Small Business?))*. Few people realize how this type of business differs from other kinds of companies that can be born in a garage, let alone the key lessons from startup history about how to steer it to success.

Are there things you can do to reduce the chances that your startup will implode? Can you learn from the collective wisdom of experienced and successful founders to avoid making the same mistakes others have?

The answer, thankfully, is yes. The lessons and guidance in this book won't guarantee success, but they can at least save you time, money, and some of the extreme stress that comes with trying to build an industry-changing startup. ○

Why I wrote this book

Startups often fail because their founders lack clear information on how to build them. I've seen many entrepreneurs and students face the same challenges and make many of the same errors. If they had known more when they started, they could have fared better.

I began working on this book a few years ago after meeting with students and entrepreneurs who wanted to deeply understand the startup journey. I saw there were plenty of books on the market that addressed related topics:

• *General business advice for entrepreneurs*
• *Stories about a single successful startup*
• *Deep dives on just one startup topic or theory*

However, I couldn't find any books that explained the full story of starting high-growth, technology companies in detail.

There really isn't a proven canon of wisdom when it comes to building a strong startup. No single person has all of the information that's been accumulated over the last half-century. The fifty-plus years of the computing revolution and emergence of the commercial internet has obviously been a huge creator of wealth and change. At the same time, entrepreneurs are choking with information overload, thanks to the scattered advice they get from content on the internet and their personal networks.

I interviewed dozens of successful founders and venture capitalists for this book and hand-picked the advice that no founder should go without. They told

At the same time, entrepreneurs are choking with information overload, thanks to the scattered advice they get from content on the internet and their personal networks.

me what they would have done differently, shared which activities they think are most important for an entrepreneur's success, and recounted vivid, true stories about triumphs and fiascos in Silicon Valley and around the world.

The insights here aren't new, but they're like golden life rafts spread across a giant ocean of blogs, tweets, conferences, and well-intentioned friends. Don't cling to that dead squid when you're sinking.

Who I am

There are so many books, blogs, magazine articles, and (literally) endless Twitter feeds on building a startup—many written by very intelligent and experienced people. You might be wondering why you should read this book.

I work with startup founders and new entrepreneurs every day. Previously, I was the Chief Technology Officer of Derek Sivers's CDBaby—before it was acquired for $22m. In the wake of Hurricane Katrina, I worked with the world's largest technology companies (on behalf of the government) to help rebuild and diversify the New Orleans economy.

As the Director of the Techstars Startup Next program in San Francisco, I work with teams who have later joined elite accelerator programs like Y Combinator, Techstars, 500 Startups, and Highway1—and (collectively) raise millions in early-stage capital. But I also work with founders at the very beginning of their journeys. I'm a Global Facilitator for Startup Weekend, and I work with student entrepreneurs at Babson College's San Francisco campus (ranked number-one for entrepreneurship in US News & World Report). I was first a full-time member of the teaching faculty at Loyola University in New Orleans, and now I teach at the San Francisco campus of Hult International Business School, where I've coached hundreds of MBA students about their new ventures.

But I'm not a venture capitalist, I've never built a blockbuster startup, and I'm certainly not a Silicon Valley insider. I make my living by taking in a lot of information and standing in front of a big classroom of students to explain it for hours. This forces me to find the best information and frame it in a way that's accessible, and also stay current in this ever-evolving world of startups.

So I present myself not as the all-knowing veteran of startups, but as an explainer and a quasi-journalist of high-growth entrepreneurship. And that's one of the key reasons this book is so valuable: you won't just be hearing from me and getting my take on startups.

There are so many books, blogs, magazine articles, and (literally) endless Twitter feeds on building a startup—many written by very intelligent and experienced people. You might be wondering why you should read this book.

Instead, you'll benefit from the wisdom and experience of many different voices. These pages are filled with insight and knowledge from the amazing founders and VCs I've interviewed, and these are the people you'll ultimately learn from.

Who this book is for

This book is for you if want to learn the basic elements of building a startup.

MAYBE YOU WANT TO LEARN ABOUT THIS BECAUSE:

- You see something that you can fix or improve in your industry or just in day-to-day life.

- You've worked as a designer or engineer for someone else's company, and you're considering building your own product.

- You've been an entrepreneur in traditional business, and you'd like to explore building a high-growth tech startup.

- You're considering investing in a friend's or family member's startup, and you want to know more about how the industry works (and whether they know what they're doing).

If you'd like to be a startup founder, you don't need to have an idea yet. And you don't need to have any funds. (Myth #1: Founders think that they need investment to start building and learning.)

You also don't need to be a developer. Historically, many founders have been software engineers, partially because building web software and apps took so much technical know-how (still true, but there are now many tools that make it easier to quickly build and scale a popular service). Today, people with all kinds of backgrounds are founding amazing startups.

And there's so much more to building a startup than coding. Design is incredibly important—some would even say it's the most important differentiator of contemporary tech companies. It's also crucial to find a business model that makes sense. While you don't need an expensive MBA to do this, it's still one area where many startups make fundamental mistakes that prevent them from making meaningful progress.

No matter what you've done in your career or whether you're still in school, you can benefit from the ideas and stories in this book. No technical knowledge is required, except how to use the internet.

Perhaps you've already begun your startup journey, and you feel stuck. The students and teams I work with can spend months (even years!) adrift in that ocean of startup advice I mentioned earlier. This book will provide you with viewpoints from experienced VCs and founders that will help you filter information, reprioritize your efforts, and find the best way to move forward.

What this book does and doesn't cover

This book will give you an overview of the high-growth startup world and then help you figure out where you want to go, lay out a roadmap, and give you a push to get started. I've tried to mix a little history, some current thinking, and direct insights from a founder or VC into each chapter.

In *Part I*, you'll learn the first steps to generating a viable startup idea. We'll discuss the difference between a startup and a small business, how startups design their business to make money, how to explore and validate business ideas, how to map out an early business model, and how to learn from your customer.

Part II will push you to get started even if you don't have technical talent, funds, salespeople, or a perfected product. You'll learn how to prototype, size up your competition, and understand how to measure meaningful growth.

> *So this book will teach you the basics of what successful founders and funders have done to create new startups.*

In *Part III*, you'll learn how and why startups get funding, what an accelerator can offer your startup, and ways to pitch your startup.

So this book will teach you the basics of what successful founders and funders have done to create new startups. But it won't take you all the way to the finish line, and because it's just one book, it can't give you all the advice and guidance you will need. If you reach a point where you've proven your business and need to start scaling the company, my hope is that you'll have a great network of investors (spoiler alert: their main value to your startup is not their money, it's their network and expertise) and advisors who can work with you to grow and improve your product. ○

HOW TO ~~LISTEN TO~~ READ THE STARTUP MIXTAPE

You may wonder why a book about tech startups is called a mixtape. A mixtape is just a bunch of different songs someone puts together to take the listener on a journey or make a statement.

I have been a DJ since I was seventeen years old. At the time, this didn't especially please my father, who was a professor of classical conducting, but I was inspired. I loved the idea of taking all sorts of different pieces of old vinyl and mixing them with new music. Every mix is different, even when the pieces are the same.

Your startup will be like a mixtape in this way. It's not a blueprint (too precise), a recipe (someone else's idea), or anything that seems linear and predictable. Every startup has its own narrative and its own unpredictable evolution. Hopefully, it's also funky.

Your startup will be like a mixtape in this way. It's not a blueprint (too precise), a recipe (someone else's idea), or anything that seems linear and predictable.

So be creative with this book. The chapters have an order for a reason, but you should look around. See how the pieces fit together and then decide how you might reorder them.

It's designed so you can open up to any page and find something relevant and actionable. It's meant to be something that you don't have to consume all in one sitting. It's also designed to be engaging and offer some visual cues to help you understand the material. You can read it in small doses on your subway commute, between classes, or for a few minutes on the couch without being lost in dense prose. (And I hope it looks good enough to be on your coffee table in the first place.)

Do these excuses sound familiar?

After working with hundreds of budding startup founders, I've heard them say a few things that consistently hold them back. Don't let them affect you.

"I just need to raise money to make this work. Everything else will work itself out."

Many companies don't need to raise money. And even if you do, funding isn't your golden ticket to success. Investors care that the building blocks of a good business are in place (if they don't, you probably should find investors more grounded in the fundamentals of the business being successful). We'll cover those building blocks in this book and make sure you are introduced to the terms and concepts. They will get you a lot further when you're answering question after question from a VC.

> **"My idea is so special that most of this stuff doesn't apply."**

I'll be blunt. Your idea is almost certainly no more unique than any other idea from anyone else reading this book. Ideas are inspiring but inherently worthless. Execution is everything, and you need to know what to execute on. We can learn from the trail of dead startups that runs from San Jose to San Francisco (and beyond).

> **"I know most of this stuff already. I read Zero to One, The Lean Startup, The Hard Thing about Hard Things, etc."**

There are lots of popular books about startups. The most famous tend to be interesting, but they are mainly philosophical, not tactical.

More tactical books like The Lean Startup can only explore one or two core themes in great depth within a single book. With all of the things you need to learn about building a startup, you'd need to read dozens of books like that, and that's likely more detail than you need at the very beginning of your journey. It is possible to read thirty books on startups before you take any action on your idea, but the prospect of patiently reading thirty books before starting work can dissuade a founder. (Most often, it dissuades them from doing any prep.)

Not everything in this book will be equally valuable to everyone, but I know that your time will be well spent considering at least a portion of the knowledge and wisdom of the many founders and investors whose experiences fill these pages. •

Ready to build something amazing?
Let's get started.

ARE YOU A STARTUP

OR A

SMALL BUSINESS?

Before we launch into the nitty-gritty of creating your high-growth startup, we need to discuss what this means and whether this is the right model for you or your business idea. High-growth tech startups are inherently risky (even more so than a typical new business); founders face an unusually high risk of failure in the pursuit of unprecedented rewards. Startups aren't for everyone, and not every new business should follow the high-growth model.

In this chapter, you will learn:

• *The definition of a "startup" in the context of this book and how it compares to a traditional new business*

• *Constraints and considerations that may mean a startup is not right for you or your business idea*

• *The conditions necessary for a startup to achieve exponential growth (necessary for a successful venture-backed startup)*

Entrepreneurship is an exciting and liberating idea. For many decades, the simple idea of "being your own boss" has appealed to people who are stuck in jobs where they don't feel a sense of autonomy or purpose, or who just don't like commuting to an office every day.

With the global economy facing recessions and with the general downsizing of the middle-tier white-collar population, entrepreneurship can become a necessity. In areas that historically have had relatively few opportunities to work for large companies, such as sub-Saharan Africa, many people are already entrepreneurs of some sort, such as independent operators bringing goods to market.

Then there's the rise of Silicon Valley. Since Intel raised one of the first rounds of venture capital in 1968, enormous wealth has been created in an unbelievably brief amount of time. In the current zeitgeist, startups have a sheen of being young and sexy. As one venture capitalist who funds software startups told me, "It's the new rock and roll."

If you've caught the entrepreneurship bug, it's tempting to dive in and get started quickly. But an entrepreneur's most critical decisions are made before the real action begins. Step back and ask yourself what you'd like to achieve in the bigger picture:

- *What kind of business do you want to build?*
- *Have you considered how it might shape your life in the long run?*
- *How long can you stay committed— one year, five, fifteen?*
- *What are you getting yourself (and your friends and family) into?*

The answers to these questions may actually lead you away from creating a tech startup and toward a different business model. There are many types of businesses you can create, and a high-growth, VC-backed technology startup (or as we'll call it, just a "tech startup" or "startup") is riskier (by design) than any other venture.

For example, perhaps you'd have a better chance of meeting your long-term goals if you built a small business instead of a high-growth tech startup. Venture capital-funded tech startups and small businesses can look similar at their inception, but they provide wildly different experiences and financial returns to their founders, employees, and investors. ○

A SMALL BUSINESS IS NOT A STARTUP

A small business gets started by an entrepreneur—but that doesn't make it a startup. While there are no startup police to determine who is using the term in the most appropriate way, a small business simply doesn't have the characteristics of a high-growth technology company. It won't disrupt an industry or provide the potential of 10x returns on an investor's money (which is an aspirational benchmark with most VCs).

And that's okay. There's a very unfortunate trend across the vast spectrum of entrepreneurship: some people look down on any business that's not ultra-high growth and highly scalable. People deride these companies as "lifestyle businesses" because they might simply grow enough to sustain the founder's lifestyle and not much more. They imply that the entrepreneur isn't serious and that the business is trivial. This is toxic for the broader world of people who want to create wealth and (hopefully) a better world by starting new businesses.

A small business is nothing to be ashamed of. Often, these "small" companies can eventually become very profitable, employ many people, and inadvertently turn into huge companies (Dell Computer was started in Michael Dell's college dorm room where he made custom PCs). And like startups, small businesses can also leverage technology in interesting and innovative ways to build a customer base and deliver a product or service.

So, what's the key difference between a startup and a small business? The framework of a small business isn't well suited to take an entirely new business idea and grow the company exponentially. It has constraints that limit it to steady, slow growth: the gradually increasing costs for labor, office space, and equipment for a typical small business. We'll look at how a software startup has much lower costs for these fixed items and why that gives it the potential to grow in ways a more traditional business can't.

"0 to 1 versus 1 to n" Peter Thiel

Peter Thiel, founder of PayPal, investor, and author of Zero to One, says that while some companies are based on known business models, the startups that are based on completely new ideas are the ones that will become giant, era-defining businesses.

1 to n companies take an existing, proven idea and simply reinterpret it. Meanwhile, 0 to 1 companies go from the absolute unknown into a new, unproven place. Thiel advises entrepreneurs to avoid 1 to n ideas and instead chase the novel ones because they create (or anticipate) the unforeseen change that can capture a huge market.

Small businesses are always 1 to n. They work with a known business model that's been proven before (e.g., dry cleaners), and they can grow (e.g., a large chain of dry cleaners in the Los Angeles metro area), but they are incapable of having exponential growth based on this entrenched model. Some 1 to n ideas can become fundable "startups" with the potential for exponential returns, but most of these (e.g., fashion design, film production) don't grow primarily by the power of scalable software.

Here's an example of a small business that initially looks like a startup idea but has constraints that keep it from becoming a true high-growth technology company.

A group of my MBA students once worked on starting a mobile barbershop to give men haircuts and shaves in the downtown San Francisco area where they worked. The customer would be able to book an appointment and make payment through an app. The idea was unique, the business model was unproven, and its operations would be supported by technology. Sounds like a tech startup, right?

Look closer, and you'll see that a mobile barbershop isn't scalable. It actually fits squarely in the small business category.

Here are a few examples of the constraints that would limit your growth if you started one:

ALL BARBERSHOPS ARE CONSTRAINED BY:

- How many barbers the business employs (You need one human barber to cut another human's hair. Robots soon, though!)

- How many barber chairs are available (You need one big barber's chair for each customer to sit in during their cut.)

A MOBILE BARBERSHOP IS ALSO CONSTRAINED BY:

- How many modified Winnebagos with barber chairs they can deploy on the road on a given day

- How many men are within a reasonable proximity of the mobile barber shop (Because you're mobile, you're less geographically constrained than a traditional barbershop, but customers are still unlikely to travel a long distance for a barber's cut. So, you're limited to serving people who are clustered together in dense cities.)

If you want to scale your barbershop and double your customers, you need to hire more barbers, buy more chairs, and buy more trailers to expand your geographic coverage.

Now, perhaps you can double your revenue without doubling your costs. You might not need to hire twice the number of barbers and buy a full second set of chairs to fit in twice as many customers. This is an idea from classical economics that you may be familiar with: economies of scale. When this works, the more you sell, the more you make per customer because you don't have to invest as much in subsequent customers (for example, eBay only had to develop its platform once, and the cost to add another auctioneer is almost zero). But the economies of scale are quite small for your mobile barbershop; having another barber cutting hair necessitates an extra salary, additional space, and a new set of tools and hair products. In other words, your costs don't go down that much as you grow the company.

If people in big cities like the idea of getting a quick cut in the financial district during their lunch break, you could have a nice business with some potential to scale. But it would be difficult, relative to a software startup, to make it grow 10x per year. Is it possible you could take investment from a venture capitalist, whose job is to invest in companies that can receive a return of at least ten times what they put in the barber shop's seed round? It is possible, but your VC would be as delusional as you and your co-founders to believe your business model could generate that kind of growth. (Not all VCs do a great job of forecasting the ability of their portfolio companies to scale.)

In contrast, a high-growth startup can provide these returns because it has economies of scale that give it the potential to dramatically multiply its customer base with only a small relative increase in costs. Let's take a closer look at them and see why. ○

THE ANATOMY OF A STARTUP

Six decades into the computer revolution, four decades since the invention of the microprocessor, and two decades into the rise of the modern internet, all of the technology required to transform industries through software finally works and can be widely delivered at global scale.

Marc Andreessen, "Software Is Eating the World"

In this book, we focus on high-growth tech startups: companies that can grow big within a big market and are dependent on software and the ability to address customers across the internet. Perhaps they sell software itself or use software to enable a solution to a problem: things to be delivered, rides to be given, hookups to occur.

These companies are the bread and butter of contemporary Silicon Valley. They can originate as skeletal code on someone's laptop and end up changing how we view our world and relate to each other. Startups are particularly attractive against the current media backdrop of dizzying technology and even more dizzying amounts of investment. They can offer services that can seem like science fiction before they become routine ("See the best route to get to work with the touch of a button!").

But startups are unsustainable companies by design. Because VC-funded startups are meant to grow as large as possible, there is no middle ground: get all of the glory or die trying. If you want to build a company that grows consistently over time and has the potential to offer a relatively stable income for you and your employees, a high-growth startup should not be your first choice. In fact, it should probably be your last.

David Heinemeier Hansson is one of the leading voices against taking venture capital money and building a more sustainable software company. As a co-founder of the popular, self-funded project management platform Basecamp, Hansson felt that sustainability was more important than jumping on the startup bandwagon.

He explains:

> *One of the big things that we believe in is to bootstrap a business. Do it in a way where you rely on yourself. We don't rely on other people giving you money . . . what we wanted to do was build a business where we would own it when we were done and where we would have a chance to base a company that could last for the next 10, 20, 30 years off that, which is just not the case generally when you go the venture capital route.*
>
> **David Heinemeier Hansson**

These high-growth startups have a few defining characteristics. First, they are based on novel ideas and have huge markets of potential customers to court.

In the hair salon business, there can be many kinds of business models—some innovative and others more familiar—and the size of the market they address will vary.

Let's look at how the market size and novelty of an idea can interact:

	Small Market	Big Market
Commodity	Local hair salon	Shampoo
Novel idea	Hairdresser desktop widget	Peer-to-peer haircuts*

*(a terrifying high-growth startup)

But most importantly, successful high-growth startups have economies of scale that allow them to grow wildly and become more and more profitable with each new customer.

As we'll see later, not all software companies are startups, but software companies have massive growth built into their DNA. Software is written just once and can be used over and over again. When the ultra-low cost of reproducing software is paired with a previously unimaginable audience online, there's a chance of ultra-high growth. (Software and computing hardware are why there is a venture capital industry in the first place. The first VC investment was made in the late 1960s in a tiny microchip company called Intel.)

Once you write the code for eBay, you just need to make sure that millions of people can quickly access the site that runs that code. Similarly, Google can leverage the investment that they've made into their search engine technology to get new users very quickly and inexpensively just by localizing to new countries, opening up markets of millions of new customers each time they make Google results available in a new language.

Other startups achieve cheap economies of scale with business models that leverage software and a platform for connecting people in the physical world. Uber and Airbnb get around the sticky problem of added costs to scale by placing the cost of the infrastructure on their partners in the sharing economy (i.e., Uber drivers provide their own cars, and Airbnb hosts own the properties where guests stay). Ultimately, software provides the leverage that lets startups grow while keeping costs down.

Of course, not all startups are software companies. For example, biotechnology companies that develop cutting-edge pharmaceuticals can have relatively little to do with the internet, yet they are high-growth (primarily because their investment in research pays longtime dividends once they go to market) and are attractive to certain venture capitalists. Cleantech companies that provide innovative, environmentally-friendly ways of using and harvesting energy are much the same: they can be highly disruptive to established industries and scale into huge markets. These biotech and cleantech startups, however, require a relatively enormous amount of capital and years of research (which introduces lots of risk) and are subject to ever-shifting governmental and geopolitical factors. Compared to software-based startups, these companies are not the sort of thing you drum up in your garage over a weekend and test with your friends (and probably shouldn't, in the case of biotech).

Conversely, not all software companies are high-growth startups, even if they can maintain very low costs as they sell more and more software (unlike our mobile barbershop, which has to keep buying chairs and hiring stylists). Sometimes software is just helpful software, and it doesn't have a market big enough for ultra-high growth.

For example, if you built a desktop widget for Windows PCs that allowed stylists to quickly track each customer's haircut preferences, this could be useful and profitable if you sold it to enough stylists. But you'd be limited by your market: the number of hair stylists there are (a common profession, but not that common), the number of stylists who use a Windows computer in their salon (less common), and how many stylists don't already have a sufficient way of tracking their client's haircut preferences (a hypothesis would be that this number is a pretty low percentage of an already small number). Perhaps they already track them in a spreadsheet or simply remember what their customers prefer. (Later, in **Chapter 7** *[Competition]*, we'll talk about how both Microsoft Office and the preexisting habits in our brains are unintentionally vicious startup killers.)

Similarly, Google can leverage the investment that they've made into their search engine technology to get new users very quickly and inexpensively just by localizing to new countries, opening up markets of millions of new customers each time they make Google results available in a new language.

So there are biotech and cleantech startups that, although they aren't software tech companies and typically need a lab and hordes of mad scientists, can have explosive growth and do rightfully attract venture capital. There are also software companies that can be solid, profitable businesses but stay relatively small (which can still mean a multi-million-dollar company supporting dozens or even hundreds of employees, like Basecamp) because they don't have a huge market for their product. Here, though, we're focusing on startups that have the potential for gigantic growth and that leverage software's ability to scale to keep that type of growth increasingly profitable. ○

GROWTH AT A ROCKET-SHIP TECH STARTUP

You can put the typical growth patterns of startups and small businesses in a visual graph form to easily see how different they are.

This is the hope of a small business: steady, incremental growth.
Most businesspeople would be happy to have a company that consistently grows and is profitable.

BUT FOR A STARTUP,

THIS GROWTH CURVE IS UNACCEPTABLE.

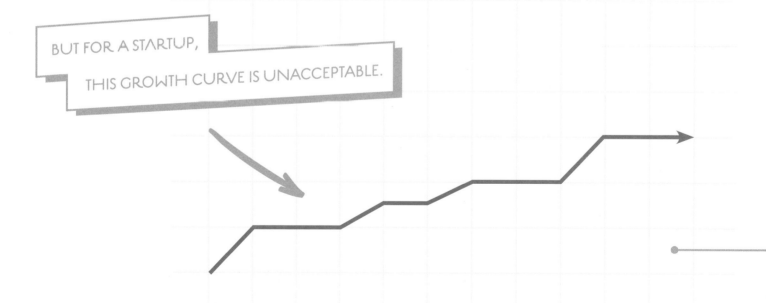

> *"A good growth rate during [the Y Combinator accelerator] is 5-7% a week. If you can hit 10% a week you're doing exceptionally well. If you can only manage 1%, it's a sign you haven't yet figured out what you're doing."*
>
> *Paul Graham*

If you start a company and have 1 percent week-over-week growth, this compounds to almost 14 percent growth over three months—the same amount of time that startups need to pass through the Y Combinator accelerator. That would be considered very successful in the normal business world, but you "have no idea what you're doing" in the funhouse mirror of startup success.

What does the growth trajectory of a startup look like?

It is a near-vertical growth slope—the fabled "hockey stick growth." Startup founders put these kinds of graphs in their presentations to investors and it's such a cliché now that a hockey stick curve triggers a reflex of knowing smirks. Nevertheless, startups do need to have the potential to grow like this if they're going to secure investment. ○

"HOCKEY STICK GROWTH"

NAVIGATING BIG MARKETS

Because of the need for explosive growth, startups need big markets to grow into, but this brings its own challenges. If you have an exciting new idea and the market seems huge, isn't that a good start? You might say, "If I can only capture 1 percent of the huge market for people wanting on-demand transportation, I'll be a massive success!"

But this is a paradox for startups: the bigger the market opportunity, the more competitive it is and more difficult to survive as an under-resourced young company.

Startups often operate in winner-take-all markets. Think of the biggest online services: Google for search, Amazon for e-commerce, Facebook for social networking, Dogster for your dog to build a social network. (The last one may not be the giant it once was back in 2005, at the dawn of social networking [for both humans and animals].) These companies don't have a lock on all of the customers they are competing for, but they're remarkably close.

That hypothetical 1 percent of the giant market you want to capture (which can hypothetically bring in a lot of money, if it's truly a big market) is almost never enough to cover both the cost of building your startup and successfully multiplying your investors' money many times over.

Here's an example of a real-life winner-take-all scenario: I spoke with an entrepreneur in Palestine who was building a ridesharing company and was planning to enter the market in Jordan. But Uber already had plans to go into Jordan. Uber could easily achieve the economies of scale to make this a relatively low-risk, high-reward proposition for them. They already had a protocol for vetting drivers, a robust app with very complex analytics, and lots of experience dealing with inevitable customer service issues.

The entrepreneur, on the other hand, had to build systems for all of these concerns from scratch, making it very tough to compete with an established startup that's growing in the same market of on-demand transportation. If she did grab 1 percent of the global ridesharing market, she couldn't spread her high costs over other markets that make up the other 99 percent of the world's appetite for ridesharing.

The Palestinian founder was launching into a big, winner-take-all market. On-demand ridesharing is a novel idea that could be a great fit for a young startup to pursue, yet Uber is strongly leading the pack globally. There's no room for her to build a high-growth ridesharing startup in Jordan when Uber's costs are so relatively low in comparison.

Could we be focused on a business model different than Uber's? Is it possible to take this big market and find economies of scale with another tech-based business model, even if it's not a novel idea? Here's an example: perhaps our Palestinian entrepreneur could create a giant confederation of taxi companies that used an app to coordinate operations. (Taxi companies have begun to use apps that are similar to Uber and allow for easier requesting and payment.)

Unfortunately, there are some immediate indicators that this idea would have a significant amount of friction compared to Uber.

First, because of regulations, taxi companies in most parts of the world face an issue of supply.

THEY ARE CONSTRAINED BY:

- How many taxis can legally operate in a particular city.

- How many drivers are available that have the necessary driver's license to operate a taxi (unlike driving an Uber, it's very common that one needs to get special training and pass a test.)

AND EVEN WITH THE APP, THESE TAXI COMPANIES ARE

LIMITED IN THEIR GROWTH BECAUSE OF:

- The number of people who need transportation in a place where the company's fleet is registered.

- Their ability to match the limited number of taxis with potential swells in demand (the chances that a rider could summon a taxi that's close by decreases during busier times because there is a fixed number of regulated taxi cabs on the road at any one time—meanwhile, Uber drivers can be on standby, and there's practically no limit to how many of them can be on the road).

- How many people are interested in riding in a typical taxi (Uber offers a range of high-end and budget rides).

The business model of Uber and its primary competitor, Lyft, can take away all of these constraints. Anyone can become a driver, they don't need a special driver's license, their fleet is intrinsically adaptive to where the riders are, and they can offer the level of car that someone may want to ride in.

This is what a novel, highly scalable business model looks like. The market for on-demand transportation is huge (and it's growing a new market of people that weren't taxi customers because of this business model), and the more Uber and Lyft grow, the more they can beat out small competition of any kind.

You can see that building a startup is very unique. Even in a big market that's filled with customers, it's very difficult to do anything except have amazing success or complete failure. And if you do find success, of course, it often means immense growth (if not also revenue, or even profit) in a short amount of time.

All or nothing. It's the most exhilarating, high-risk path of entrepreneurship. In the chapters that follow, we'll look into the key areas that you need to understand to increase your odds of success as a startup founder, employee, or investor. ●

STARTUP

REVENUE

MODELS

Startups need a mechanism to generate repeatable revenue. Your revenue model is the vehicle that injects revenue and growth into the solution they're looking for. This chapter explores the most common revenue models on which many highly successful tech startups are based and looks at the pitfalls of some of the ways that founders try to derive revenue.

You'll discover:

• *The advantages and pricing options for Software-as-a-Service (SaaS) business models*

• *The difference between peer-to-peer and on-demand marketplaces and how some businesses are more suited to one or the other*

• *When in-app purchases or advertising may or may not be appropriate for your startup*

STARTUP REVENUE MODELS

It's not enough to just uncover an underserved market with an unaddressed problem. Startups need to test and refine the right business model for a solution to be successful.

"Business model" can mean different things to different people. The Business Model Canvas is a method from *Chapter 4 (From Plan to Canvas)* to map the nine building blocks that form the components of a business, the Lean Canvas being a version especially adapted to startups. In this chapter, we're looking at the specific mechanism in the business that brings in revenue. While a full business model would involve everything from partnerships to competition, we will narrow in on popular ways that startups turn their innovations into cash-generating machines.

Because every company has a business model of some kind, let's avoid the basic tenets of business models that could apply to every business and focus on the things that are specific to startups.

There are a handful of startup business models that dominate. Some startups try to have a unique business model as their competitive advantage, while others stick to a well-worn path that's proven reliable for other startups that have served similar customers (e.g. there are numerous models for selling software to businesses—the enterprise market).

Let's start with some typical startup business models:

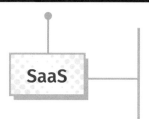

SaaS

Software as a Service (or "SaaS") can't happen without the internet and the web. And it's been the most disruptive business model to affect the world of software since the dawn of the internet.

SaaS is so ubiquitous now that you probably don't even think about how much you use it. Consumer applications like Gmail and Facebook are SaaS, for example. In the simplest terms, it's when you interact with cloud-based software in your browser or via an app.

Before the dawn of SaaS, software was either distributed on physical disks or run "on premise"— meaning on a server physically located at a company.

Thanks to recent developments, SaaS startups now also have a fighting chance in the B2B market. The reasons that made it so difficult to previously compete with enterprise software giants like SAP and Oracle are, in many ways, reduced or eliminated with open source and on-demand server capacity in the cloud. There are ever more startups building SaaS products because of these low barriers to entry.

The innovation of SaaS is that software can be updated anytime and maintained centrally by the company and distributed to everyone when the change is made. And the business model is that the customer pays for a subscription instead of a single upfront fee. You're not buying VisiCalc (the first spreadsheet software) in a box off the shelf, you're paying a monthly fee to Microsoft, Google, or a startup like Smartsheet for your company's employees to access an online spreadsheet.

Pricing for SaaS companies

It's typical for a SaaS company to offer several tiers of their service. A beginning tier might allow just one user with relatively limited functionality, a middle tier with more users and more bells and whistles, and so on.

Beginning in the mid-2000s, SaaS companies began offering a "Freemium" tier of their service. This is an option where the user can have minimal functionality or usage (e.g. only one project in a project management app) without paying for a subscription.

The idea was simply to lower the barrier for someone to try the application. The SaaS startups hoped that people would get a taste of the Freemium tier and then soon upgrade to a monthly paid plan for more users, projects, integrations with other apps, etc. The offer was straightforward and compelling to new users: you don't need to enter your credit card, and you can use this "free" tier essentially forever.

But the ground is always shifting beneath the feet of the ultra-competitive SaaS market. Many SaaS companies are now eliminating the Freemium tier, since it hasn't converted users to paid plans as quickly or effectively as they'd hoped. The growing consensus is that Freemium can show too little of a product's value (because of limited features) and that users were given the wrong incentive: make the free tier work for you so that you don't have to pay for an upgrade. There's another simple, timeless reason: once customers are already using your service, it's probably too late to ask them to buy. ○

Marketplaces

Marketplaces are hot in the startup world. Maybe that wasn't the case for the first consumer-to-consumer marketplaces, like the global garage sale on eBay or the plain-text (often all caps) potpourri of Craigslist. But those two sites were functionally advanced for their time and ushered in the promise of a more connected, person-to-person economy in the 1990s.

Airbnb is the breakout success that's made peer-to-peer marketplaces both en vogue and highly profitable (and whetted the appetite of investors hearing pitches for the next "Airbnb for X").

There are a few terms that get used when people talk about services like Airbnb and Uber, and it's important to differentiate them:

Peer-to-peer marketplace:

This is where an exchange of value happens between two users, and the company is in between, collecting some kind of fee. (Craigslist is slightly unique in that most of the connections it enables are free to users, with the exception that it charges for job postings.)

Sharing economy:

Person-to-person lending of goods. It can have a central hub (like an app that facilitates the connections being made), but it doesn't have to incorporate a fee. For example, the site couchsurfing.com brings in money from offering an optional premium tier of service. (For the purposes of understanding business models, just remember that sharing economy [also known as peer-to-peer, since the transaction involves two users] services are a subset of marketplaces.)

On-demand:

Using an app, you can summon something: a car ride (Uber, Didi), a meal (EAT24, Postmates), or someone to take your dog for a walk. But you're not asking another user on the app to do this, you're just requesting it, and the company sends someone who gives rides or delivers lunches all day.

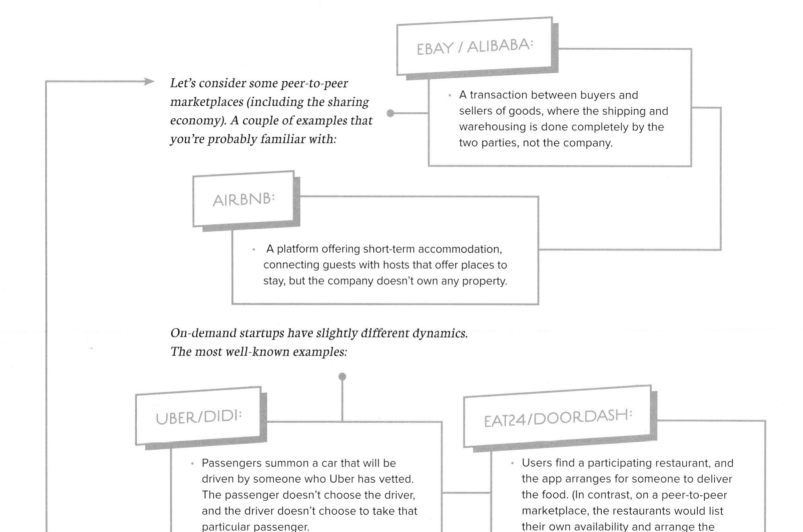

Let's consider some peer-to-peer marketplaces (including the sharing economy). A couple of examples that you're probably familiar with:

EBAY / ALIBABA:

- A transaction between buyers and sellers of goods, where the shipping and warehousing is done completely by the two parties, not the company.

AIRBNB:

- A platform offering short-term accommodation, connecting guests with hosts that offer places to stay, but the company doesn't own any property.

On-demand startups have slightly different dynamics. The most well-known examples:

UBER/DIDI:

- Passengers summon a car that will be driven by someone who Uber has vetted. The passenger doesn't choose the driver, and the driver doesn't choose to take that particular passenger.

EAT24/DOORDASH:

- Users find a participating restaurant, and the app arranges for someone to deliver the food. (In contrast, on a peer-to-peer marketplace, the restaurants would list their own availability and arrange the delivery themselves.)

An accepted rule of thumb for both peer-to-peer marketplaces and on-demand services is that you must have supply first. It's logical: if you don't have anything to offer the customers you've lured in, it's a waste. And if you don't really know and understand the supply side of your business (sellers/drivers/hosts), you will continually frustrate the buyers/users by having an uneven pool of what they're interested in purchasing.

Why does the difference matter between peer-to-peer and on-demand marketplaces? If you're a peer-to-peer marketplace, you have the Herculean task of persuading buyers and sellers of the same thing to engage with your service. (Many startups have filled a room with bespectacled data scientists and statisticians and still haven't found the right formula for having the right ratio of both buyers and sellers at the same time.)

Why does the difference matter between peer-to-peer and on-demand marketplaces?

You have to get both sides of your marketplace to do more than just log in once and give it a spin, like a utility piece of business software. They need to be engaged for your marketplace to have value: fill out a profile, upload photos, and be responsive to messages they receive from the other side of the table.

If you're an on-demand startup, you still need to build a robust supply of people (soon, robots?) who will do things like pick up laundry or deliver fresh groceries, but the benefit of Uber controlling exactly who will pick you up is that they can better control the quality of the supply. Before you drive for a ride-sharing service, you need to go through screening and training—there is currently no equivalent for renting a room in your home. Airbnb relies on their onboarding training and guest ratings to try to avoid negative host issues.

If you do control the supply of workers and undertake to match them with customers needing your startup's service, you just have more to manage. You can't just flip on your auction website and acquire sellers through digital channels but never meet them in person. This is the trade off as an on-demand: you have better control of the supply, so you have a more reliable service and can hopefully charge a higher premium for the service, but there is more work involved.

With some business ideas, you may not have a choice of whether to be a peer-to-peer marketplace or an on-demand service. For example, ridesharing has only been successful as an on-demand service. Sidecar, a ride-sharing marketplace, was an early entrant into the market in 2011 and allowed riders to choose from a list of nearby drivers. Even though Sidecar raised over $45m, its marketplace approach to ridesharing didn't work and they closed four years later.

Marketplace pricing

Two-sided markets like these enable things to happen. A marketplace can add value and succeed when the two parties connecting on the platform wouldn't have otherwise found each other. For example, a seller reaches people interested in his 1970s Star Wars action figures on eBay or a specialty t-shirt printer uses Alibaba to find clients who need a batch of a unique design.

If marketplaces can provide this type of value, they can justify taking a percentage of the transaction. The startup will have to consider its fee structure, for example:

Who pays the fees to the service, the buyer or seller? Or both? (Or, in the case of on-demand marketplaces, is it more opaque how much of the transaction comes from the buyer and service provider in the platform, respectively?)

Does the fee vary based on the size of the transaction? (True for Airbnb, not true for eBay)

Marketplaces are not a new idea. A job board like Monster is an example of a long-time successful online marketplace. Employers are always seeking ways to connect with the best candidates, and people are always looking for the best job opportunities and like to browse even when they haven't decided to move on to a new job.

Some business models come into vogue for a while based on a one or two successes but don't get considerable traction when the model is applied to other industries.

While online job boards and marketplace-style ecommerce sites have endured, it's unclear whether there will be another Airbnb or Uber that brings the concept into a web-enabled mix of the online and physical worlds.

In-App Purchases

Video games were just like software before the internet hit its stride: you walked in a store and bought a cardboard box off the shelf with a DVD inside (or if you still remember reading the news on paper, a stack of floppy disks). Later, you could pay to download the entire game online— a one-time price and just one chance to monetize that user until the next box in the series was finished and put on store shelves.

It's not easy to convince a user to pay for something before they see it and try it out. Since startups have basically zero brand since they're new and unproven, this problem is compounded. So the "Freemium" model that SaaS companies adopted helped bring in paying customers by first letting them take the software for a test drive.

Instead of a big feast of features and extras that users buy all at once, startups can sell the meal bite by bite. It can look a lot like Freemium: users are in the app, they can experience it and see what it's about. But they can't see it all or do it all.

For each extra morsel of access (such as tools and tokens in a game), you charge a small amount. It's not a recurring payment. It focuses on that moment when the user is ready to have things like:

- *More photo filters*
- *Fertilizer for their virtual farm*
- *Extended forecasts for surfing conditions*
- *Offline access to notes and saved articles*

Instead of a big feast of features and extras that users buy all at once, startups can sell the meal bite by bite.

These can be one-time fees or recurring. Just like Freemium enterprise software, the goal is to find the balance between delighting users with what's no cost and putting an extra benefit on the other side of a small transaction that feels inconsequential.

Zynga[2] has been the biggest example of selling incremental in-app goods like these. They raised over $800m, had the largest Initial Public Offering since Google, and acquired thirty companies on their quest to build an empire on streams of small purchases made in their games like Farmville and Mafia Wars. ○

Advertising

Marketplaces and Software-as-a-Service are two ways that high-growth technology companies trade value with their customers. It's the most direct way that customers bring in revenue: by paying cash for something.

But getting someone to loosen the purse strings and type in a credit card number can be extraordinarily hard. This difficulty persists even after you've proven the problem, made them aware of the product, and convinced them to use it.

SaaS startups tend to target businesses (they are "B2B"—business-to-business). Businesses don't just sign up for a new piece of software because they think it might be helpful or entertaining; they do it because it could become critical to the company's success. They are, as a class of customers, more motivated and more likely to punch in their 16-digit credit card numbers for software than a consumer might be.

Products that sell to consumers, "B2C," often need network effects to reach critical mass and scale. Asking consumers to pay for some kinds of software is possible—video games alone have proven that—but startups live or die by the rule that you don't want any barriers to adoption, especially if you need to achieve network effects for your startup to offer value to your users. If your startup is a platform that gets more value from having more active and engaged users, asking for payment just for being on the platform can cool growth tremendously.

If your consumers probably won't pay, an advertising-supported service is a logical option.

Traditional broadcast media have survived on an advertising model for decades. Television and radio sell advertising to companies that want to reach their audience, and the consumer pays nothing for the content. The broadcaster is, in effect, selling time with its audience. For a certain amount of money, the broadcaster will interrupt the experience of consumers for 30 seconds to play an ad.

The first commercial websites used the old media model. They had blinking banner ads at the top of the page for large brands or perhaps products that could roughly match with the site's intended audience. However, there were no meaningful ways to track whether the ads were effective or whether the ad was really appropriate for that user, much less whether there was a better ad to show them and what it might be.

It's a problem that goes back a long time. Sometime near the turn of the 20th century, John Wanamaker, a member of the merchant class of Philadelphia, made a profound statement: "Half the money I spend on advertising is wasted; the trouble is, I don't know which half."

Online advertising was initially a blunt and crude instrument that had no way to target users other than choosing what site the ads might run on. But that started to change when search engines could offer ads based on your searches, and social networks built the ability to serve ads to specific users based on their interests, location, and the attributes of the people they're connected to. The same cloud technology that allowed a company like Salesforce to completely disrupt their industry also enabled consumer sites to have the same functionality of a desktop computer. The first social networks, Friendster, MySpace, and Bebo, were primitive web applications that gave an interactive experience.

These types of targeted advertising are the primary revenue drivers for both Facebook and Google. You might not think those small text ads are their most important product, but they account for the lion's share of their financial success. What you search for, what stuff you are thinking of buying, and which other sites you like to visit are all a golden trove of data for companies who want to pinpoint the consumers they hope will be interested in their product.

So, advertising moved from being a simple way to make money (and a crude way to target consumers) on a website, to being a viable way of targeting users that commands very high ad rates from advertisers. It has built some of the largest technology companies in the world.

Should my startup use ads?

Successful ad-supported startups have one thing in common: they must achieve massive scale. Internet advertising rates traditionally move in a single direction (namely, down), so you need an extremely high amount of users being served ads for them to support your startup. Few have succeeded. ○

Network Effects

Network effects are built when more and more people contribute to a system—a marketplace like Airbnb is an example. Having the right amount of hosts across Europe means that when a couple is planning a long summer vacation, they'll have enough options for each country they'll visit. If Airbnb mainly had hosts in Southern Europe and very little supply in Northern Europe, the value to that couple would decrease. Then the couple might start looking at hostels with private rooms or less expensive bed-and-breakfasts, and the startup loses potential business, as well as lowering their ROI for acquiring that customer.

Business Model Traps

The Dim Prospects of Selling Data

Many founders struggle to figure out how to develop a business model that could generate serious revenue. Especially with B2C startups like apps, the writing's on the wall that consumers won't pay.

The founder imagines many users who are engaged with the app. Let's think of a fantasy sports app: users around the world can make their dream rosters and the teams play each other. Because there are so many options for football fans to have an online fantasy league, if the startup tried to charge its users, it would likely be a self-imposed death sentence.

If a startup can't sell the app to the users, why not sell the users themselves? The app collects a lot of data, and the founders think it's likely to be valuable to some company that found a way to profit from this kind of information. Maybe a soccer league wants to know more about the people who might attend their matches, a broadcaster might want to figure out what kind of people tune in every week, and maybe a sporting goods manufacturer is looking for new ways to target potential customers.

The basic idea is true: companies want to know more about their customers. But they don't want to know just any information about them, they need it to be something actionable. It needs to be something that can directly help them sell to these people, which is why ad targeting based on consumer preferences and browsing history are so lucrative.

In the football app, there might be two kinds of data:

USER DATA

- Name
- Email
- Facebook info (since the user might log in with their Facebook credentials that could contain demographic information, depending on which permissions the app asks from its users at signup)

APP DATA

- Frequency of logins
- Time spent in the app
- Actions taken in the app (did a user make a lot of trades?)

User data is valuable: these are potential customers for someone. However, you shouldn't just sell your users' information to another company so they can spam your users without their consent (speaking to the generally accepted best practices in the developed world, which vary by country).

So you can't sell this user data. What's left is the data from your app.

It's possible that you could resell aggregated anonymous app data (this sort of thing happens all of the time with retargeting on the web). But is your app data worth anything to a sportswear company that would like to sell more jerseys? Would the mass market telecom in the countries where your customers are benefit from knowing about the actions in your app? They wouldn't, at least not for your startup.

You could tell them all about how many player trades users made, how that correlates to their winning or losing streak, and whether users tend to pick players that are more from their home regions. But while this might be useful to one or two companies, it's unlikely to be enough to base a high-growth business on. There's not enough potential in the data for an investor to think they'd have a chance at a big multiple of their investment.

There are exceptions. If your app catalogs consumer preferences, real-time sentiments about news and entertainment, and how these things relate to the people they know and the people that those people know, you could have a trove of data big enough to build an advertising platform.

This is what Facebook did after years of collecting unprecedented amounts of consumer data, and it's not easy to achieve such incredible engagement and scale.

There are very few chances to compile meaningful data at scale. The odds are better to look for another avenue than selling data from your app.

The short-sightedness of an Exit-Focused Approach

Founders should be in for the long haul. Building a successful high-growth company can take five to ten years. Building a startup that ultimately fails can end up taking just as long.

We have three basic outcomes for a high-growth startup: death, acquisition, or an Initial Public Offering. An IPO is rare and death is common, so founders gravitate toward thinking of being acquired. It's glamorous to think of a Google or Microsoft wanting to buy your company for an obscene amount of money and seeing yourself on the front page of Techcrunch.

But that cannot be a substitute for having revenue. In the first dot-com era, the naïve idea of "accumulating eyeballs" meant that startups were just trying to get people to visit their sites. (The idea that it would eventually turn into valuable advertising revenue on essentially generic sties didn't work out.)

Acquisition is based on many things. But this is most likely to happen when you have built something of value that the other company can amplify in a way that would be impossible for you—the proverbial "taking it to the next level."

Planning from the beginning to build something and then sell it also means that you're not invested in the business, you're invested in an outcome. The founder who works only toward acquisition won't have the internal persistence and drive needed to put in the long days to get the company where it needs to be.

Basing your startup's future on the idea that it will be acquired is toxic. Not surprisingly, it rarely works out. Focus on a problem that you're passionate to pursue fixing, and follow the satisfaction of delighting users first. ○

Your choice of business model will ultimately be the fuel in the tank of your startup, and you'll need to choose well for meaningful growth. The vehicle itself, however, is the problem your business solves.Whichever business model is right for your startup (whether you adopt one from this chapter or create something completely new), without being able to first find great problems and test them, the startup won't even get off the ground.

In the next chapter, we'll look at ways to find startup ideas you can be passionate about. After that, you'll learn how to build a set of hypotheses around your startup idea and test those with customers for maximum impact. ●

FINDING YOUR

STARTUP

INSPIRATION

"A great flame follows a little spark."

Dante Alighieri

> Without a strong idea based on a problem that customers urgently want to solve, superb engineering or killer design won't move the needle. In this chapter, we look at methods of coming up with a problem worth solving for your users.

We'll cover how to:

• *Build up your "idea muscle'" so you can regularly generate new ideas and avoid being too critical of them*

• *Move beyond your own head, to discover problems people are looking to solve*

• *Find the right balance between your personal passion and your customers' needs*

• *Use the principles of Design Thinking to validate your startup idea*

FINDING YOUR STARTUP INSPIRATION

Sometimes, people have moments of epiphany. In the normal course of life, they are struck by an insight into a problem that needs to be fixed: a process that could be better or a customer who could be happier. (The person having the lightbulb moment is often also this dissatisfied customer.)

Those moments of inspiration can spur us to build our imagined solution. Too often, though, entrepreneurs think of the finish line too early. They get stuck on the endgame without understanding and focusing on the root problem they hope to solve.

And an entrepreneur's inspired idea, no matter how great, doesn't matter if it doesn't match up with a potential customer's judgement of whether it solves a problem that's worth fixing.

So, if you want to create a startup around an exciting idea, you'll first need to uncover the problem itself. This is not a natural way to start for most entrepreneurs; they instinctively want to figure out the whole thing on their own and have a vision for how it should work from beginning to end. Unfortunately, founders who jump into the execution phase too eagerly, without validating their idea by researching underlying customer needs, are almost always disappointed when they launch. They either realize that they created an ineffective solution or that no one had the problem in the first place.

But if you find a problem worth solving, you have the foundation for a killer startup. Here are two examples of acute problems that turned into successful startups.

Before *Google*, the web was a sprawling mess that was organized by humans on a site-by-site basis. If you wanted to find a great site on fly fishing, you had to visit a "search directory" where one of Yahoo's editors might (or might not) have put some decent links into a category like "Recreation>Sports>Fishing>Obscure Fishing>Fly Fishing." Now the web is a sprawling mess that's organized by Google's automated robot army. The value in Google's search engine is that it's built to serve up the most relevant results for "what is fly fishing?" The goal is to help you find the most relevant site (or ad) by doing as little investigation as possible and with the smallest number of clicks.

Before *Tinder* hit the scene, online dating was a slow process that involved writing and replying to lengthy messages. In a lot of ways, it felt more like making pen pals than actually dating. Tinder gives its users an experience that emphasizes the immediacy of real-world dating behavior, like making snap judgements about whether you're attracted to someone from across the room at a party. Instead of writing sonnets to someone on a dating site after reading their page-long bio, you instinctively swipe left or right on Tinder for a quick up-or-down vote.

As an entrepreneur interested in building useful products, you can continually get better at seeing the issues waiting to be solved all around you. Your own issues can be a wealth of insight into the issues faced by other people who are somehow similar to you. And there are also other people's problems, which we might not even be aware of or fully understand. We need to train ourselves to find them.

The Passion Warning

Passion in a startup cuts from both sides of the sword. If you have so much passion about your idea that you can't listen to feedback, you can career into non-responsive product development and ultimately, failure.

Having too little is also an issue. Customer input is a great tool, but you do have to care about the problem. You need to have the burning passion to get out of bed and work on solving that problem when nothing's working, your competitors are trouncing you, and your bank account is dwindling with no revenue or funding in sight..

Solve a problem that your customers have and that you are passionate about, not just one of the two.

There are lots of methods for finding user problems, with pragmatic steps that anyone can apply. Two simple frameworks that have been useful to my students are based on the philosophies of startup thought leaders James Altucher and Paul Graham, and they have taken hold because of their simplicity. After we've had a look at those, we'll talk about a method pioneered by a design firm that sets aside your opinions and outlook while you root out other people's problems.

Be an Idea Machine

Entrepreneur and best-selling author James Altucher built a number of software companies, and like any serial entrepreneur, he's had many failed businesses and bad ideas along the way. But coming up with bad ideas is actually a good thing; it's the step you have to take before you can uncover an idea worth pursuing.

His advice is to become an idea machine by writing down ten ideas per day on cheap waiter's notepads.

Why ten? To push your limits. Most of us can think of a few ideas off the top of our heads. That's easy. But getting to ten can feel like a stretch. Why waiter's notepads? Because it's cheap to buy a lot of them—no excuses for not being action-oriented.

But coming up with bad ideas is actually a good thing; it's the step you have to take before you can uncover an idea worth pursuing.

Altucher compares it to exercising a muscle: you have to develop and practice the ability to think of new ideas, and the best way to do that is by pushing yourself to come up with more ideas than seems possible at the moment. It's like consistently lifting more weight at the gym than you think you can handle. That misery will eventually translate into building muscle mass—or in this case, quicker impulses to crank out ideas every day.

"Note that when you exercise in the gym, your muscles don't start to build until you break a sweat. Your metabolism doesn't improve when you run until you sweat. Your body doesn't break down the old and build the new until it is sweating.

"The poisons and toxins in your body don't leave until you sweat.

"The same thing happens with the idea muscle. Somewhere around idea number six, your brain starts to sweat. This means it's building up. Break through this. Come up with ten ideas."

James Altucher

He doesn't expect you to write ten amazing ideas, just ten new ones. They can be bad. But you have to push through the process to stop your brain from prematurely critiquing the ideas (which it does to try to save you from embarrassment).

"The way you shut the brain off is by forcing it to come up with bad ideas."

And these ideas don't have to be specific to any one industry. Altucher recommends that you allow yourself to come up with ideas that aren't even business ideas. Those adjacent thoughts might spark something interesting or at least keep your idea muscle limbered up.

Paul Graham's "How to Get Startup Ideas"

As the co-founder of Y Combinator, Paul Graham has seen a lot of startups. Some of the most successful companies in recent memory, like Airbnb and Dropbox, have come through his venerable accelerator in Palo Alto.

In his seminal essay, Graham thinks about the biggest tech companies in the world: Google, Facebook, Apple, and the like. He identifies three common themes that they all shared at their humble beginnings:

- *The founders needed the product.*
- *They could approach the problem and build it themselves (or get reasonably close with an ugly but functional first version).*
- *Other people didn't realize the problem was worth looking at.*

Based on these characteristics, Graham advises the would-be entrepreneur to "notice" a problem, something you observe "organically." Look for the things in your life and work that are frustrating, those situations where you find yourself saying "this could be better." Your first-hand experience gives you a unique vantage point and insight that an outsider just can't understand as well as you.

One thing Graham and Altucher share is that they don't judge startup ideas too early. Altucher advises to "let your brain run wild," and Graham says to stop yourself from trying to predict whether your idea can become a big company. Later in this book, there are methods for talking with customers, which can help you figure out whether you've found an idea that anyone cares about, but for the time being, focus on generating ideas that meet Graham's criteria without projecting into the future.

The value of other people's problems

The downside of relying on yourself for idea generation is that you're limited by your own perspectives, cultural worldview, and day-to-day experiences. Engineers are notorious for coming up with elaborate solutions to issues that only they perceive as painful user problems. (How inefficient you think a piece of software is usually varies based on how much you obsess over software.)

The downside of relying on yourself for idea generation is that you're limited by your own perspectives, cultural worldview, and day-to-day experiences.

From a cultural perspective, Silicon Valley and the established startup world has been criticized for being too focused on the needs of the "developed world," and more specifically, on the needs of affluent American males.

Increased global exposure to startups and growing diversity within the startup community is changing that. More and more, the future is being built across racial, gender, and geographic lines. From an investment point of view, there are also many opportunities for companies to serve populations that aren't wealthy men (overwhelmingly the current demographic of Silicon Valley investors). To ignore these opportunities isn't just myopic; it leaves money on the table, since startups must travel down undiscovered roads in search of big markets, which is harder to do if you're looking in the same place as everyone else.

After the dot-com bust of the early 2000s, the party was over, and there was a lot of sober talk among investors and founders. If the informal motto of the boom was "build it and they will come," but during the bust, there was a growing understanding of how important it is to work with customers to uncover their problems and reconcile them with a founder's startup idea. The new motto became "get out of the building," meaning that founders shouldn't rely on their self-generated opinions of what their customers need and instead do the hard work of getting out and learning from them (this phrase was coined by Steve Blank, the father of Customer

If the informal motto of the boom was "build it and they will come," but during the bust, there was a growing understanding of how important it is to work with customers to uncover their problems and reconcile them with a founder's startup idea.

Development, who we'll meet in *Chapter 4 (From Plan to Canvas)*. The founder might have experienced an issue that triggered an idea, seen it happen to someone else, or even just thrown a proverbial dart at the dartboard. But the actual voice of the customer—the one whom these solutions were supposedly built for—was often missing.

Why Design Thinking matters

In the mid-2000s, the new trend was to "do your homework" on customers before running with a startup idea, and different opinions about how to do this started percolating in the startup world. Around this time, a design firm called IDEO developed a rigorous and methodical way to understand their users' problems and were focused on designing products and experiences that truly met customers' needs.

IDEO's method is called Design Thinking. Other wildly transformational frameworks from the post-Bubble, pre-Facebook/Twitter era, such as Steve Blank's Customer Development, start with a founder's assumption about a customer problem. Design Thinking, on the other hand, throws out all assumptions and asks the founder to simply receive information about a user's needs straight from the source.

At its core, Design Thinking encourages you, the person hoping to start a company, to give up authority of knowledge. It asserts that you shouldn't assume that you understand anything about your customer's needs, and that those romanticized "founders' epiphanies" can't give you the answers, let alone a proper understanding of the problem you're tackling.

Instead, the stages in the Design Thinking process allow you to uncover your users' problems as they relate to a general issue you're investigating. The focus is on developing empathy, an orientation toward another person's experiences in a given situation. A global community of design thinkers has developed and shared many practical ways to implement these stages.

After a day of (often awkward) interactions, the students return to campus with a huge swath of information that describes all sorts of real-life problems they hadn't considered.

In a master's-level Social Innovation class I teach, my students use Design Thinking as the primary tool for validating new ventures. They come in early on a Saturday and are instructed to go out into the streets of San Francisco to talk to strangers. (Some of them are so freaked out by this idea, that I always see a few looks of terror the morning I spring the assignment on them.)

They don't talk to people about a specific startup idea or even a problem they've identified. And that is the point. It's a blank canvas, and the only predetermined frame is the subject matter (e.g., access to healthcare). While this provides a vessel for the conversations, it leaves immense room for people to guide my students toward a problem.

After a day of (often awkward) interactions, the students return to campus with a huge swath of information that describes all sorts of real-life problems they hadn't considered.

These interactions out in the field are the essence of the first stage of Design Thinking: "Empathize." This involves not just engaging with users but also immersing yourself in their experiences and observing the context in which they encounter problems.

The next phase of Design Thinking is "Define," in which you scope and pinpoint a user challenge that emerged during your initial exploration. Then comes "Ideate," where you and your team brainstorm as many solutions as possible without poking holes in them (just like Altucher's ten judgement-free daily ideas).

Once you've found a problem—however you came across it—don't get too attached. The final two stages of Design Thinking are "Prototype" and "Test," which we'll revisit in later chapters. If you learn from your potential customers that they indeed have the problem you've identified, then you can start work on a possible solution and search for the holy grail of startup founders: problem-solution fit and product-market fit.

The biggest strength of Design Thinking is that it gives you a structured way to find out what your customers struggle with and how you can provide value. This important initial step gets you closer to the user and removes a barrier of assumptions that can lead you down a path of wasted time and energy. If more founders utilized Design Thinking practices, the startup world might have more ideas that truly address a user's core needs, not just ones that entrepreneurs assume are worth solving. •

Design Thinking Resources

There are several great resources for learning more about this method. Both the d.school at Stanford (formally known as the Hasso Plattner Institute of Design) and IDEO itself have largely open-sourced their materials on Design Thinking.

The IDEO site DesignKit.org has a wealth of curated videos and examples. The nonprofit OpenIDEO runs active Design Thinking challenges that crowdsource solutions online through a platform that anyone can join. Anyone who creates an account on OpenIDEO can join a team and contribute to ideas that tackle problems like water scarcity, food waste, and more.

FROM PLAN
TO CANVAS

"Everyone has a plan until they get punched in the face."
Mike Tyson

As you now know, high-growth startups don't work on the same principles as businesses based on relatively incremental growth. Startup founders need to employ more fluid practices that allow them to change direction at any time, making a traditional business plan obsolete almost as soon as the ink dries on the page. In this chapter, we introduce you to the idea of a business canvas—a more flexible planning solution that adapts as your startup grows.

We'll introduce you to:

• *The reasons business plans and most new ventures don't mix*

• *How the Business Model Canvas and its startup-focused cousin, the Lean Canvas, revolutionized the way businesses understand themselves*

• *How a canvas is ideally suited to startups because of your ability to monitor and update your plans as the business evolves*

DEATH OF THE PLAN, BIRTH OF THE CANVAS

For a long time, business plans have been the dominant way of communicating new business ideas in academic competitions and investment circles. These thick, formal documents paint a picture of the business in about forty-plus pages of dense narrative and charts full of things that the author thinks will happen once the company is off and running. And both of these aspects are why business plans don't work well for startups: not only are they long and tedious reads full of assumptions, they aren't innately geared to test those assumptions.

> **"Startups are in search of a repeatable, scalable business model."**
> **— Steve Blank**

There's a mismatch between startups and conventional business plans. Startups search for new and unproven ideas. A high level of risk, then, is built right into the startup founder's journey. The reason it has any appeal to investors is because the potential rewards attached to that risk are also very high. On the other hand, while any business plan still involves risk, the business plan format asks founders to write up their assumptions as implied fact. The impetus has been to sell the dream of what customers will like, how much they're willing to pay, and how much effective marketing will cost, with few tools baked into the format to help incrementally prove or disprove those assumptions.

Business plans don't work well for startups: not only are they long and tedious reads full of assumptions, they aren't innately geared to test those assumptions.

Why Business Plans for Startups Don't Work

I don't want to completely write off the old-school business plan. There are many people who have gotten a great deal of value out of it and for good reason. If you were going to start a chain of dry cleaners in the 1970s in an area of the United States that had relatively few of them, you could make a lot of pretty decent assumptions about that business because you wouldn't really be innovating. Since you would just be adopting an existing business model to provide a familiar service, you would have lots of prior examples to draw from. You could look at the growth of dry cleaning across the United States to see which demographics tend to use dry cleaners, and you could understand the costs involved based on other dry cleaner businesses. With that kind of information, you could probably make decent assumptions about what your marketing costs might be (or more relevant to startups, the cost to acquire a customer).

Of course, just because you were going to open a business similar to one that had succeeded elsewhere doesn't mean all your assumptions would be correct. Even if you did have a lot of data to base them on, the market has never been that stable. But you would have enough to reassure a potential business partner or investor that there's a fair chance of success.

However, startups have much less data to base their assumptions on, so a business plan for a startup would be mostly based on pure speculation, not data.

Since technology companies can make more money with fewer costs—someone just needed to write and maintain the code for TripAdvisor and make it available to millions and millions of users—they can scale dramatically. That makes them attractive businesses, but it's harder to predict what will happen with them compared to a local chain of dry cleaners.

So, what would happen if you tried to sell your startup idea with a business plan? Let's imagine that, instead of a walk-in dry cleaner, you're building a startup that provides on-demand dry cleaning. Your assumption is that there is a high demand for dry cleaning that isn't being met because busy professionals in dense, urban areas find it too inconvenient to bring their outfits to a brick-and-mortar dry cleaner. Maybe they live too far from one, or maybe it's practically around the corner but they just never find the time. Either way, you have a solution that should appeal to them.

You could write a business plan about this concept, but as soon as it came off the printer, most of its projections would be incorrect because you'd inevitably not understand the finer mechanics of the business model on the first try (to say nothing of whether it catches on with users at all). And it's not because you weren't diligent with your research on the dry cleaning business or because you were sloppy in your calculations; it's simply because there's never

You could write a business plan about this concept, but as soon as it came off the printer, most of its projections would be incorrect because you'd inevitably not understand the finer mechanics of the business model on the first try

been a successful on-demand dry cleaner. Anyone else trying to start a business like this would also be throwing darts with a blindfold on. Building an innovative idea into a startup involves validating a number of hypotheses. And those hypotheses (or the next set, or the set after that) need to be validated as correct to be successful.

An alternative solution for startups was desperately needed.

Business Model Canvas

Alexander Osterwalder spent the early 2000s studying business models while earning his PhD in Switzerland. After gathering information on the components of business models, he and his thesis advisor, Yves Pigneur, formulated a nine-component Business Model Canvas. In their book, Business Model Generation, Osterwalder and Pigneur show their process of mapping a business using those nine components.

The Business Model Canvas was a revolutionary update to the business plan. Instead of compiling forty-plus pages of neatly presented charts and bullet points, you take sticky notes and write down hypotheses of how your business fits into the nine boxes, representing what Osterwalder and Pigneur saw as the key components of a modern business.

They built the Canvas to represent the most important aspects of any business at any stage of its lifecycle. Who are the customers? What's the overarching value proposition to each set of customers? What costs will the business need to incur? What are the revenue streams for the business? What channels do you use to reach your customer? (The Bullseye Framework, explained in **Chapter 8** *[Growth and Traction]*, is a great method for testing out different channels.)

The Business Model Canvas and Business Model Generation have been wildly successful. Because the Business Model Canvas was essentially open-source from its release, people have been free to modify it and share their variations. Using the Creative Commons copyright license, anyone can take it and remix it into something of their own. There are dozens of canvas models that have been based on the original, but only the Lean Canvas has managed to build a popularity rivaling the original, which it achieved by addressing the specific needs of startups.

Key Partners

Key Activities

Key Resources

Value Proposition

Customer Relationships

Channels

Customers

Costs

Revenue

The Lean Canvas

Ash Maurya was working on startup ideas in Austin when he recognized the transformative potential of the Business Model Canvas. It gave founders and entrepreneurs an opportunity to move away from abstract business plans and into something more tangible and iterative. Approaching the Canvas with a startup's quest for a problem-solution fit in mind, he realized it would need to be modified so that those nine boxes full of sticky notes could test hypotheses related to the many unknowns early-stage startups face.

The Lean Canvas keeps four parts of the Business Model Canvas—customer segments, value proposition, cost structure, and revenue—but adds four of its own, which are specific to high-growth software startups. Instead of a "partners" box, the Lean Canvas has a "problem" box. In the original canvas, you place a sticky note with the name of a company that would be a key partner in getting your business done.

This is basically an action that wouldn't make sense for the company to do on its own—like a bank partnering with an ATM manufacturer instead of manufacturing their own. While this would be a valuable step for an established company, startups have something far more pressing: proving that there is a problem worth addressing.

First and foremost, you want to find and validate a meaty problem. After you've used the interview techniques in *Chapter 5* (*The Customer Rules*) to learn which customers have this problem (and noted those findings in the "customers" box), you can then move to the "value proposition" box.

The "value proposition" is the high-level benefit a startup is offering its customer. This can be tricky for founders to grok: the value proposition is the benefit, and the solution is the way that it manifests. So it's only after the problem, customer, and value proposition have been established (or at least guessed at) that you move to putting in and testing ideas for the "solution" box.

Problem

Top 3 problems

Solution

Top 3 features

Key Metrics

Key activities you measure

Unique Value Proposition

Single, clear, compelling message that states why you are different and worth paying attention

Unfair Advantage

Can't be easily copied or bought

Channels

Path to customers

Customer Segments

Target customers

Cost Structure

Customer acquisition costs, distribution costs, hosting, people, etc.

Revenue Streams

Revenue model, life time value, revenue, gross margin

Product ⟵   ⟶ **Market**

The Business Model Canvas includes a "customer relationships" box to map customer interactions via, for example, personal service and online support. Again, while this can be very important for an established company, a startup will still be trying to figure out how it can survive. For that reason, Maurya replaces the "customer relationships" box with one labeled "unfair advantage." Since startups are so easy to build and ideas are worthless (execution is what's valuable), you need to figure out what unique and valuable advantage your startup has over any competitors who are also trying to solve the same problem.

When you use a Business Model Canvas or Lean Canvas, you don't write on it, you always use sticky notes. Why? Because nothing is set in stone.

The Lean Canvas also replaces "key resources" with "key metrics." It's true that the "key resources" box is applicable to any kind of company, including startups. However, as we will see in **Chapter 8** *(Growth and Traction)*, what your software startup really needs to find is the "One Metric That Matters." You need to continually test different metrics to discover which are the most meaningful indicators of growth for your startup.

How to Use a Canvas

As you can tell by now, a canvas is fundamentally different from the business plan. It's a living, breathing document. When you use a Business Model Canvas or Lean Canvas, you don't write on it, you always use sticky notes. Why? Because nothing is set in stone. Everything we put on any kind of business mapping canvas is a process that needs to be continually tested and proven.

Sticky notes are a constant in co-working spaces and accelerators for a good reason: they reflect a mindset of continuous change and iteration in startups. Business plans can give you the constrained feeling of having the future charted out ahead of you, regardless of whether it's right or wrong—you don't want to feel beholden to that. Using a canvas to track and update your understanding of your startups builds your tolerance for uncertainty and change that's a constant with high-growth ventures.

Your Lean Canvas focuses on your relationship with your customer, which means that if you have more than one customer base, a different canvas is necessary for each. If you're building a two-sided marketplace, for example, you should make a separate canvas for both the supply and the demand aspects of your business. If your dry cleaning startup connects consumers and dry cleaning stores, you need to determine the value proposition, the problem, and the potential solution for each of those customers.

Using a canvas is a great way to keep your team and stakeholders on the same page even when things are shaken up. If your team has been at work measuring the metrics in your app and finds that you're tracking the wrong one, put the correct one on your canvas and share it with your investors. If you realize the kind of customers you're addressing has changed, make sure that is reflected on your canvas, allowing your team to see the problem your startup will solve.

In the next chapter, we'll look at the value of talking with customers, the evolution of customer development, and some specific tactics for getting the right information onto your canvas. ●

THE

CUSTOMER

RULES

*"What we anticipate seldom occurs;
what we least expected generally happens."*

Benjamin Disraeli

As a successful startup provides a great solution to a problem, it's essential to learn from potential customers to find out whether your solution works and even if the problem really exists. Too many founders invest time, effort, and cash into a solution for a problem that only matters to them. In this chapter, we encourage you to "get out of the building" and find out what's going on in your customers' minds.

This is where you'll discover:

- *Why it's worth resisting the temptation to try to understand your users from the safety of your workspace*

- *How the Customer Development Process fits into your startup journey, putting the customer at the center of every stage of your business*

- *An introduction to Ash Maurya's Lean Canvas and interview techniques, which together can uncover valuable information about what your customers care about, without introducing any ideas of your own*

- *Why this can move you closer to problem/solution fit and product/market fit*

THE CUSTOMER RULES

As a budding founder, you will hear over and over that you need to understand your customer. Whether you're considering product design, user experience, or how much your startup should have a presence on Snapchat, knowing your customer is absolutely critical to your decision-making process. It's essential to consider your customer throughout the entire process of building a high-growth startup, especially during the earliest stages.

Since you are trying to establish a new business model and you don't yet have any customers who depend on your service and with whom you have a dialogue, it's difficult to gauge your potential customers' interest level. And yet without knowing whether anyone cares about what you're working toward, you're firing shots in the dark.

Get Comfortable with Your Customers

There's a historical tension between traditional engineering culture and interacting with customers. The stereotype in Silicon Valley is that engineers hide away in their garage to build software, thinking they know exactly what their customer wants. After spending months—or even years—developing a product they are sure customers will flock to, these isolated tinkerers discover that they more often hear the sound of crickets than of applause.

This was the disastrous refrain of so many startups in in the late '90s dotcom bubble. Even though they had big venture capital checks and some even had colossal debuts on the stock, there were many product launches that flopped because they were just sure they had a golden business on their hands—and they largely didn't do enough work with customers to understand if that was actually true.

There are a couple of key reasons the entire team, including engineers, need to get comfortable with talking to their customers. First of all, everyone who works for a startup does almost everything. You're multifunctional, not necessarily because you want to be but because there are constant fires to put out and surprises around every corner. Major corporations have enough personnel to set up dedicated departments where necessary; you don't. So every member of your core team needs to be flexible enough to jump in and help put out whatever fire is threatening to burn your shanty down.

The stereotype in Silicon Valley is that engineers hide away in their garage to build software, thinking they know exactly what their customer wants.

The second reason is that, as a founder, you are trying to build the absolute best product to serve your customers' needs. You might be able to assess those needs if one team member goes out to speak with potential customers, but every single co-founder having direct contact with customers makes the product development process that much richer and more informed. Even if your specialty is building complex algorithms or crunching terabytes of data, you will benefit from understanding the minds of your customers. Every decision made by a startup affects the product that ultimately has to delight your customer, so get comfortable putting yourself in their shoes. If you do that, every decision you make about how to implement a feature will at least be an informed decision to some degree. You won't always be right all of the time, but you will be a lot less likely to frustrate your users or leave them with that look of a confused dog cocking its head to one side because it can't understand why you've done such a strange thing.

It's not just programmers who avoid talking to customers—most people aren't comfortable with it. My students get nervous before executing the first phase of the design-thinking process, which is to go out and talk to people about their problems. They're not nervous because they can't

Major corporations have enough personnel to set up dedicated departments where necessary; you don't.

comport themselves, they're nervous because they're setting themselves up for the rejection of their idea. But the rejection is where the benefit lies, using first-hand customer feedback to start proving or disproving the endless hypotheses that go into a startup idea. You need to obtain genuine, unfiltered feedback and insights from your customer. If no one cares about the problem or solution, you need to know that as early as possible.

With increasingly accessible tools to build software and the fact that prototyping tools are dead easy to use, it's very tempting to just lock yourself away and build your idea exactly as you envision it. Resist that temptation. Building a startup is hard work, and this is when founders should get the first taste of how the hard work is hard but pays off. By not talking to customers and going into a self-imposed coding/design black hole fueled by cheap pizza, you might save yourself from the short-term pain of rejection or disappointment, but you'll also be neglecting one of the most meaningful (and free!) things you can do for your startup. ○

The Customer Development Process

If anyone is the godfather of getting out and talking to customers, it's Steve Blank. Blank is a serial entrepreneur with both big successes and big failures. He coined the influential idea that founders should "get out of the building" and have in-person interactions with the people they think will be interested in their products.

Blank calls the road that leads from talking with your potential customers to scaling your startup the "Customer Development Process" (or the "Four Steps to the Epiphany"). The first half of the process is the "search" and the second is "execute." The two components of "search" are most relevant to early-stage startups: customer discovery and customer validation. (The second half of the entire Customer Development Process, "execute," comes after customer validation, when you build and scale your startup into a full-fledged company.)

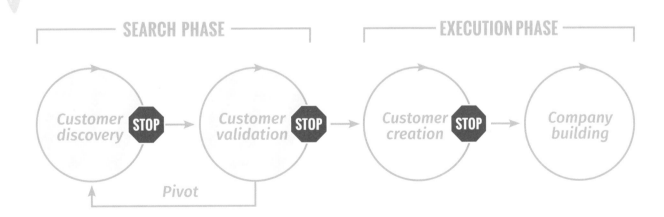

SEARCH PHASE — EXECUTION PHASE

Customer discovery STOP → Customer validation STOP → Customer creation STOP → Company building

Pivot

Customer discovery involves figuring out whether anyone has a problem you think you can solve. You build hypotheses based around your customers' needs and wants and how those perceptions form the basis of your business idea. Then, you test those hypotheses by interviewing potential customers.

We'll talk in a moment about the practicalities of getting the information you need, but customer discovery helps startups achieve the first key milestone in its journey: problem/solution fit. As the name implies, this is an indication of how close you are to solving the problems you've proven that your customers experience. You need to know whether they think your proposed solution validates their problem and more importantly, whether they will use the product (ideally, more than once). Of course, this won't ensure that the product you release will stick. But you will at least know that potential users responded positively when they imagined using your product.

Customer validation comes next. This is where you take everything you've learned from your interviews and put those learnings to the test by releasing a product (but that doesn't mean a "prototype," as we'll see next chapter) and using it to achieve the second key milestone: product/market fit. Of course, even with a product informed by the hard work of sitting down and listening to users, it still may not thrive in the market. But the odds are a lot better. ○

A 'startup' is a company that is confused about

1. What its product is.

2. Who its customers are.

3. How to make money.

Dave McClure, 500 Startups Co-founder

Practical Steps to Your Epiphany

Founders can usually get their heads around the concepts of problem/solution fit and product/market fit, but then what? They're often confused as to how to move toward testing their hypotheses and learning from their prospective users. Whenever a student or would-be founder asks me about this, I always recommend Running Lean by Ash Maurya, the creator of the Lean Canvas. It's an extremely tactical book on understanding your customer that has become a revered and invaluable resource in the toolkit of anyone testing a new startup idea.

You should start by telling a story to provide your interviewees with some context, and you will want to document their responses diligently. And bring along a co-founder to be an interview partner, so you can compare what you each observed after the fact.

Maurya lays out two templates for interviews with customers: one to determine the viability of your hypotheses about customer problems (the problem interview) and the other to assess the viability of your imagined solution (the solution interview). Running Lean breaks down how an interview might be structured, down to the minute. In both, you should start by telling a story to provide your interviewees with some context, and you will want to document their responses diligently. And bring along a co-founder to be an interview partner, so you can compare what you each observed after the fact.

The Problem Interview

The Problem Interview is entirely focused on asking about and understanding customers' problems, and it's the complement to filling out the first box in the Lean Canvas: "problem." There's no pitching whatsoever at this point. This deserves repeating: don't pitch in the interview. Don't even talk about what your product might be. Founders struggle with this; they're understandably eager to share the glorious vision of the product they're spending their precious time on.

But if you tell people about your product, many of them will simply tell you that your idea sounds cool. This feedback is essentially worthless. It's a wise maxim from the fifty-four hour scrum of Startup Weekend: don't ask ice cream questions. If you ask someone, "Do you want some of this ice cream?" the answer is always yes. Everyone loves ice cream. If you ask a question like, "What do you think of my app?" (which you shouldn't

do), the answer will be, "It's cool!" or, "Sounds great!" People also love being agreeable to strangers they're having a quick coffee meeting with.

So you want to find out whether your potential users actually experience these issues that you're trying to solve. This is where your startup immediately begins to save resources and move as quickly as possible. You're investing in a hopefully decent premise of what the problems are before you try to sell them on your would-be solution, and not how clever or well-designed they think your product is in the abstract.

When you're sitting down face-to-face with your potential users and asking them about the problems they experience, you need to pay attention to more than just their words. You don't just want to know if they have the problem; you really care about how much it affects them and how much enthusiasm they have about the prospect of solving it (a startup can be born from a problem that people have given up on solving—your startup can step in to show a new way after people have given up). When someone tells you that they do, in fact, wish they had a more convenient way to hire and manage dog walkers, make sure you read their facial expression and try to get a general feeling of whether or not they really care. Time is limited, so we deprioritize problems that we don't imagine we can solve. When someone you're interviewing lights up when you mention a certain issue, you're probably onto something meaningful.

The Solution Interview

Next comes the Solution Interview, which moves toward validating problem/solution fit. It's tough to know exactly when to move on from the Problem Interview, though. You may find that your solution interviews flop, and you feel the need to return to talking with customers about problems again. (A common rule of thumb, though arbitrary, is that you need 100 strong problem interviews to move forward with working on the solution side.)

Your goal in the solution interview is to figure out what your app's most important features are. In other words, which components of your product will most meaningfully address your users' problem?

In this round of interviews, there are a few consistent guidelines you will want to follow. First, as with the problem interviews, always work to have coffee meetings with people in person and never rely on online surveys. Your human brain is much better at reading nonverbal cues than any computer, and the output of an online survey is efficient but flat numerical data—perhaps good for Unilever to gather sentiment on flavors of toothpaste, but not for seeking hidden disruptive opportunities.

What is a pivot?

When the product you release isn't gaining traction from your target market (or anyone else, for that matter), at some point, you have to concede that it's just not working and rethink your game plan. This is called a pivot. Pivots can happen in the early stage of building your startup, but they can also happen way, way down the road after many large fundraising rounds.

Groupon had a great pivot early on when it realized it would be stronger at organizing people around daily deals than around social causes. Unsurprisingly, two-for-one pizzas have proven to be more attractive to consumers.

For the interviews themselves, you want to have quick demographics for each person. These are best when they aren't just primary indicators like gender or age. Seek out quickly measurable quantitative questions from your interviewees. If, for instance, your food delivery app is targeting people who are too busy to cook because of their demanding careers, make sure the people you interview all have demanding careers. Ask how many times they go to the grocery in a month or how often they cook—simple numbers that allow you to compare your interviewees and see if a characteristic is skewing the results of the more in-depth interview questions.

In the Solution Interview presented in Running Lean, you follow a similar script to the Problem Interview, but this time, you've earned the chance to talk about the ideas you have that can solve their problem. The Problem Interview involves directly asking the participant how much they care about the problems you're presenting them with. The Solution Interview involves a demonstration of some kind, which you follow by asking the participant how much they'd be willing to pay for the product. o

Putting Theory into Practice

The customer discovery process is designed to find a genuine problem and identify the solution most likely to solve it in a way your customers will like. But hypothesizing about doing something and actually doing it are two completely different things (just think about all the times you intended to do X and wound up doing Y when the day came). Even if your customers like and praise your solution, it doesn't mean they'll necessarily use it once it hits the virtual shelves. That's where product/market fit comes in. When your first barebones product is released into the wild (as a Minimum Viable Product, or MVP—see the next chapter), you start measuring what your users do and how many there are. This is essentially Blank's idea of seeking customer validation by releasing the product. The Pirate Metrics and One Metric That Matters frameworks in Chapter 8 can help you set goals and measure progress.

It's tough to say exactly when you've reached product/market fit. Like success itself, different people measure it differently. But just because it's fuzzy and subjective doesn't mean it doesn't matter. Startups have more pressure from investors to not just show a problem and solution but also demonstrate compelling product/market fit (however they define it) before they invest. The access to open source tech and cloud infrastructure make startups easier to build, so there's less preventing a startup seeking investment from showing product/market fit. (Since last year's impressive growth curve can be this year's flatliner, sophisticated investors are continually raising the bar in fundraising).

Working toward product/market fit comes after problem/solution feedback, but there's one step in between the two. You need to build a something tangible, whether it's an early version of the workable application or a simple representation of the functionality you will offer your users.

The next chapter will dive deeply into how to build effective prototypes and MVPs to more quickly and effectively understand what your users are interested in. Most of all, you're working to reduce the amount of time you spend developing early versions of your product and to not get stuck tinkering in the garage too long, even after you've gone out to learn from customers. ●

DES TRAYNOR

Co-founder
Intercom

With a background in user experience, Des Traynor leads marketing and strategy for Intercom, one of the fastest-growing and most innovative communication startups to connect a business with its customers.

ELLIOTT ADAMS Intercom is very successful because it's so unique and because it's solving a problem people didn't realize they had, in a sense. How did this come about?

DES TRAYNOR In 2007, the four founders of Intercom had a consultancy called Contrast, and we were very much inspired by this Basecamp style of having a consultancy and building a side product.

The project was called Exceptional, and it had thousands of users and was making money. It wasn't a smash hit, but it was definitely popular. We were just four founders in Dublin, and the problems and the pains we felt all trickled out of Exceptional. Obviously, being in Ireland, you're not in amongst your customers.

EA Sure.

DT I often thought Dublin looked like a street in San Francisco where we had more customers than we did in all of Ireland. We had this physical divide from our customers, but it went so much deeper than that. In 2007–2009, the web and startup world wasn't very mature. There was no Stripe. A lot of technology was missing, so most people's understanding of their customers was either an email list, which wasn't all their customers, or it was a PayPal dashboard, which was actually a list of active subscriptions. Everyone was widely out of touch and out of sync with reality in the sense of what people were doing with your product. We had thousands of customers, and we didn't know who the hell they were. And finding the customers

who used us a lot would involve asking Ciaran, the CTO of Intercom, "Okay, can you pull an SQL export so I can get all these email addresses?" Then, if you wanted to talk to those people, you take this new export, run it into a Campaign Monitor and you write them an email, and then all their replies go into your Gmail. There was no good, structured way of dealing with six or seven hundred people replying. It just occurred to us progressively that there had to be a better way. The language I use to describe it now is not perfect, but it's a lot more mature because we've been marketing Intercom for five years. But at the time, it was a very raw intuition that this just needs to be easier. Talking to your customers was a nightmare. The real and frustrating thing was that just talking to only your active customers was a seven-step process.

EA Was there an inspiration from anyone in the enterprise realm?

DT At the time, we were actually quite inspired by a coffee shop in Dublin we were at, a company called 3FE, 3rd Floor Espresso. They were just starting, and Colin, the guy who runs it, was the most in-touch-with-his-customers kind of person we'd ever seen. I realized over time, Colin was not dealing with email lists. If he wanted to try out a new bean, he was not sending people SurveyMonkey links. He was just asking people, "Hey, how's that coffee?" Which, today, we call in-app marketing, or in-product marketing. He was talking with people in a store about the thing they were consuming in the store.
The very first iteration as Exceptional had this little star, which is our logo, that was in the photo of the

product. One day, the star had a little note pop out that was apologizing for downtime. It was just like, "Hey! This is happening!" We realized it was so much easier to talk to our customers than anything we did before. From there, we built in a way to respond. We thought, what if our customers could reply? What if we could message some, but not all, of our customers? What if we could message them only at certain points of the day? What if we could do all of that through email? Today, you can sort of see how Intercom rolled out of that. But the key realization was knowing who your customers are and how talking to them is probably the most important thing you do as a product creator, so it needs to be really, really easy. That's what Intercom is: our contribution to making it easy.

EA With all things in this space, when you guys get success, everyone notices. Everyone's like, "Let's build our own Intercom, let's add our own Intercom."

DT Yeah, "Let's rip off Intercom."

EA Sure, or make Microsoft's version of Intercom.

DT Yeah.

EA So, just generally, how do you stay competitive in that way?

DT When we think of competitors at Intercom, what we actually think is there are a few direct actual pixel-per-pixel ripoffs. It's very uninspired and an awful waste of human capital. It really disappoints me. But for the most part, when we think of actual, credible competitors, it's rarely the whole Intercom thing. It's like, oh, we're like a help desk, but now we've added in your little bubbly thing. Or, "Hey, we're email marketing, but we've added in a way to push an in-app message." So, people compete with us as a help desk but not as a marketing tool or compete with us as a marketing tool but not as a help desk. Our vision is basically making a tool that can help a business person do everything that needs to be done. That often leads us to times where we're doing things that look slightly

and they had their own original slant to begin with, so we obviously respect them. But our question is, how can we make business owners, product managers, support managers, and frontline staff feel more connected and know every need-to-know to do their jobs? We only really think of it from that point of view. What is the job they're trying to do, and how do we make it as easy as possible or as fast as possible or as cheap as possible for them to do it? And that's kind of it. I know it's not a great answer as in, "Well, we have

DT Oh, yeah. That's very much on the road map. You can actually do it today, but we are going to make it easier. But the stuff that's exciting to me is anything that can make the human connection richer. I think our product team is way more likely to look at Snapchat for inspiration than a helpdesk system. That said, we're very aware. Inside every company, there are two products. There's the innovation, and there's the table stakes work functionality. When you start, you may only focus on innovation because you need to get your brand out there. You need to sort out what you're doing and what you're about. I think for the last while, we've definitely been doing a bit more of the latter.

"Inside every company there are two products. There's the innovation and there's the table stakes work functionality. When you start, you may only focus on innovation because you need to get your brand out there."

irrational. We might spend months building a really great emoji picker. Our whole belief is that messaging is the way forward. Messaging is getting expressive, and anything that becomes the normal way for humans to communicate with other humans is what Intercom needs to do.

So, the way we stay competitive is by not looking at it like, "We need to take care of Zendesk or Help Scout." I mean, they're all great companies with great products,

this one little tactic that gets us ahead of competitors," but that's honestly how we think about it.

EA You're not just building a ton of random stuff. You're just doing what you do really, really well.

DT Yes.

EA What's exciting for you as a next channel or next step? Do you have GIFs on the road map, for example?

How could we use video to connect businesses and customers? How could we use audio to connect businesses and customers? How could we use annotations and drawings and heartbeats from a watch? What can we actually do that will make people really feel connected with a business or with a customer? That's the tale of two products inside of things.

EA Do you do follow-up through these other unique channels?

DT We're actually working on that right now. The best way I would phrase it is the way we tend to think about these things is by what feels right. You're interviewing me, and at the end of all this, we are going to conclude the interview. What would feel more natural? We just say, "Hey, how was that? Was it okay?" Or would you send me a survey tomorrow or an email later on, or would you shoot me a text message? The reality is, different things are appropriate. If I had to just mic drop and leave, you are not going to come running after me saying, "How was it?" So, I think the way you have to think about these things is by what is the most natural way. Ultimately, our mission is to make internet business personal. Personal means appropriate to the person and the circumstance. If you're having a live chat session, and we were shooting messages back and forth, and I answered your question, an email kind of feels weird because it's an orthogonal direction to come in at, as opposed to just a natural conclusion. I'm like, "Hey, Elliott, just checking in. If this answered everything, can I just ask you to fill out this form?" And a little form pops open. Can you fill it out in context? I could argue that would work better and perform better when it's actually the right thing to do.

EA Right.

DT Versus other circumstances, where we could be talking over the course of three days while we're trying to figure out some complex issue on your side, and at that point, maybe an email is more appropriate That's honestly how we think about it. I don't know where I'll fall out on this exact thing. Maybe there will be options, maybe there won't. Who knows? But I think the guiding principle is always what feels right from a personal perspective.

EA So, different channels make sense for different customers and situations?

DT Absolutely, we have no opinion on channels. We've created one proprietary phenomenal channel, which is the in-app stuff, but we absolutely support email, we support Facebook, and we support Twitter. We don't really mind how businesses and customers want to communicate. We just want to make it great on all sides. And we're about to add some SMS capabilities soon as well, but your analysis is totally correct: different mediums for different people and different circumstances. To give you a very simple example, you could start a chat, but then it gets really serious, like, "Oh, well, the order's going to be $4,000." You might want to loop in your CEO, and that might happen by email because maybe that's how they work. We think it's dangerous to take an opinion on channel because obviously, we have b2b customers, b2c customers, we've got marketplaces, enterprise, mobile apps. We don't get to decide. We do our best to make sure that all the richness of Intercom is available in all the various means, but we can't build an emoji picker into your email client. Hopefully, you already have one, but that is genuinely how we think about it. It is, to the best of my knowledge, the only actual omni-channel communication system for businesses and customers.

EA Are there any thoughts on helping your business customers have a sense of what channels work for what customers?

DT Our best guidance is that we have seen a significant increase in performance when you talk to people inside your product, specifically when you're trying to get them engaged and show them your new features. That just makes sense. If you're in my coffee shop, the chances of me getting you to try coffee is much higher than me emailing you about coffee, right?

Similarly, the chances of you getting someone to download your book are much greater when they're on your site. There's a lot of intuition and actual data that backs up in-app outperforms, but it's not perfect for all circumstances. You can't talk to inactive users, for example.

EA And are you integrated with services where users seem to be migrating, like WeChat or WhatsApp?

DT No, not yet, but they're all things we look at. When we look at integration partners, we look for either a large volume of requests on our side, or we look for it to be a good experience for the end user. Our customers go through us, and whenever that makes sense, we're into it. That's where our Facebook move came from, and WhatsApp could be a candidate, but again, the story's yet to be written about WhatsApp. Well, actually, how formal or how serious they want to take customer service as a channel, if you like. But for sure, if it's relevant, we'll be there. ●

JON STROSS

Co-Founder
Greenhouse

After college, Jon Stross found his way to San Francisco and began working inside of startups, which led him through acquisitions and an IPO. He started Greenhouse to help businesses better hone their process for finding the most crucial asset they have: their employees.

ELLIOTT ADAMS You've done everything from baby websites to enterprise sales software, how did you land on tackling recruiting with Greenhouse?

JON STROSS That's a good question. I've never been one who's about the whole domain thing. It has to be the thing that I know everything about. I mean, I don't know squat about pregnancy or babies. I have a baby, but I still don't know anything.

As we were figuring out our ideas and brainstorming, we interviewed tons of companies and people in pursuit of a different business. What we saw over and over again is when asked what their biggest challenge was, every leader would say recruiting people and talent. "It's the biggest barrier in my business. I can't get the people I need."

In response, I would ask them what they were doing to solve that. And they'd say, "Oh, we're doing this and we're doing that." Well, that's not going to work. And so we both sort of realized that my co-founder Dan (Chait) and I had each had this experience in building teams, even though we weren't recruiters.

EA You'd done that when you were expanding Baby Center after it was acquired by Johnson and Johnson?

JS I had to create this whole system. How do I hire editors and salespeople in twenty countries? I mean, I don't know anybody in Kuala Lumpur.

I made a whole system to find them, interview them, hire them, onboard them, and manage them. Dan's partner

had built a huge engineering firm, and they were hiring programmers in New York, London and Sydney. And so, we both built these recruiting machines and we realized it's not rocket science. There's no secret. It's hard, but once you do it, it's this huge weapon, and you know you can quickly and consistently bring on the very best people. Most companies don't have it, that was the business idea right there.

I also knew we started from that problem statement of more and more companies realizing that people and recruiting are strategic advantages, not an administrative function to be managed for cost. Once a company realizes that, what tools do they need to help them achieve their goals? We eventually realized that we had to build what's called an applicant tracking system, but we didn't start from there. We didn't start from this place of applicant tracking systems being terrible and "I'm going to make a better one," which is where all the rest of them started from. But there have been hundreds of these things, and they typically start from a recruiter starting a business and saying, "I hate my ATS. I'm going to build a better one." And so, they would build something that's kind of incremental or is a reaction to their old ATS.

EA How did you approach it?

JS We started with the problem statement of: "I don't really know what an ATS is." I don't know what it does. I don't know why people hate it, but I know that most companies are terrible at recruiting, so by definition, it's not solving the problem I'm going to solve.

> "The problem we're solving is not solved. Whatever the tracking systems are doing, they're not solving that, and that kind of led us down the path of creating a very different product."

EA I'm trying to imagine what happened before you had this epiphany. What was the conversation that led to this?

JS We kind of knew we were going to do a business product. We weren't going with a consumer idea. We were brainstorming different ideas and going in and talking to people with the question of, "What are the biggest problems?" You hear this every time. We were going down the path with a couple different ideas, and eventually, we decided those ideas were not good. We weren't passionate about them. They weren't coming together.

We kind of stepped back and said, "What do we keep hearing about?" Yes, everybody struggles with talent. One of the biggest disconnects in business is how much people say talent is important and how bad they are at it. And so, why don't we help people be good at recruiting? And that's kind of opened up this very rich vein that we've found ourselves in.

EA So, you went in without trying to solve the applicant tracking issue. You just went in and were kind of broadly hearing what their issues were and then trying to find a thread through that, is that right?

JS Yes. We were very naïve about the applicant tracking system market. We knew it existed, and we knew everybody hated their ATS, but we didn't know why. I don't think I've ever used one. We figured that the way we define the problem—where the problem exists is that everybody's so bad at recruiting. The problem we're solving is not solved. Whatever the tracking systems are doing, they're not solving that, and that kind of led us down the path of creating a very different product. Eventually, we did have to go build all the ATS stuff that every other ATS had.

But it helped us build a very different opinion in the product, which allowed us to have a very different positioning, and that was very helpful right out of the gate.

EA Once you found the problem, how did you make a decision as to how you could do this better?

JS Most of it was in my co-founder Dan's head. He had built this recruiting operation at his previous company, and so he pulled it apart, found some commonalities, and figured out what was what. Then we read books and

blog posts and did all this research to find out what good recruiting looks like. It's not that mysterious. You can talk to the folks at Google, and they will tell you they tried all the algorithms and none of that stuff worked. It's like a basic structured interview. There are basic factors that you should follow. Read any of the books. They all say the same thing.

Why doesn't everyone just do that? We thought, "Oh, that's the problem to solve." So, we went through a whole process, then, of doing a startup as lean as we could. We built the first product prototype, literally, in paper. We sat down with people, with all these note cards and flashcards, and built the experience in our heads out.

We had people that we talked to that in ten minutes, you'd see the lightbulb go on, and they'd say, "You could do it that way? I think I'm going to change how I recruit because of the last ten minutes."

EA Wow.

JS Actually, anybody who thinks about it a lot will come to the same conclusion. You should write down the criteria that you're looking for in the person, per each interview, and then you should figure out which of the criteria you're testing for.

As you're preparing to look at job applicants, you should prepare an interview beforehand that tests for those criteria. If it's a behavior or personality trait, ask behavioral interview questions. If it's a skill, ask them to demonstrate the skill. If it's a qualification, ask them to

prove that they have that qualification, and then verify it again later. You can structure out a process where suddenly, every recruiter knows their role. Every recruiter prepares what it is they're looking for and how they're supposed to find it, and for every interview they do, every candidate they meet, they do the same interview. It takes all this pressure off the interviewer, and it actually provides a much fairer way to interview.

After we built a paper version, and we saw the light bulb go on, we went to General Assembly, and we said, "Can we teach a course called How to Make Hiring a Strength of Your Company?"

Just to see if anybody would show up, right? So, they posted it, and the next week, thirty people showed up.

EA That must have felt encouraging, right?

JS We were amazed. We thought we'd better come up with something to say, and so Dan got up there and basically did a song and dance for three hours. People thought it was amazing. And two years later, some of those same people have said they bought our product, which is so cool.

That class at General Assembly was basically where we did informal user testing of what stuff works and what doesn't, and we saw who was interested. People showed up from small companies, big companies, recruiters, hiring managers, all different places, and we taught it a couple of times until we felt like we had kind of milked that dry.

We figured out that we had something there. At which point, we said, "Let's start the company." But all that was before we had a company or a name. Once we decided to start the company, we went through the whole song and dance of raising money, hiring people, and building a product.

Even with all that planning that we did, all that customer development, research, and making sure we really thought this early version of the product was the right thing, we pretty quickly—shockingly quickly—had a product that frickin' Pinterest bought. They said to us, "You guys don't even have a website." We were like, "Yeah, we didn't build a website yet. We're still building our website, which is kind of crazy." And eventually, they said to us, "We're going to dump the industry leader for you guys." Like, holy shit!

EA Wow.

JS Our early ramp was shockingly fast and easy. It just happened. We had all this scale, and people loved it. We raised all this money, even though early fundraising was hell. But once we got through that, we were living on inbound leads. Since we didn't have a website, people would have to approach us in order to see the product they'd heard about. We didn't even have salespeople.

EA That's a great story of really nailing the customer need.

JS What we found is that you've got to figure out your unique setting. Who the hell needs another applicant tracking system? But you need to figure out that unique thing that makes somebody want it. From there, once

you have product-market fit and you want to go scale, figure out how to scale marketing, sales and product, and customer stuff and everything.

> "Since we didn't have a website, people would have to approach us in order to see the product they'd heard about. We didn't even have salespeople."

There's sort of a playbook by price point, whether you charge $1,000 a year versus $10,000 versus $100,000 versus $1,000,000. There's no right or wrong answer, but whatever price point you're at, there's a playbook. Some VCs completely get that, and they know exactly what to look for. They know who has it and who doesn't, and which things are going well and which things aren't. A lot of VCs don't have that, so we were pitching to a lot of folks who were not SaaS investors, just general investors.

Social Capital and dedicated SaaS investors like Benchmark and Thrive, they asked such good questions and they understood the dynamics of the business so well. The metrics that they asked for were really different than generic VCs. When they talked to me, I could see why they were asking for the things they were asking for, and there were a bunch of things that were good about our business that we didn't even realize because we didn't know the benchmarks, you know?

EA Do you recall any of the things they asked for that you were surprised by, but then saw their relevance later?

JS I think there was one … probably Series B or C. They were looking at what the average contract length of the renewal was. They said that when people sign up for twelve months and then come back to renew for thirty-six months, that's a really good sign, and they noted that people do that with us all the time. At the time, we just thought it was cool. But now, a couple of years into it, we can see that it's really great when people do that.

At the beginning, when you're doing renewals and you're on this huge growth curve, the amount of renewals you're doing at any time is tiny because it's basically a function of where you were a year ago. And it's clear, in any month, you're way bigger than you were a year ago. And so renewals seem so small, but a couple of years into it, you realize you are set to renew $20 million. That's a giant business. ●

LOIC LE MEUR

Co-founder
LeWeb

Loic Le Meur has been a well-known bridge from Europe to the rest of the startup world, most notably for his pioneering LeWeb conference. He was an early investor in LinkedIn and Evernote, among many other startups. He's taken his experiences from building LeWeb to create Leade.rs, his platform connecting the people shaping the future of technology and more, with avenues to spread their message.

ELLIOTT ADAMS I'm interested in how LeWeb came about and its effect on the European startup ecosystem.

LOIC LE MEUR LeWeb started in 2003 and was definitely the first in Europe. The other thing that existed at the time was Web 2.0 in the US, and we were definitely the first English-only tech conference in Europe. There was no TechCrunch Disrupt. TechCrunch Disrupt was launched three years later. What that brought was a very special atmosphere of early adopters. It was special because it was all English, despite the fact that it was in France, so it became truly European and included eighty-five countries and 4,000 people.

EA Wow.

LL Then for years, LeWeb was the oldest, and basically that first impact was that a lot of our attendees got inspired and launched their own, which is great. So, conferences like Slush or even Web Summit, which is now way bigger, got their inspiration from LeWeb. Now there are maybe a hundred tech events in Europe, all English, the same way. Before that, it was mostly local, so you would do your own events in Spain in Spanish, in France in French, and so on and so forth. So, that's the first thing. Then the second one is obviously the many successes that came from LeWeb. The first to come to mind is that Uber was invented there, and—

EA Sorry, Uber was invented there?

LL: Yeah. Travis Kalanick and Garrett Camp, the two co-founders, they were there and could not find a cab, and it was snowing. They created Uber right there. That's where they decided to launch it as a business. The other one that comes to mind is Waze. It won our startup competition, and I think there were only ten people. Two years later, they were acquired by Google for a billion dollars.

> **"The other one that comes to mind is Waze. It won our startup competition, and I think there were only ten people. Two years later, they were acquired by Google for a billion dollars."**

I'm not trying to attribute that to us, but it definitely helps. The other one is that Fred Wilson discovered and invested in SoundCloud at LeWeb. Now SoundCloud is a huge success. That's where Alex Ljung, the founder, established his funding.

EA So, it's a platform in that way.

LL Yeah. It's a platform for success, and you'll see what I'm trying to do with Leade.rs. That's basically

where it's coming from. People and events have a huge impact on discovering the entrepreneurs and inspiring them. I'm not saying we gave the idea to Travis and Garrett, but a lot of people get inspired by meeting other people and listening to the stories of other people. The other thing that it does is put a light on them so they get featured in the press, they get interviews, and then they get funding. So, I gave you the example of SoundCloud for funding. A number of things that have happened in ten years also generated, that I know of, ten weddings. People met there and got married.

EA So, one overall point here is that this created a forum for a lot of people who were not in California, right? This seemed to very much impact the internationalization of the industry.

LL Exactly.

EA You said it was the only English-speaking event that really had prominence at the time when you began.

LL All English. It was a good sign my first year that the French president and the Senate were there. They asked, "Why is it not in French?" But I held it in English. It's international or it's not.

EA And you felt like it'd run its course?

LL No, we sold it and it became something different, so we decided to stop. It's good to start from scratch and do it differently. I think it did what it had to do, though. It inspired a lot of events. Now there's a hundred tech events in Europe.

And so Leade.rs is the tool I actually dreamt of while I was curating LeWeb. I've dreamt about that app or tool as my two hats: one hat is the speaker, myself, and I probably invited 2,000 speakers on stage over those ten years at LeWeb. I've always thought that there was a tool to be created for speakers to know what they are invited to. If you're invited to LeWeb, or you're invited to Slush, here's what it is, here is who went and who goes as the audience. Basically, information about the event. If it's free, why should you care? If you're invited to TED, you don't ask for money, because it's the best exposure in the world. But if you're invited to that SAP event in central Germany, it's maybe not that much for your reputation, but they say they pay you $20,000.

Between those two, there is a whole range of events, and it's very difficult as a speaker to be aware of what to do because it's difficult to promote yourself or know if they're good or not. So, number two, as an event organizer, the way I would discover people is by going to TED and going to Davos. That's why I love doing it. I get to meet people all day long. I would read the site and then I would add them to a Google Doc. From that Google Doc is how I would record people I've met and want to invite to future events. That's how TED does it too.

And then you hold your event, and everything goes into the trash, and you start all over again next year. There is no central database of speakers to begin with, so what Leade.rs starts with is a Netflix of speakers. Basically, we're building a database. We have 2,000 profiles in it: everybody who spoke at LeWeb.

EA So, it's like a LinkedIn for events and speakers to connect?

LL There is much more than what you find on LinkedIn. There are videos and photos, where they spoke, and their affiliations. So, there are young Global Shapers in Davos, for example. We added, like, a hundred affiliations, like Nobel Prizes and Fortune 40 under 40. Basically, I did my homework by adding all of mine, and now we're starting to invite curators of events all around the world who have the same problem, showing them the tool, and saying, "Hey, I'm solving my own problem, and I know you have the same. Would you like to contribute? Here is my network. I'm giving it to you. Do you want to add

> **"And then you hold your event, and everything goes into the trash, and you start all over again next year. There is no central database of speakers to begin with, so what Leade.rs starts with is a Netflix of speakers."**

yours?" We are already working with twenty-five of our event organizers.

So, SXSW—we have an official Leade.rs session there for a thousand people. At Singularity University and Web Summit, we have Leade.rs sessions in all of those events, so right now, it's confidential for curators, if you see what I mean.

What we're building next is a booking system. Inside, you'll be able to say to the event organizer: "I want AI. Here is who we have on AI. I want to see if they're available." You select them, and then you have a booking system which is very much like Uber, where instead of an Uber driver, it's a speaker. We're going to enable a whole long tail of speakers who, before, would have never been discoverable.

EA And is the platform accessible both ways? Can an event open up submissions, and I can say, "I'd really have something great to talk about at that event, let me pitch them"?

LL Both sides. We decided we are the partners of the leaders. I call them leaders, not speakers, because speaking, for me, is just the first step. For example, if you're a shitty event which has a bad reputation, we won't let you contact everybody. We want to bring quality; otherwise, it's going to be a mess. But just

to give you perspective, where we're going, speaking is one. Then we'll add press requests. We'll book interviews, press interviews, etc.

EA And you have all these different enterprises you might be engaged in but you're not in business with.

"We decided we are the partners of the leaders. I call them leaders, not speakers, because speaking, for me, is just the first step. "

You can't be doing all those things on your own, right? It's almost a new profession, in a way, to be this multi-sided. Maybe Leade.rs is one way of doing it, right?

LL Absolutely. This is all enabled by online tools. People can just become brands themselves, something that was impossible before. We're starting by trying to disrupt all the agents' businesses, which is very old fashioned, has intermediaries, and is not efficient. I've not met a speaker who likes his agent.

EA It makes sense to me, and it seems like this is almost a new archetype. For example, say you're a scientist at a university. You don't just put out papers,

you write a trade book, and you also do some speaking and some consulting.

LL Exactly. You see where it's going. It's speaking, press requests, book interview requests, then maybe someone will

want to write a book themselves. Then, we find a way to help them with editors, and maybe they want to raise funding, whether they're social entrepreneurs, they need donations, or they need to be connected to business angels like we did with Alex Ljung and SoundCloud. The long-term view is a platform for success for those people, helping them be discovered. This is going to be my next ten years, like LeWeb took about ten years. It's going to take time. ●

TESTING YOUR SOLUTION

"Striving to better, oft we mar what's well."
William Shakespeare

With a clear indication you've found a desirable solution to a problem in your customers' lives, it's time to start testing the market with prototypes and Minimum Viable Products (MVPs). Although the two terms are often used interchangeably, each has unique features and a specific function in your startup's journey. In this chapter, you'll learn their respective value.

We'll show you:

• *The differences between a prototype and an MVP*

• *Four examples of prototypes that can effectively demonstrate the value of your product to your customers, and how to use them to evaluate your product's effectiveness*

• *The key characteristics of an effective MVP*

• *How to design an MVP that is small, affordable, and quick to release*

TESTING YOUR SOLUTION: PROTOTYPES AND MVPs

If you want to make sure your startup is on the right track, you need to talk to your customers. You don't want to jump in too soon without gathering some evidence and validation of your hypothesized customer issues. In fact, you shouldn't spend too much time building your solution, especially the initial version. Silicon Valley is littered with dead startups whose founders spent too long tinkering in the garage and didn't, as Steve Blank would say, get out of the building.

It's true: interviewing customers is much more grueling and monotonous than choosing a cool logo. But the same amount of diligent incremental work needs to be put into how you learn from customers about the product that you hope can solve their problems. The learning process is put on steroids when you make iterative versions of your product before you get the satisfaction of having something in the market that lives up to your dreams.

Like many concepts in the startup world, the terms "prototype" and "MVP" are often used interchangeably, but they shouldn't be. Both are early representations of your final product (if you ever build the final product), but a prototype is trying to show the potential of the product—it's not a functional version. It might not be as slick and optimally designed, but it will at least demonstrate the value proposition in some way. A Minimum Viable Product (MVP), on the other hand, is a very basic version of your product. Unlike the prototype, it will only include the essential features.

> **Like many concepts in the startup world, the terms "prototype" and "MVP" are often used interchangeably, but they shouldn't be.**

Building both prototypes and MVPs happens as soon as you have validated your customer's problems and are nearing the end of the search for the problem-solution fit, and MVPs specifically start you on the road to establishing product-market fit. After countless interviews with customers, you've established what their problem is. You walked through the specific problems you believe they have, rated them, and used that information to validate your hypotheses, perhaps by putting together a Lean Canvas. That's where building and testing prototypes and MVPs comes in. The MVP can also give you an early sense of whether you're headed toward product-market fit because, unlike a prototype, it's released out in the wild and has the chance to gain traction through these early and ugly iterations. O

Prototype

When most people hear the word "prototype," they think of the first working version of your product, but that's not the case. A prototype is only a representation of the final product experience that conveys the value of the solution you plan to offer your customers. Prototypes are useful for gathering qualitative data from the reactions and impressions of your customers, but with certain kinds of prototypes, you can also gather some quantitative data.

Here are a few different approaches to prototyping:

The landing page

A landing page is a simple, one-page marketing website that provides only the essential information. Laying out all of your product's selling points on a single page is a great way to test a customer's interest. When they visit the page you have the chance to explain what your product is, how it works, what it can offer them, etc. You can use headlines, graphics, or embed an explainer video (detailed next).

A landing page often includes a "lead magnet," or an incentive provided in exchange for the user's email address. This can be a related product, such as a promotional ebook you've written about the industry, or it could be something simple, like basic notifications of any updates about your product.

The primary way to quantitatively measure the effectiveness of your landing page is to compare the ratio of unique visitors to email sign-ups. However, that is only a binary comparison and doesn't give you data that's complex or vivid.

Explainer video

Most well-funded startups have a slick video presentation, full of custom graphics, that walks the user through every step of how the app works and its benefits. You can build one of these explainer videos for your product by using simple online tools made for this express purpose, such as PowToon.

The key to making an effective explainer video is storytelling. Even though your goal is to demonstrate the features of your product, it should feel more engaging than reading a list of product features on a web app's pricing page. Customers know what problems they are having, so you want to engage them in a narrative.

Acknowledge their problem, highlight their pain, and then demonstrate how compelling your particular solution will be for people like them.

One advantage of creating an explainer video is that it can be repurposed for several different uses. It can sit on your landing page, or you can email the link to prospective customers. It's also a really good idea to have it prominently featured on your social media feeds. You can then use your website analytics to see where traffic to a landing page originated from, for example, and how much of that is from a given email campaign or social media post.

> *Customers know what problems they are having, so you want to engage them in a narrative.*

Feature-rich prototype

Wireframes and mockups are sketches of your software's functionality, showcasing the features that users will interact with in the application. You can make a representative wireframe by going low tech and drafting with pencil and graph paper. For a mockup, where you want to show the elements exactly as they should be in the application, there are loads of intuitive and inexpensive software platforms, like InVision, that make it easy to create something that looks like a polished software product.

Whichever method you use, don't go overboard with the features. It's very easy to create a mockup of your app that has all the important components without overdoing it with the bells and whistles. You want the people evaluating your feature-driven prototype to base their reactions on the few critical features that you're trying to test now, and not get distracted by all the functions tied to less crucial hypotheses that you can test later. Think back to your earlier customer interviews. What were the problems most relevant to your users? Those are the only ones your wireframe or mockup should seek to get feedback on.

While a landing page lets you collect quantitative data by measuring how many people are interested enough to share their email address, your feedback from your wireframe or mockup will be qualitative since you're putting it in the hands of users, but you'll be manually recording their reactions and feedback. This is your chance to show off your product vision to the public. If it's an interactive software mockup built using InVision (that shows the user the experience but doesn't actually work), let them explore it, and pay attention to what they are drawn to.

Crowdfunding

Using a crowdfunding platform like Kickstarter or Indiegogo is a very direct way to test customer response to your product (in its conceptual form) before it is finalized. Crowdfunding is not a common strategy for funding software products because they have such low capital costs. Hardware and software devices, on the other hand, have done very well on these platforms. In fact, this book was funded through a Kickstarter campaign in October 2016, resulting in over 300 backers funding the project at over 350% of its original goal of $5,000.

Crowdfunding is a very intense process. Kickstarter and Indiegogo are great platforms, but you shouldn't expect the crowd to come to you. You'll need to bring your own crowd to light the match. That will spark further interest and spread to people outside your circle of contacts. In the spirit of moving fast and continuously learning, it's worth considering whether a Kickstarter page campaign could be essential to building momentum for your product or whether it would be more of a distraction. Again, it's less likely that a software-only project would benefit from the time and investment it takes to set up and promote a crowdfunding campaign.

Whether it's a crowdfunding campaign to build awareness and test the profitability of your idea or just a simple landing page to find out how many people will trust you with their email address and take the time to sign up, the overall goal of a prototype is to gauge interest. The point is not to put something out that is as usable as your product will be, but to express how it can solve your customer's problems. Use your prototypes to firm up your problem-solution fit, and then you can build an MVP to further validate that you've found the solution, and start gaining traction toward product-market fit. O

Minimum Viable Product (MVP)

"If you're not embarrassed by the first version of your product, you've launched too late."

Reid Hoffman, co-founder of LinkedIn

Unlike a prototype, an MVP is an early version of your software product. The prototype approximates and suggests, whereas a product actually demonstrates.

Three Basic Characteristics of an MVP:
Marty Cagan is a Silicon Valley thought leader on the subject of building products. He believes that MVPs should be three things above all: valuable, usable, and feasible. What this boils down to is that, in his words,

"People choose to use it or buy it; people can figure out how to use it; and we can deliver it when we need it with the resources available."

In the first instance, customers need the option to actually use it. The landing page prototype gives you an idea of what the product could be and gathers interest from prospective customers. A set of mockups only depicts the user journey through the application using static images. An MVP, however, actually gives people the opportunity to interact with the product and even to potentially edge the product out into the marketplace without any additional interaction or cajoling from you, as would be needed if you were showing them a series of paper mockups.

Users will be trying out your MVP by themselves. Since you're not going to be there to hold their hands, your users need to be able to intuitively grasp the concept of the product on their own. You'll need to work with good software engineers and user experience designers to build a good MVP. An MVP needs to be like all good design: 99% invisible.

"Ninety-nine percent of who you are is invisible and untouchable."

Buckminster Fuller, architect and inventor of the geodesic dome

You want your users to quickly and easily understand the series of steps they need to take in order to achieve the goal of the product.

There are two parts to the idea of an MVP being "feasible": you can build it in a short amount of time, and you're able to put it together quickly with whatever resources you have access to (e.g. design and engineering talent on your team, not an outsourced development firm). All startups have limited resources, even those with lots of funding or revenue. But it is certainly not just money that is limited.

There are only so many hours in a day, and you can only expect each person on your team to work productively for a fraction of them. There is also a limited amount of time any team member can put into these projects without distracting from other tasks that are important to the startup's viability and growth. Deciding which tasks are most critical and which ones can be put aside to focus on building your next MVP is a tough management call. You're better off getting an MVP up and running instead of wasting time fundraising too early or chasing investors that are only half-heartedly interested because you haven't shown any traction, but other cases might require you to use your judgment and hope it's sound.

How Minimal Should Your Minimum Viable Product Be?

You want people to understand how to use your MVP without any coaching, you want to get it out to the market as quickly as possible, and you want to be able to measure engagement with your product through usage and revenue. So now you have to ask yourself what features you will need to include in your minimal version to achieve those outcomes. There's an inherent tension here. If you include too few features, which is possible, you may not be able to properly gauge the market's interest in the product. On the other hand, include too many, and not only do you risk making your product less intuitive and engaging for users, but you also won't be able to get it to market quickly.

Brandon Schauer, former chief executive of groundbreaking software design firm Adaptive Path, has a great analogy that can guide you when building your MVP. In his well-known talk, "Cupcakes: The Secret to Product Planning," Schauer compares the two methods to two different approaches to selling a wedding cake. A startup releasing an MVP is a lot like a baker trying to convince the soon-to-be newlyweds to hire them to create their wedding cake. Both the founder and the baker are in the same situation: they need to figure out the best way to let potential customers get a preview of what the final product can be.

You're better off getting an MVP up and running instead of wasting time fundraising too early or chasing investors that are only half-heartedly interested

Method #1: Test Cake

Schauer breaks down the cake preparation process into three steps. First, the baker will prepare the cake itself. Then, they will add filling to the cake. Finally, the baker will spend a lot of time decorating the cake by piping intricate patterns using icing.

If you think of your MVP in this kind of linear cake-building process, then you have two ways to approach it, neither of which are terribly appealing. First, you could build a complete product. That would likely do a great job to entice customers—just imagine the baker giving you a full, three-tier wedding cake that you can sample—but you would spend an incredible amount of resources and it would take a very long time to get to market. This approach would, in effect, defeat the purpose of building a minimal viable product.

The second linear approach would be to start building your final product but release it as soon as you've managed to create something usable. This would be like the baker going through the first step of the baking process and presenting you with the dry cake that will serve as the base of the completed product. You can probably see what's wrong with this approach: no one likes dry cake all that much. If the baker presents you with a dry slab of cake as a way to convince you to hire them to create the centerpiece of your wedding, chances are you'll be looking for a new baker. Likewise, if you give your potential users a barebones version of your product, one that might barely resemble your vision, they're not likely to be convinced that you have a great user experience and interface coming just around the corner. In other words, you'll get the product to market on time and on budget, but there will be nothing to differentiate it and it's unlikely to build a groundswell of early adopters.

Method #2: Test Cupcake

Another option the baker has is to build small. Instead of giving you stage one of the cake creation process (the dry slab of cake), they can bake a cupcake. Baking a cupcake is a lot less resource intensive than creating a full wedding cake, but it gives the customers a great idea of what they'll be getting out of the final result: it's small, but it's still a delicious baked dessert with yummy filling and sweet icing on top. The baker doesn't have to put a team on making full-size preview cakes, and they don't have to lose customers by presenting them with an uninspired slab of dry cake.

This is really the best way to think of your MVP. It needs to be small, affordable, and quick to build, but it still needs to give your users a real sense of what you're offering. You're trying to gauge interest, so you need to put out a product that lets you figure out whether they are intrigued by a product like the one you are offering, only bigger.

> *It needs to be small, affordable, and quick to build, but it still needs to give your users a real sense of what you're offering.*

What's understandably difficult from a founder's point of view is letting go of the complete vision of the ornate wedding cake and being willing to put out the much less beautiful cupcake. You need to be able to get over this perfectionism. Success in startups requires being able to move fast, put things to market, and iterate them quickly. You can't wait around for the fully polished version of the product; by the time you release it, it will likely be too late.

These steps of solving for customer problems and learning about what users will engage with are tough, and they don't happen in a vacuum, but the hard work of testing and learning saves you precious time. It's essential to move as quickly as possible as you compete with all kinds of forces in the market that can get in the way of your startup's growth. In the next chapter, we'll look at the different forms of competition that your startup is likely to face. ●

ASSESSING

YOUR

COMPETITION

"Ignorance is the softest pillow on which a man can rest his head."

Michel De Montaigne

This chapter explores different sources of competition for your customers' attention, including the less obvious status quo solutions your customers have already found. Your startup will have to anticipate and overcome these challenges to have a chance of success, but it's not all bad news.

Here you'll discover:

- *Threats from "existing alternatives," taking into account the cost of switching to your product from whatever your customers already use*

- *How you are likely competing with larger, more established technology companies, as well as other startups solving the same problem as you*

- *Cost-effective ways to identify sources of competition for your startup*

- *How to use your competition to generate new ideas or evaluate whether you're on the right track*

ASSESSING YOUR COMPETITION

There are many forces that might draw people away from being your customer. Founders often just focus on companies with similar products, but there are other types of competition that can steal away your potential customer's attention.

The biggest form of competition is the existing alternatives. These are the things that people might already be doing to solve the problem your product is designed to help them solve. Existing alternatives are especially dangerous because they lessen the need for a customer to explore different products that could solve their problem, and increase the effort required to craft a customer acquisition strategy that will lure them to your new solution.

Threats from existing alternatives include:

You're fighting the mediocre status quo

For a startup building enterprise software, the biggest competition can simply be Microsoft Office and Google Drive—particularly spreadsheets. Since spreadsheets can essentially act as a relational database (rows of entries with columns of attributes), people use them not just to make accounting statements but also as ad hoc databases of information.

What this means for your startup is that they are probably less inclined to want to learn (and pay for) a new piece of software that will, in many cases, just feel like a shiny front-end to a simple database.

Let's think of an education technology (or "edtech") startup. They've come up with a grading tool that allows teachers to create assignments with descriptions, enter the amount of points possible, put in each student's results, and get their overall grade based on how much each assignment is worth.

Granted, this is not a pitch that would send a horde of tech journalists scrambling for an exclusive story, but it might sound attractive to a teacher: get rid of paper, compare students easily by assignment, and have an instant snapshot of what each student's grade is. The trouble is, of course, that this offers very little that can't already be done with an Excel sheet.

If time is the most precious resource (because it is finite and nonrenewable), asking for a customer's time is a huge ask.

In the early days of SaaS, before Google Drive was released, there might've been a stronger case for this startup because it could offer online portability. But today a startup must offer much, much more to go beyond a functional hack in Google Sheets. Since customers don't normally have the luxury of taking the time to compare all their options, those who need a business productivity tool are likely to simply reach out and grab Google Drive. By the time your app tries to find these ideal target customers, they've been using Drive in this stop-gap way for months or even years.

So you're asking them to change their behavior. You're asking them to try something new on the promise that it might be better, but by how much? You think it's a lot better. But first, they have to commit to learn the software before they can even decide whether it's ultimately worth the time and effort to switch.

Switching Costs

If time is the most precious resource (because it is finite and nonrenewable), asking for a customer's time is a huge ask. Switching costs are the things that would make it painful for a user to switch products. For a software startup, one example of a switching cost for their potential new users is that those users would have to get their data out of their current application (or their customized spreadsheet) and move it all into your new app. (If you did have a good solution for migrating their data, you'd need to make it obvious to the time-constrained customer this could happen easily and painlessly.)

Another example of switching costs that potential users of your app might face is the cost of learning new software, just like in the example of different spreadsheet solutions above. Added to this is the time they've already either sunk into formatting that blank spreadsheet into a bespoke, if clunky, tool or invested in training their employees to use the software that you're asking them to move away from. Plus, business customers especially will be cautious about a potential negative impact on their productivity or even worse, problems with their ability to please their customers as a result of your app.

Switching costs also apply to consumer apps. If you're an active Facebook user, you've been putting more and more of your data into your profile, plus building a larger and larger catalog of connections to people you know. To move to another social network, you'd have to recreate the content and connections that you'd been building up gradually.

This is an example of a high switching cost for a consumer that is prohibitive because Facebook has built such strong network effects. With a platform like Facebook, value increases as more people join and contribute, building ties across the network that can't be easily replicated because so many individual actions go into that giant mesh. Switching away from Facebook's incredible web of connections would be a very painful switching cost for your users if you tried to build a Facebook competitor. (Many credible teams have tried in vain to get past the user's switching costs to move them away from Facebook, often by offering a value proposition of better controls on privacy, but none have succeeded.)

The giants and the swarm

> **"A big company might study you for three months, then approach you and tell you they want to invest in you or partner with you or buy you, then vanish for six months, then come out with a directly competitive product that kills you, or alternately acquire you and make you and your whole team rich.**
>
> *Marc Andreessen, co-founder & general partner at Andreessen Horowitz, in "The Moby Dick Theory of Big Companies"*

While habit and convenience are real barriers to adoption for a startup, there can be real danger from existing players who might not be doing what you're doing yet also see big potential for the problem space that you're working in. Simply put, the largest software and web-enabled technology companies in the world are in the business of staying on top of the biggest opportunities in the world so their software empires continue to grow.

In 2006, Jack Dorsey and Evan Williams were working on a side project at their podcasting startup that became Twitter. They slowly built it up, had nice growth in 2007, and by 2008/09, people started to really notice (the Ashton Kutcher vs. CNN "race to a million users" formally ordained Twitter as mainstream and beyond the realm of the hacker hoodie). Along the way, they had a couple of so-called "micro-blogging" competitors, but none were able to build meaningful network effects.

Something more interesting happened as Twitter continued to grow (and eventually IPO on the stock exchange in 2013): they faced no strong competition from older and larger tech companies, and by the time any of them tried to jump in the fray, it was too late to stop Twitter. Google launched a short-lived product called "Google Buzz" that was essentially Twitter on top of Gmail, but it never caught on. (And while anyone can play Monday morning quarterback, it's unclear as to why Google's incredible customer reach through Gmail didn't push Buzz to success. The only thing that's for sure is that Buzz wasn't Twitter; it was Google trying to be Twitter.)

Twitter would face two huge adversaries if it launched as a fresh new startup today: the so-called "Big Five" technology companies and countless smaller competitors (there might be more Twitter copycats now, since the technological barriers to launching a fast Twitter clone are so much lower than in the mid-2000s).

The Big Five previously seemed content to dominate their own well-defined area of the tech landscape: Amazon for ecommerce, Google for search and ads (even phone tech), Facebook for social media, Microsoft for Windows and Office, and Apple for high-end computers and smartphones. Now they are competing to some degree on almost every major front. Facebook's ad business is a strong second to Google's. Google's Android smartphone OS has dramatically impeded the total dominance of the iPhone. Google Drive is gaining on Microsoft Office. Microsoft's cloud offering is targeting Amazon's hugely successful cloud computing platform. The list goes on and on. There is seemingly little room for a startup in these existing, established sectors.

For any new technologies, the Big Five are all pushing forward strongly. Using artificial intelligence and machine learning for voice recognition, for example, is something all of the Big Five are heavily invested in (e.g. Apple's Siri, Google Assistant, Alexa from Amazon, Microsoft's Cortana, Facebook's own voice recognition software).

As soon as you have an interesting idea and start pursuing it, it's likely that many other people around the world are also working on this. They don't know about you yet, and you don't know about them.

So an also-ran social media service with no perceivable product innovation (unlike Snapchat's user experience, which was wildly innovative before it was slowly mimicked) isn't going to rattle the cage of the Big Five these days, but if anything grows fast enough, they can take notice. And when they do, the three most common outcomes for startups who suddenly are on the tech world's radar are: get acquired, die, or eventually do an Initial Public Offering on the stock market. (These are also, not coincidentally, the primary outcomes of raising venture capital.)

Assuming that you're flying under the radar of larger competitors because you haven't hit a strong growth curve (or you're simply being underestimated), you still have company. There are many reasons it's easy for anyone to found a startup now, including cloud computing, open source tools, and simply better access to information. This is exciting to new founders because the means of production are so close at hand, but it's also a stark reality that you probably need to dig deep to find any true advantages in these areas (if you do, remember to note them in the "Unfair Advantage" box of your Lean Canvas so you can test them).

As soon as you have an interesting idea and start pursuing it, it's likely that many other people around the world are also working on this. They don't know about you yet, and you don't know about them. Neither of you might truly make it to market with a strong product, but others will if the space you're working in addresses a problem that's meaningful enough that people are willing to endure the costs of switching away from however they're solving that problem right now.

Time matters again: getting to market and growing fast are more important than ever. We've discussed the importance of getting started, but once your product is truly ready to be released, it's all about growth. O

How to Identify Competition for Your Startup

The status quo and big tech giants looking to expand are both real threats, but you shouldn't forget the obvious question of your direct competitors. It's important to know if anyone else is attacking the same problem using the same approach you are.

While you may not be able to readily identify any competitors, if you're in an industry or problem space that's meaningful, there are almost always more competitors than you initially think. You just can't find them because, like you, they are in early, semi-stealth mode. So, you have to turn over rocks until you find similar Protean startups crawling through the early-stage muck.

Here are some ways to discover and evaluate startups who are doing what you are:

The easily-overlooked Google search

This might sound ridiculously obvious. But you'd be surprised how many founders fail to find what's in plain sight by doing a simple search query the right way.

When you search Google, start with your overall value proposition. For example, if you are a subscription-tracking platform that helps customers know how many online subscriptions they have going at any one time, choose a search query your user might use. Don't search for the technical way that you offer it or the slightly unique way that your service solves the problem.

"Subscription tracker" is better than "monthly subscription bank account integration alerts."

And think of what's on the customer's mind when they go to search for a solution. "How do I keep track of monthly subscriptions?" can be better than "how to set up alerts for dormant subscriptions."

This might sound ridiculously obvious. But you'd be surprised how many founders fail to find what's in plain sight by doing a simple search query the right way.

Searching for a pulse on Twitter

Active startups that are moving forward and building a brand with customers will have some Twitter activity. It may be just one post or retweet a week, but they know they need to have something. Even as the usage of the service shrinks overall, Twitter still dominates the tech world's communication and acts as a de facto journal of record. If a startup hasn't posted to their Twitter in a year, something is up. There could be founder discord, money running out, or it's an early sign of death. (They could be lying low before a pivot, but it would be unlikely to not still try to engage users on Twitter in the meantime.)

The encyclopedia of Product Hunt

Every day, dozens of new apps, technologies, books, and other creations are posted to the startup world's daily leaderboard, Product Hunt. Its popularity is fueled by the desire of techies and investors to be the first to know what apps and services are launching that very day. In this way, it's as current a stream of what's coming out as you'll find online.

The site does some recommendations ("apps similar to X") but is also very useful as a search engine for startups. For the bill-tracking app, you could search "subscriptions" or "bill management," for example. Since it's limited to only Product Hunt listings, these simple queries have a decent chance of unearthing startups that might be directly competing with your solution.

There are also "Collections," where users group together products from the site into lists. This can be a great way to find products addressing similar problems as you or just operating in the same general industry or to the same customers, even though the solution might be very different than yours.

The giant cocktail party of AngelList

AngelList can be really helpful for a startup to find an investor and for investors to build their bets on the shoulders of more experienced (or at least famous) angel investors, which is one reason why there's so much activity on the platform.

Because it's so valuable to both startups and investors, you can find lots of young startups on AngelList who might be working on something in your space. But the picture isn't complete. Some startups throw an AngelList profile up as an afterthought and could be much more engaged than their profile shows. On the flipside, some startups are trying to use AngelList as their calling card—faking it until they hopefully make it. They've filled everything out, added photos and a video, listed their advisors, and generally have tried to make themselves seem active and alive.

If a competitor does share a lot of information on their profile—which is rewarded on the platform when you're looking to court investors—there's plenty to investigate: the background of the founders, their investors, and the other AngelList users who "follow" them. All of this can be a clear indication of social proof, the amount to which the people who align themselves with that startup are reputable and experienced.

The bottom of the app store sea

Both Apple's iTunes and Google Play are filled with millions of apps. Not always startups, these are often the product of one or two people who threw something together, often with a pretty mediocre logo, and submitted it to the crowded bazaar of an app store. The worst of these might have just a few downloads and a review or two, but they are still of great value to you in your search for signals around the problem that you're trying to solve.

While working on your subscription tracker, you search the iTunes Store and find an app with the unfortunate name, "What Did I Sign-up For? I Can't Remember, AGAIN!" Maybe it has a pixelated image of a stressed-out face encircled with flying dollar bills. Nothing about this app signals product or marketing savvy, but it does sound a soft beacon that other people are thinking about people losing track of how many subscriptions are billing their credits cards each month.

So look around: did anyone seem to download this app and rate it? How are the reviews? Reviews can have great insights; people say things like, "I really want to track my subscriptions, but this app is super buggy and I hate the logo being on my home screen." The problem could be there but the execution isn't yet right. O

Your Competitors Can Find You Too

Ultimately, the biggest danger for startups isn't mimicry, it's obscurity. You might have a fear of competitors (including the Big Five) finding you, but you frankly need to get over it if you want to survive. Unless you are selling to a very small number of very high-volume/high price-point customers, your customers will need to find you eventually. You can't expect to drive the outreach and stay in "stealth mode."

You can decide when and how to open the kimono, but it has to happen. And your competitors will find you the same way that you found them.

But don't lose hope. Startups think they need to be first to market; this is more often wrong than it's right. Competition can actually clear a path for you, make mistakes that you don't have to make. You might be in a race to scale up against a competitor who is almost identical (e.g. Uber vs. Lyft), but each small step they take before you do can be an advantage or a setback for them. For the monthly bill tracker app, a small competitor in the app store may have several reviews that consistently hammer a desire to get special alerts when a new subscription is over a certain amount. This misstep by the competitor can be a chance for you to move up user-defined alerts on your product roadmap.

Startups think they need to be first to market; this is more often wrong than it's right. Competition can actually clear a path for you, make mistakes that you don't have to make.

Your competition can show where you might be doing something right (if there's a trend toward a problem you're focused on) or where you're either doing something wrong or being radically innovative. You can't really know, so take the actions of other startups in perspective: they're just as prone to making mistakes and spending time on the wrong customer issues.

It's also worth remembering that a crowded and contested market can mean there's really something there worth fighting for. That's not always the case, but it can at least signal that other people see the issues that you do and consider them worthy of an investment of time and effort. This should reassure you that you're on the right track.

However, while it's important to look honestly at what competition you have, you shouldn't allow it to dictate every choice that you make. A better use of your time is to focus on growth and turning early users into ecstatic evangelists. Since growth is the foundation of a startup, choose to be action-oriented toward building and delighting your user base. We'll look at some ways to think about how to grow your user base in the next chapter. ●

GROWTH

AND

METRICS

"Never mistake motion for action."

Ernest Miller Hemingway

How do you know whether your startup is growing?
More importantly, how do you know it's growing in the right direction?
Exponential growth is a primary goal for a startup, but it's easy to get
lost in "vanity metrics" instead of assessing your progress in the areas
that really count. This chapter dives into introducing valuable metrics
for startups and how to identify which ones should matter to you.

You'll learn:

• *How virality rarely happens by accident and why going viral offers no guarantee of success*

• *How, in the face of almost unlimited data, to identify the One Metric That Matters
  to your startup's success*

• *The five stages of Pirate Metrics, with suggestions for valuable metrics that tell you
  how your product is performing or contributing to your growth*

• *How to identify which acquisition channels work best for your product*

GROWTH AND METRICS

Startups have one job above all else: to grow. If your goal is to be a large, high-growth company, this will be crucial to your success. You need massive growth to attract investment, build highly beneficial economies of scale, and achieve network effects for your platform.

Traction is growth.
The pursuit of traction is what defines a startup.
Gabriel Weinberg & Justin Mares, Traction

There is a common misconception that high-growth startups grow by virtue of striking the mythical match of virality. But "going viral" without a plan or system to measure massive growth happens very infrequently, usually due to plain old luck. This myth of easy virality complements another one: "If you build it, they will come." There's a reason you speak with customers; identifying a problem and proposing a solution that users can get excited about is the basis of building momentum for your startup. It won't guarantee your success, though. As you're trying to grow your startup, issues like competition, market size, and simple lack of revenue or funding can still put your success in danger.

As described in **Chapter 7** (*Assessing Your Competition*), startups face competition from both direct competitors and indirect sources like a user's solution. It's often this indirect competition that is the most brutal. The opportunity cost of researching every single available option is astronomical for anything but the most extreme problems in life, so the consumer will simply settle for something that works well enough. This product is the best as far as they know (or care). It succeeds not because it's truly the best, but because it's the one that seems to be the best given a limited set of options.

Market size can also be a problem. High-growth companies need to expand at a rate unparalleled to any other kind of business, and they need a market big enough (measured by the number of potential customers or the potential amount of spending in that market) to accommodate that growth. Software companies that begin playing the role of a high-growth startup can soon discover they're selling to a market that doesn't have the capacity to help them grow exponentially.

Finally, the founders of a startup must be able to acquire their customers at a cost that allows them to have fast-growing margins. Any startup can reach consumers if money's no object, but no business can continue to spend more than it makes. A founder's job, and part of growing your startup, is to acquire and keep consumers at an affordable cost, ideally approaching zero.

So, just as the inspired founder who hasn't spoken with any customers before launching stands a high chance of having a product nobody cares about, the founder who doesn't know how to effectively reach their customers has a product that no one ever hears about. O

Which Metrics Matter?

Successful startups use metrics to measure growth (as all businesses should, in a way that's relevant to them), but software companies need to make sure they use the right ones. The problem with building a software startup is that there are so many options of things to measure. Everywhere you look inside your application, there are countless roads to travel, but few of these are actually worth measuring. Most of them won't be important indicators of what truly causes your business to grow.

Think of these useless indicators as vanity metrics. As the name suggests, these can make a startup feel good about its progress without actually indicating anything meaningful.

If you're building a web app, for example, there are many tempting vanity metrics. You can open Google analytics and see, hour by hour, how many hits, unique visitors, or page views your site is getting. You can see exactly how much time people are spending in the app. If you have a product in the app store, then downloads are of course exciting, as are ratings and signups within the app. A founder could be forgiven for being excited about seeing this early engagement, especially when it's from new customers and in real time. But as thrilling as it can be to watch people sign up for your app or rate it in the app store, this surface-level activity is probably not directly correlated with the metrics that move the needle on your company's goals.

> *Everywhere you look inside your application, there are countless roads to travel, but few of these are actually worth measuring.*

You might be thinking, "If startups need to grow, then aren't these improving metrics exactly what we should be looking for?" And it's true, growth matters—a lot. But startups shouldn't be measuring mere growth; they need to focus their efforts on a single, meaningful metric. O

The One Metric That Matters

So, which metrics matter for your startup? In *Lean Analytics*, Alistair Croll and Ben Yoskovitz develop a framework for determining the important elements of user behavior in your application, what they call the "one metric that matters."

The bedrock issue you want to identify is the single number in your application that most contributes to your success. Once you've determined what this measurement is, you make all other questions and metrics that appear in your product secondary. Collectively put on blinders for anything else that could distract from this core focus, as long as the team believes it is still the best indicator of growth. The benefit of using this one metric is it allows the entire team to align their efforts around product development and testing, leading to concentrated results and faster learning.

While it can seem like tuning out everything except a single measurement would make the development process more rigid, Croll and Yoskovitz argue the opposite. They say once that single metric is decided and agreed upon, it actually encourages experimentation. It gives the team a sandbox to work inside and makes them think creatively about how to push this number up—hopefully with a novel and extremely low-cost user acquisition tactic.

So now we can see what's wrong with instinctively looking at typical metrics like downloads and site visits without investigating their relevance to actual growth. These measure initial interest in the product, but not its ability to meet the customer's needs. It's easy to be satisfied knowing that people are looking at your site and signing up for your service, but that's only the beginning of what your engagement with your customer should look like. O

Metrics for Pirates

Dave McClure, co-founder of the startup accelerator and early-stage venture fund "500 Startups," developed a framework for the five stages that software startups need to shepherd their customers through. Playing off the phonetics, McClure has cheekily dubbed this approach "AARRR: Metrics for Pirates." The funnel starts off wide at the first step and gradually narrows as fewer and fewer users stick around and make it to the later stages of the customer journey. Here are the five stages your customers go through, starting with the top of the funnel:

This is the first step in your funnel—the initial connection between you and your customer. Through whichever channel successfully brought this customer to you, they are in some way engaged with you and your product (they have visited your site, downloaded the app, etc.). Users enter this first stage of acquisition on first contact with your product, but you also want to get them to come back repeatedly (which is where the later Retention stage comes in). Every successive step down the funnel asks for higher levels of commitment from the customer, and more customers drop off between each step.

Getting customers to your site is one thing, but getting them to sign up is another. The drop-off rate rises as you begin asking users to engage. Of the people who have poked around your product in the acquisition stage, only a small percentage can reasonably be expected to sign up, and an even smaller percentage will give you their credit card information in the final stage of the funnel, Revenue.

Retention

There's still a real danger of losing users almost as soon as they have formally engaged by signing up on your platform or downloading your app. After you've activated a new user, you need to take steps to keep them on board. Startups can raise retention by developing targeted email campaigns, for example, based on their users' relationship with the product, and building an ongoing conversation with their users to keep them active and engaged (and for community-based sites, contributing to the activity, which adds to the value for all users). Otherwise, the time, effort, and money spent getting users through the top of the funnel is wasted.

Metrics for retention

One key retention metric is churn rate, which is the rate at which users leave the app. Another is simply the engagement a user has with the product: how often do they return, how much time do they spend in the app, and what actions do they take while there?

A product with stronger retention has the chance to increase these retention metrics because there's a snowball effect. If users are coming back to the site and contributing to the community, building more virtual farms, or messaging more and more friends in the platform, they are less likely to leave because they're continually building more value into their experience.

Referral

The viral coefficient

The Referral stage is measured best with a metric called the viral coefficient, which at the highest level, calculates how many users are brought into the product by existing users. Like the alternator that keeps your car running, your viral coefficient can continually propel your growth. To find the optimal way to keep this number up, systematically isolate the groups of users and user behaviors that drive referrals.

Your existing customers can be your best channel for acquiring new, potentially great customers. Satisfied users will recommend your product to people they suspect will get value out of your service. These existing users are effectively handing you free prospects who have all the characteristics of a quality user for your product. Effective referral mechanisms, then, are gold. Although this is a peer-to-peer referral process, it is a kind of virality. Others are often built painstakingly by design, requiring a lot of testing and refinement with live users; the referral process, on the other hand, is what is known as a viral engine (see sidebar).

Revenue

Whether or not Referral happens, Revenue is the end goal for any customer who enters your funnel. You will likely spend money acquiring a new customer (even if you don't use a paid tactic and just amortize the cost of your development over the number of users), so you need to retain them long enough to cover your costs—and then hopefully long enough to make a large profit. O

We did anything possible just to get revenues so that we could grow and be a real business.

Mark Pincus, founder of Zynga

CAC & TLV

Once you have customers in the Revenue stage of your funnel, there's a critical calculation that all startups have to face: can we acquire users for less than the revenue they generate? Startups often don't spend enough time considering this crucial combination of two metrics: the Cost of Acquiring a Customer (CAC) and whether it costs the startup less than the Total Lifetime Value of a customer (TLV) they receive.

Many VC-funded startups fail because they spend incredible amounts of money trying to get more and more users, often because they hope it will spark virality and then result in cheap acquisition. Unfortunately, this doesn't happen, and they can end up spending far more on ads and other Traction channels than they could ever make from those users.

Choosing the Right Channels

Whatever metrics you decide to test, you will need a similar focus on the channels you use to acquire users in the first place. In Traction, Gabriel Weinberg and Justin Mares put forward a framework for finding the right channels to build traction. They know that startups tend to promote themselves through the same channels as other startups, like search engine optimization, content marketing, and online ads (aka SEM, or Search Engine Marketing). While these tactics can (and do) work for startups, high-growth companies often leave valuable and more cost-effective tactics on the table.

Weinberg and Mares list nineteen marketing channels that startups should consider. Some of these are unlikely to really pay off for the majority of startups, like offline advertising and trade shows. Startups with a relatively inexpensive product that they sell to a large number of users, for example, won't get much out of exhibiting at trade shows, given the low TLV compared to the expense (and remember, we're focused on pure user growth, not other potential goals like partnerships that might happen at a conference). But all of these can work for some startups as their primary channel for acquiring users.

The Bullseye Framework

Just like we don't really know what our customers want until we learn from them firsthand, we also don't know, without testing, which channels are effective at acquiring customers. Weinberg and Mares advocate using a framework for testing marketing channels that they call the "Bullseye Framework." It's a simple but effective way of narrowing down and building a consensus around what channels you're going to test, with similar benefits of team focus and alignment that come with the One Metric That Matters:

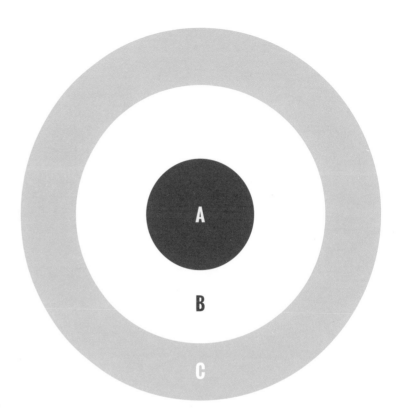

WEINBERG & MARES'
BULLSEYE FRAMEWORK
A - *inner circle*
B - *promising*
C - *long shot*

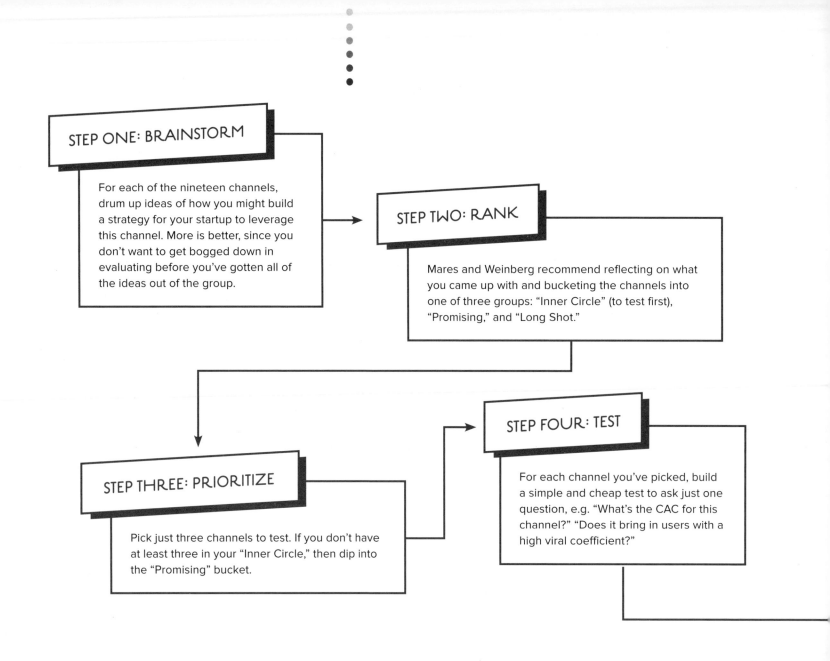

STEP ONE: BRAINSTORM

For each of the nineteen channels, drum up ideas of how you might build a strategy for your startup to leverage this channel. More is better, since you don't want to get bogged down in evaluating before you've gotten all of the ideas out of the group.

STEP TWO: RANK

Mares and Weinberg recommend reflecting on what you came up with and bucketing the channels into one of three groups: "Inner Circle" (to test first), "Promising," and "Long Shot."

STEP THREE: PRIORITIZE

Pick just three channels to test. If you don't have at least three in your "Inner Circle," then dip into the "Promising" bucket.

STEP FOUR: TEST

For each channel you've picked, build a simple and cheap test to ask just one question, e.g. "What's the CAC for this channel?" "Does it bring in users with a high viral coefficient?"

STEP FIVE: FOCUS

This is much like Croll's "one metric that matters": once you think you've found the right thing to focus on, double down on it with all of your efforts to see how useful it can really be.

Growth is necessary for a startup and in a perfect world, is compounding and constant. But the reality is that growth is a moving target. In your first year, growing users by 5 percent each month can be electrifying—until you talk to an angel investor in your sector and realize that you need a minimum of sixty million active users to begin to monetize your advertising revenue model.

So the imperative to grow is as big as the imperative to build something useful. It's possible to build something useful that no one ever uses, and it's possible to build something relatively useless that's pumped up to grow but then doesn't ever really establish virality because delighted users are few and far between.

You meet the imperative to grow by constantly recalibrating and testing to determine the most important metrics for your startup (whether it's CAC, viral coefficient, churn rate, or one of the many others) and finding ways to improve those metrics and gain traction. The experimentation of customer development continues through the entire life of a startup, both because you always need to understand what your customer wants and you need to seek it out, and because as a high-growth startup, you can never grow too much. ●

RYAN HOOVER

Founder
Product Hunt

Ryan Hoover's passion for tech and startups grew from an email list into one of the main hubs of startup activity on the internet. Product Hunt's daily dose of the newest productivity tools and online oddities is built around a passionate community that rivals most others online.

ELLIOTT ADAMS I've heard the first version of Product Hunt was an email list, how did it all start?

RYAN HOOVER It's actually a little bit ironic that I'm at AngelList now, because they also effectively started off as an email list. Product Hunt began as email, and the inspiration was that I like discovering new apps, new products, new things. My friends and I were always sharing these things, but we were sharing them on social media and text messaging and group chats, and I didn't know of any place online where there were other people who were all sharing these new products together. There was no single list of "here's what's new and cool in tech." The idea was pretty simple: how can we share these things on the internet with other people? The easiest path to do that in the very beginning was to build an email list.

I'm not an engineer, so even if I wanted to, I didn't have experience building Ruby on Rails apps or anything like that. So, I was sort of forced to be creative, forced to do something simple, and using email is kind of a great pathway to do that. But it's also still to this day, as much as people say they hate email, it's a great engagement channel. It's a way to deliver content to someone on a daily or weekly basis within their existing workflow versus building a website. They have to remember to go back to a website. In the early days, when you stumbled across a website, you rarely remembered to go back, even if you liked the experience.

EA If I'm sick of my Facebook, I just don't go to Facebook. But if I get sick of my email, it's because I have to be in my inbox all the time, right?

RH Yeah, exactly.

EA So, you were putting out a daily email with new products that people had submitted. Is that how it worked?

RH Well, I was actually using a service called Linky Dink. Ridiculous name, awesome service. The way it worked was I would basically invite these collaborators and people that would get access to be able to share links. Every day, it would automatically aggregate those links and then send that out to all the subscribers. I didn't actually personally have to choose the things. I didn't have to assemble the email. It was all automated from the very beginning.

All I did was invite the people. They were a combination of venture capitalists (because they were people who were always looking at new things every day), founders, and other people in technology that were in the ecosystem, who were always exploring and curious to find new things.

EA Obviously, it caught on quickly. How did it grow?

RH In the beginning, it was actually all people I had as either friends or people I'd built relationships with in the prior months or years. So, in the very beginning, I wasn't actively looking for people that were outside my own network. It was just people that I knew already. That's how it started. Fast-forward much later—the community grew and went well outside my network. That was very organic, but we did many things to facilitate that growth and build that community early on.

EA When did you decide to make the jump toward having a website?

RH It was maybe two or three weeks in. It was cool. People were using it and emailing me about how useful it was. After some weeks and multiple data points of "there's something here … people seem to like this thing," it was at that point when we realized we could turn it into something more than just email lists.

Email is great, but you're very limited by that structure. You couldn't really engage in comments and discussions because the curation mechanisms weren't there. The talk form itself is very limited. We couldn't inject other types of content. At that point, I realized we could turn it into a website and build something that people are familiar with. We didn't want to re-invent a new type of way to interact with people on the internet, but we wanted to look at what works in Reddit, in Hacker News, and on other platforms that people are familiar with, and model it after that, for the most part. It was also things like using the messaging mechanism and comments, and things like that were really pretty straightforward and technically a very easy thing to build, at least in the very beginning.

EA You said you had some organic growth, but there was also some awareness building. I'm curious what some of that stuff was.

RH We launched the site, and what I would actually do would be to look at who was signing up, and I would manually email a lot of people that were joining Product Hunt in the very beginning. When you sign up for a service, you get an automated email that says, "Hi, I'm the founder of the company. I'm so glad you're here…." I mean, we see these all the time, and we all know that it's automated and it's fake. It's not that I think it's a bad thing to do that, but it's definitely fake authenticity.

I would email dozens of people a day, and in the intro, it would be very clear that I was a human, and I would mention something like, "Oh, you work at Techstars" or whatever, and something else that clearly couldn't be automated.

What it did was build the base of our community and started growing it in a way that was kind of like when you go to a house party and you see a bunch of people that you know. There's some familiarity there. It's a more welcoming experience if you know all the people

> "It also made them feel a lot more welcome, more so than any other service that you sign up for, and that was the tactic in the very beginning."

EA That seems like a lot of work, but I assume it was worth it?

RH What that did was build some rapport, or it at least made Product Hunt more memorable for people. It also made them feel a lot more welcome, more so than any other service that you sign up for, and that was the tactic in the very beginning. Then over time, I would reply as a follow up on those email threads or reach out to people who were using Product Hunt often. Frankly, it's a very non-scalable tactic.

What we would do is ask if anyone they knew would like to register in Product Hunt, anyone that's also in technology that you think would like this as well. Because if they were using it, they'd clearly value it a little bit. So, we'd just ask them if they want to introduce me or forward it along to two other friends of theirs. Again, these are things we'd do that are not scalable.

there versus a random group of people you have no direct connection to. In many ways, it's best to build a community by enabling the community to invite and grow within itself organically.

EA That's awesome. You guys put in a lot of sweat equity.

RH Yeah, and it was, again, not scalable, but it's also the best way to grow an early community. Just certain elements of Kevin Kelly's article on a thousand true fans. In some ways, you just need to hit some sort of critical mass where it feels like there's enough activity, enough engagement, and a healthy discourse, and that's all you need to get to the next level. Very few communities get to that point, or if they do, they end up churning out users and they don't continue to grow. We also know that people are going to join that are never going to come back. No matter how great of a product you build, you can't have 100 percent engagement all the time, so you constantly need to grow the community as well. ●

VU VAN

Co-Founder & CEO
ELSA

Vu Van assembled an incredible team of artificial intelligence and machine learning specialists to help build a way to help people with their pronunciation when learning a new language, based on their native tongue. Her startup, ELSA, has big ambitions to change how people learn language, and she's been using ingenious methods of spreading the word about her startup since day one.

ELLIOTT ADAMS I know you were in Stanford's StartX program when you were in our first batch of the pre-accelerator program that I ran in San Francisco, but I wasn't sure of when you started raising money. Did you bootstrap for a while?

VU VAN When I started out, I bootstrapped for a few months. That was when I hired some people and paid out of my own pocket, but I didn't pay myself. I used my own money to pay for them for a few months. Then, I decided to raise angel funds by the friends and family round, so we called it a pre-seed. We raised about $250k then.

We used that money to pay others. I still didn't pay myself. I used that money to pay for others, until I needed to raise money again. So, I raised the another round about nine months after the pre-seed. That's when I started paying myself.

EA I know when you were in Startup Next, you were getting a ton of users on board. How you were growing your user base at first?

VV Before we released the product, we had a landing page, and we had about 7,000 people sign up on the waiting list within a week. I think that was the initial traction of the database that we had. Then, we did a few rounds of beta testing before we released the app. In the first release, we only opened for a few thousand people to test it. We had those people on the waiting list, and we said we'd email and test those few. When we publicly released, we were at SXSW—we launched onstage. We were the winner at SXSW that year, so I think that gave us some initial publicity, and we got 30,000 downloads in the first 24 hours.
EA Oh, awesome. How did you get 7,000 people going to the landing page in the first place?

VV Well, I started a Facebook campaign, and I called it "Love My Voice." I just wrote a note on Facebook about my journey of learning English, including some of the special moments in my journey learning English growing up, and how my voice matters. We hashtagged #LoveMyVoice, and then I started getting a few friends of mine joining the campaign. Just within the first twenty-four hours, I started writing people, asking, "Hey, can you write something about your English learning journey? #LoveMyVoice #ELSA"

> **"We got about a thousand people or so to sign up on that waiting list very quickly, because we just asked these people to post it on their Facebook post, which already had a lot of traffic."**

Back then, nobody knew what ELSA meant. We just had the name, but that's nothing, right? We just said to hashtag those two, and then just post it on your page. The campaign was really well received. We somehow got a lot more people writing about their stories than the few people that I asked for. I asked people who had a lot more followers or friends or influences, right? We got quite a bit of people doing these campaigns. We probably got around 100 in the first two days or so. People wrote very inspiring stories. Lots of people were sharing with that hashtag.

When we then came out, we just piggybacked on this campaign, and we said, "Hey, now ELSA is out to help you perfect your voice," or whatever. I can't remember exactly, but we just came out with a tagline, and we said, "This is the website." We had a very simple landing page. The

landing page said, "Hey, my name is ELSA. I'm here to help you speak English like an American," and then, "Sign up for early access." We just shared that one out. We got about a thousand people or so to sign up on that waiting list very quickly, because we just asked these people to post it on their Facebook post, which already had a lot of traffic. I think that's when we noticed people were actually signing. Initially, we only told people that we had access for about a thousand, but we had more than a thousand people signing up.

We figured out that we should do a referral, so we just changed the campaign twenty-four hours later to say, "Hey, now you're number 1,100 on the list. Refer five friends to be part of the VIP and escape the line," or whatever. That campaign worked extremely well. So many people started sharing. Just imagine 1,000 people sharing to five—we could get to 5,000 pretty easily. I think that's how we got 7,000 people on the waiting list.

EA Sure.

VV We said, "Okay, now the waiting list is closed." We had the first 7,000 people, and that's how many we needed to do beta testing and to get feedback with those first users for it to be meaningful for our MVP. ●

DON
DODGE

Developer Advocate
Google

Don Dodge has had ridden the startup rollercoaster many times, perhaps most infamously at Napster. As a Developer Advocate at Google, a special advisor to Google Ventures, and prolific angel investor, he keeps very close to the startup world and can be found judging pitches and meeting with founders at conferences and developer meetups around the world.

ELLIOTT ADAMS I haven't met many developer advocates that work alongside the full spectrum of building high-growth companies, it seems like you have a pretty broad interest in startups.

DON DODGE Yes. Well, I am also an advisor to Google Capital and an advisor to Google Ventures and an angel investor myself in forty-six companies. So, I spend a lot of time at startup conferences and seeing new companies and finding companies that can either partner with Google, or they could be an investment for Google or in rare cases, an acquisition. So, it's sort of my job to go out there and be an advocate for these startups back to Google, to bring the message of what Google needs to do in the product, in terms of features, to be successful with emerging companies.

EA I was reading up on your background, and I didn't realize this before, but your were part of Napster?

DD Yes, the original Napster.

EA Do you mind talking about how that came about and what that experience was like?

DD Sure, but before I do that, I was Director of Engineering at AltaVista, one of the first search engines, and my group invented what we called "multi-media search" at the time. It's hard to believe, but seventeen or eighteen years ago, in 1998, you could not search for an image or a photo or music or video because the technology to do that did not exist. So, my group invented the image search. We started with image search, then video search, and then music search. As part of

doing that work, I was always looking around to see what the competition was doing, and there was this new thing called Napster that no one had really heard of, but they were doing music search. And I thought, oh, this is interesting.

EA Was AltaVista metadata-based, or it was actually looking at file content?

DD To reveal the secrets, the way that we did it was we were already indexing the page with everything on the page and doing nothing with some of this metadata. If there was an image, it might have a file name or it might have some attributes around it or words that describe it. We just started using all of that data that was on the page to try to identify what the image was because back then, you couldn't. There was no other way to do it.

EA So, it might be "EiffelTower.JPG", and you made an educated guess on that.

DD Right.

EA So, then you saw Napster, and they were doing search and—

DD Right. So, as we were finishing up the music search part of the equation, I saw Napster and Scour and CuteMX, and others like them. I was always looking around to see what other companies were doing, and it turned out that Napster was two blocks down the street from AltaVista, and the recruiter in HR that I worked with at AltaVista was the girlfriend of one of the founders of Napster. So she said, "Hey, you should go to Napster

and help them out." Shawn Fanning and Sean Parker were eighteen years old at the time—eighteen—and just trying to get started. Long story short, I went over to Napster when it was just eight people, and then it took off like a rocket, and the rest is history.

EA I think there was something in your LinkedIn profile about that period of time, how you held on for dear life, or something along those lines.

DD Yeah, it was a rocket ride, and there were no ways to plan for it. I remember Eddie Kessler would order servers for the backend server part, and he thought he was ordering enough servers to last us for a year, and they would last us three weeks or a month, and he'd have to buy more and have to plan the capacity on something that you really could not plan. It was a rocket ride.

EA You know, that's a great anecdote that speaks to you totally, completely computing with cloud.

DD Well, it didn't exist then, so we had to build our own infrastructure. There was no Google Cloud or Amazon Web Services that would scale for you. You had to do it yourself.

EA Sure, since you guys were not even renting, you were buying servers.

DD Yeah.

EA Were you co-locating them in your facility?

DD No, we had a hosting service that would give you rack

> ## "Well, right. I think it's never been easier to start a company, but it's never been harder to build a business."

space, and you'd put your servers in there and manage them and that kind of thing.

EA I'm not sure I can think of, off the top of my head, another young company in 2000 like Napster that had that kind of consumer-driven growth.

DD Yeah, AOL took a long, long, long time. It was very slow growth. Steve Case is a personal friend of mine, and he's told me about the first ten years of AOL. They grew very, very, very slowly, and it was only in the eleventh, twelfth, thirteenth year that they took off. But at the time, and I think for a long time after, Napster was the fastest-growing web business ever.

EA That would seem to be the case.

DD There were just no corollaries. There were no other examples to say, "Oh, okay, we can plan based on this or that." It just grew so fast that we had to just hang on for dear life trying to make it work. And to some extent, Twitter was the same way. I don't know if you recall when Twitter launched the Fail Whale?

EA Oh, I do.

DD I mean, Twitter would crash several times a day. So, I would guess that the early days of Twitter were like the

early days at Napster, where it just grew so fast, there was no keeping up with it.

EA So, if at the time there was no precedent for that kind of growth in the consumer web—

DD No.

EA —and utility computing from Google—

DD Didn't exist.

EA Yeah, it wasn't there at the time. When did Google get into that business?

DD Google started building its own servers and its own data centers almost immediately, but nobody really knew about it because it was under the covers and it was only for their own internal use. It was not until much later when Amazon did the same thing, and Amazon started providing Amazon Web Services that Google decided, "Hey, we could do that too because we're the best in the world at building data centers, and why don't we—we have to build that infrastructure anyway for our business, why not just build it even bigger and provide Google Cloud Services?" So, it was somewhat later, but at the time of Napster, there was nothing you could do. Nothing that was scalable.

EA What's exciting to you with all of the young startups you see pitch these days?

DD Well, I think young companies can start cheaper than ever before because we have these cloud services and all kinds of free services to get started. Back in the day, to start a company, you had to raise $5 million and be in development for a year or two before you ever got to market. That was the traditional approach.

So, it was a long, hard road, and you had to raise significant money to do it. Now, going to consumer—and I think largely because of smartphones, which really came about in 2007, 2008, and really hit their stride in 2010—you are able to start a company with almost nothing. You could bootstrap it with almost nothing and get something working and get it distributed on a mobile platform for nothing, basically, and get enough traction to then go to investors to say, "Hey, I need some money to scale." So, that's become the new normal, where investors expect that these founders will start the company, build the product, get the initial customers, prove out the revenue model, and then ask for money.

In one sense, those are very high hurdles to meet. In another sense, it is very inexpensive and cheap because you don't have to pay anything up front for these services to get your company going. So, a couple of tech founders that are great coders can do it all themselves without any money.

EA And so, that is table stakes today?

DD Well, right. I think it's never been easier to start a company, but it's never been harder to build a business.

So, it's very easy to start a company and there are thousands of them started every year, but because the barrier of entry is so low, the hurdle to get to a point where you actually have a business, where you have customers that pay, is harder. And I think that is where the problem is. There are lots of startups that have interesting ideas and they can build a product or a working prototype and get some initial customers, but they don't know how to scale it. They don't know how to identify their target market, how to advertise, or how to do customer acquisitions in a cost-effective way to get to the scale that they need. And that's a really difficult problem that a lot of startups overlook.

EA So, as an angel, again, table stakes are much higher. If someone says to you, "I built an app," you're probably not impressed by just that statement.

DD No, not at all.

EA If someone comes up to you and says, "I'm doing X." Is there an "X" that impresses you today?

DD No, I am never impressed with an "X" or what the product is. I'm more impressed with the team. Where do they come from, what is their background, why are they the ones to do this, what special experience or issues did they have earlier so that they completely understand this problem?

EA The jockey, not the horse.

DD Right, it's the jockey, or the team of jockeys, that's number one. Number two, what's your go-to-market strategy? One question I always ask is, "How do you get to $10 million in sales?" It's a simple question, but most startups have spent so much time thinking about the product and the features and the competition and the blah blah blah blah, they really haven't really given much thought to do the math—"How do I get to $10 million in revenue? How many customers do I need to do that? What price do I need to sell it at? How am I going to target that market? What is the customer acquisition cost going to be?"—just going through those simple calculations to get a rough idea of how much it takes to get there.

EA I think you might put a lot of startups on their heels, right on stage, don't you think?

DD Here's one for you. Back in the day when this started to emerge, all startups—well, not all, but many startups were advertising revenue-based. They were going to build an audience, monetize the audience with advertising. And I say, "Great. Great idea. Let's go through the math. How many pageviews do you need to make $1 million?" And they had no idea what the CPM rates were or what the ad rates were, and how many pageviews or how many customers you needed to make just $1 million. And when I took them through the math, they were stunned. They could not believe it. They just assumed that you build the product, you create an audience, and you monetize it with advertising. Done. No, not done.

EA Startups who say, "We're not going to charge for this. We're going to sell the data." Do you hear that a lot?

DD Sure. That's the next version of, "I'm just going to monetize with advertising." "Oh, we are going to monetize the data." "Sure, yes, great idea. Let's go through the steps how you do that." And they just don't know. They assume that it just sort of automatically happens, like advertising automatically pays for this audience that you created. So yes, it's a very workable idea, data. I'm invested in several companies that that's their business, selling data. And it's a model that works, but it's much more difficult than people realize, and you need much more scale than most people realize.

EA Scale for one and I assume domain for the other.

DD Yeah.

EA In-app data from a medium-sized game maybe won't move the needle, right?

DD Right. I mean these founders are jumping for joy if they have a 100,000 downloads. They think, "Oh my God! This is awesome!" Yeah, it is kind of awesome, but it's not enough to make money. If you want to sell data or if you want to do advertising, you need hundreds of millions, not hundreds of thousands. So, I think it's the age-old problem in a different context today than it was fifteen years ago. It was all about creating an audience and monetizing it with advertising. Now it's creating an audience and trying to upsell or sell the data to someone, but the scale that you need to do that and the quality of the data that you need is much harder than it looks. ●

KRISH SUBRAMANIAN

Co-founder & CEO
ChargeBee

With his co-founders, Krish Subramanian left his corporate technology job and has turned Chargebee from a small startup in Chennai into a booming SaaS player with funding from top-tier VCs. His crisp thinking and dedication demonstrate that it's possible to build a formidable high-growth startup outside of Silicon Valley.

ELLIOTT ADAMS I'm wondering if you could explain when you guys saw that there was something valuable you could offer customers with Chargebee?

KRISH SUBRAMANIAN Sure. We started with this in late 2011 when Braintree was in existence but Stripe hadn't launched yet. That's when the four of us came together to start building a company. The three other guys had been part of the AdventNet company's transformation into Zoho as a cloud-based company from mid-2005 to 2006. They spent over a decade building products there, and one of them was my college classmate during my engineering days. Through these ten years, I had been, from the sidelines, watching this global company built out of Chennai, and transforming into the cloud.

We just wanted to build a company together. It was not about one particular idea. We didn't really say, "Okay, this is the problem I faced earlier," and so on, even though we had faced this particular challenge at some point.

We could see that there were two or three problems, which are repetitive for most products, the convergence of three things. One, the cloud was taking off in a big way by 2010-2011. Number two, people were building either cloud first or mobile first. The third was that the revenue model was definitely subscription, so there was some kind of a recurring revenue relationship with the customer.

Then more and more companies were global, and interestingly, with the convergence of these ideas, we could see that the infrastructure of products that they used to run your operations needed to change. It could be a monitoring system, it could be operations, and so on.

EA You were right on top of that wave.

small scale. Now, they have two choices. One is to say, "I can build all my billing systems on top of a payment gateway," because Stripe gives you some confidence for subscriptions to charge a little bit, but not confidence of building an invoicing system that you can keep on building with the available resources internally. Or you can say, "I need a billing system that will enable me to scale." It could be when you go global: do you

"They're all small things, but hundreds of small exceptions add up to make it so that it becomes a dedicated product within your core product."

KS And existing systems like Quickbooks or Xero are not built for collecting payments from ten thousand customers without throwing people at that problem, right? If you have a SaaS product—you have too many changes coming in throughout the day, not just in a month, where your customers are being prorated, it's either you go to a self-service model, or the inherent nature of the pricing model that allows the prices to vary on a regular basis. Now, this is not a problem where you can throw people at the problem, where we can all can hire a bunch of accountants to solve.

When it comes to how these companies collect payments, operating with customers in probably 150-200 countries, all that needs to be done even at a very

want to be able to co-collect payments with customers with a credit card? It could be bank transfers, wire transfers, paying with PayPal, etc., because your customers have varied preferences in which they like to be charged.

EA Sure.

KS Then, when you're more upstream, you want to be able to collect payments from customers who say, "I want to be able to pay you with net 30 or net 45. You need to send me an invoice in advance. Issue me a credit." For pretty much every one of these exceptions, when you're giving a discount, all these things now get in the way of customer experience if you are not able to do it immediately. It could be that you go back to your CTO team or a developer, or you need to have a couple of developers who are available for your sales guys to say, "I want to issue this coupon to the customer, how do I do it?" Now they need to hand them the exception and tell them how to do it: "Go into Stripe, and since you don't have admin access, so here is a common ID to use. You create a coupon for February 10, and you can set limitations as to when the coupon will apply."

EA That's a heavy burden for one customer.

KS They're all small things, but hundreds of small exceptions add up to make it so that it becomes a dedicated product within your core product. Where you are spending that product management time to take care of customer experience, right? Your customer experience with billing comes from how well they are able to interact with your product and how well you can enable them to do things as and when they want it. That is what Chargebee offers as a plug-in-and-play solution, where you plug in the Chargebee and you straight away are able to deliver a global experience to your customers with a superior billing module that you don't have to keep up based on exceptions.

You don't have to build your billing after you experience an exception. The developer team has been documenting all the exceptions over the last four years and trying to capture as many scenarios as possible so that you are able to deliver your support, sales, marketing and finance. So, the exception becomes the norm, right?

EA It sounds like you've gotten to a compelling product, but can you share more about the early days?

For a decade, I'd been thinking about wanting a startup. We had already planned in a frugal way, we actually just kept away, saving money for starting up later. So, it helped that for two years, we were able to bootstrap the company. Our ten years of savings were put aside, and we decided to bootstrap the company.

EA Wow, that's incredible. I haven't heard of many teams putting aside that kind of cash beforehand from their salaries.

> **"So, it helped that for two years, we were able to bootstrap the company. Our ten years of savings were put aside, and we decided to bootstrap the company."**

KS We decided to just build a company together. Initially, we didn't plan or even know whether we could build with other people's money, meaning you could take venture or something, right? So, any actual work experience gives you the buffer of savings.

KS We never planned for actually raising capital at all, but after one or two years, you realize that the nature of the product is such that the category we picked, which is vertical SaaS, where the solution has to go really deep to make a solid case for every vertical, right? It's not like where you build one helpdesk or one CRM, which serves most markets. It those cases, universities can use it, car-sharing services can use it, and even SaaS companies can use it. A helpdesk or a CRM can be that way, but a billing system needs to be very specific to every vertical. I need to make a solid case that says, "Here is the best billing system for SaaS," "Here is the best billing system for e-commerce."

That makes it very challenging for you to actually go across horizontally. By the nature of the service now, you are going deep into one niche and then solving it very well, which means that it takes longer and is harder for you to solve the problems, and that requires upfront capital. We realized that after a year, plus the idea where nobody likes to trust four guys building a new product out of somewhere random in Chennai, or the U.S., with their mission critical processes.

So, bringing on somebody like Accel Partners as an investor backing us adds more credibility, right?

EA Yeah, of course.

KS So, we found that Accel US had partners here in India, and some of our customers were backed by Accel. Through that network, they vouched for us,

and then that in turn became a long conversation. We got to know them very well, and we found that they were challenging our product and market assumptions very interestingly. They were also investors in Braintree, and so they were actually wondering if we were a feature and not a product. They were asking the questions of Braintree about our service, and by asking if this is a feature on top of a payment gateway, because Braintree also offers subscriptions: "Why do I need this?"

They kept asking the same question to our customers who had Braintree plus Chargebee. They also asked the Braintree management teams if they would actually double down and go on to build a billing system themselves. That's when the clarity emerged that we had something unique to build a business that wouldn't be easily challenged.

We took money from Accel, we raised two rounds of funding. The angel round was immediately followed by what we—Series A. We raised $1.2 million in total, followed by a Series B with Accel and Tiger Global a year after that, and another $5 million. But most importantly, access to capital is available pretty much anywhere in the world. However, the best way to actually get them is through customers, if you

are able to win customers anywhere in the world, and those customers are actually backed by some of these investors. There is no better way for you to get the word out.

EA That's so interesting. It's a customer acquisition channel for you at some level.

KS I've always viewed investor conversations as also a way to get customers. If you don't get money ideas, get some customers. ●

GEORGE ARISON

Co-founder & CEO
Shift Technologies Inc.

In addition to being a political scientist focusing on post-Soviet transition, George Arison has been an innovator in transportation. He founded Taxi Magic, an on-demand transport company far ahead of its time, and is now focused on Shift, which introduces a new model for buying and selling used cars.

ELLIOTT ADAMS Taxi Magic is especially interesting because you guys were ahead of the curve, right? You were ahead of this idea of on-demand transportation.

GEORGE ARISON Yeah.

EA What's the origin story of that company?

GA I was traveling a ton as a BCG consultant, and we'd take taxis all the time because I didn't have a driver's license, and so when you would arrive in some random town or city and try to take a cab to your client, to get up here, that was really too much. So, I wondered if you could use an app on a phone like a Blackberry to book a taxi.

I had a mentor and a friend named Tom DiPasquale, who had started a company called Cookbook, which was then bought by what was then Concur. And as a result of that, Tom's technology was used by Concur as the primary way to do all the travel bookings and expense management. What Tom was saying was that the vast majority of expense that is done in cash is ground transportation, and it's a very idiotic situation because it's where a lot of the fraud happens. So, he was really into this idea of whether you can use mobile in some way to create a more electronic receipt and electronic payment trail for ground travel. Those two ideas kind of coming together is what started Taxi Magic.

I think one of the things was we fundamentally thought that we knew what the right answer was when we got started, and that was not the right thing. In terms of how to approach it, we should have learned our way into the product a lot more than we did, and I think that's something really critical. We wasted a ton of money and a ton of time on stuff we thought was right, but then it turned out the product was being used very differently or features were not being used at all. Now, granted, agile development and the user feedback method was not as prominent back then as it is today.

So, that's number one, and number two is that we didn't focus enough on building a strong enough technology stack to make all this work. As a result of that, our ability to innovate when we were being out-innovated by someone like Uber was a lot slower. Thirdly, I think we didn't go full stack because we wanted a simple software product, versus Uber and Lyft, who are not a simple software product. I think

that was a mistake because we were very dependent on taxi fleets to provide the service, and they were doing a pretty terrible job at that. That's kind of the three big things I tend to usually focus on in terms of lessons.

> **"We wasted a ton of money and a ton of time on stuff we thought was right, but then it turned out the product was being used very differently or features were not being used at all."**

EA I assume some of those lessons carried over to what you did with Shift.

GA For sure, and in some ways, we may have over-corrected at Shift a little too much in some cases and now are correcting ourselves because that's just the reality. The answer is never as cut and dried one way or the other. But yeah, Shift was built in a very different way. Before the company was even started, I spent a ton of time testing the initial product idea and discovered that what we initially were thinking was going to be the product was actually not going to work because the consumers didn't think about that product first.

So, we started out by really being interested in lending and how to enable lending in non-dealer transactions when cars are being sold or bought, the reason being that it was a pain point personally for me, and I had lived through that experience. Secondly, it seemed like a huge market opportunity because no one else was doing that. But it turns out that there's a reason why it's like that. People don't think of the loan first, and those that do are not the customers you want to offer a loan to anyway since they're the least likely to pay their loan off. We tested our way into knowing those things and that it was not the right product before we had any tech team or a business or a company incorporated in any of that. So, we really redid the product through user testing really early, and that generally has been the approach that Shift has taken to product development.

GA Initially we didn't, but in the beginning, the thought was to not even have any touching of the car. That all the Shift product would be around the lending and the warranty and offering a guarantee on a car. Say you had a car you were selling, and Jamie wanted to buy that car. Shift would inspect your car, certify it, attach a warranty to it as a guarantee. You would still be responsible for selling the car, and you would still be responsible for finding Jamie as a buyer, but then when Jamie felt ready to buy this car, through Shift, you'd be able to offer financing to Jamie to buy that car. That was the initial product idea, and then the more we spent time with users, it became clear that the users actually wanted the car off their hands, and they wanted a more augmented set of services than the ones

the UberX experience, so that analog is number one. And then number two is, we then had this idea of a test drive delivered to you, which is kind of how we got started. That evolved over time, as well, so we initially were sending out a very expert person to do the test drive. This was a highly paid, very knowledgeable person who knew a ton about cars, who'd come out to your house or your office or whatever. That was a very good experience for customers, but we found we would run into a whole bunch of different issues.

Number one, it was very difficult to optimize their time because they would spend so much time on the road, and you could maybe fit in two test drives a day, but you could never break even on two test drives a day. It was too expensive. Secondly, it was very hard to train them because they were on the road so much, and so the variability between the high-quality performance and the medium-quality performance was so high that it just didn't work, and a medium performer would drive down the average for everybody.

So then our president, the man who started Taxi Magic with me, Toby Russell, said, "Okay, what can we do to transform this to a place where we keep this unique and kind of secret sauce of test drive delivered

> **"We tested our way into knowing those things, and that it was not the right product, before we had any tech team or a business or a company incorporated in any of that."**

EA How did the customer experience evolve? My understanding is that you send out a rep, is that correct?

that we offered them. They kind of wanted a much more Uber regular or UberBLACK experience, versus to the customer, but do it in a more optimized manner where the costs are not as crazy and the quality of the customer experience is not suffering because of the difference in the quality of people providing the service?"

So, we tested our way into a model where we have a person on the phone who is the expert, like a sales rep, basically, and then a driver, who is just the regular driver, delivers the car to the customer for a test drive. So, now the customer gets the test drive experience but also is getting an expert. He just never meets the expert, so the expert's not spending time on the on the road anymore, and instead is able to help many more customers by phone. The end result of that has been that our conversions on test drives to sales have gone up by over 10 points. Before, we'd be converting 32-34 percent test drives to sales conversions. Now we're in a kind of a 42-45 percent range.

EA Wow.

GA Number two, our customer feedback actually has gone up as well, because now everybody is getting the best person, and it's easier to train everyone because they're all in one office at the same time. So, our costs have come down because we can optimize schedules,

and our utilization is way better this way than we were able to do in the old model. Now, we tested our way into doing that where we had this idea; we did it for about five percent of customers, then we grew it to fifteen, then we grew it to twenty, then we tweaked it. We concurrently built technology to support it, etcetera, etcetera, etcetera, and over the course of Q2 and like, Q3 and Q4 last year, we made this huge change, and in January, converted the business to this model. So, that is definitely a very different way of doing things than Taxi Magic used to, and I think it's a more effective way to be successful with building a business.

EA Could you dive into that a little more? For Shift, how did you and your investors come to define product/market fit?

GA That's a tough question. There's a Supreme Court case in which Justice Scalia writes this great line, "You'll know it when you see it." It applies to this as well. You have product/market fit when you see it, and you don't when you don't see it. There's not an ironclad rule about that.

This business is different than a lot of businesses because the value of the transaction in our space is so

massive, right? We make $3,500 a car sold in terms of revenue when we do a transaction. Think about how many Uber rides that is. Uber makes maybe about a dollar fifty per ride, so you're talking about an insane number of Uber rides—about 2,300 Uber rides to make up one car revenue. And so, you don't have the luxury of lots of volume to judge things because it's just not possible to get to that kind of volume without additional capital. But I think you wonder if it's working. For us, the single biggest thing was people giving us cars. It was very clear, obviously, you could sell a car. Forty-five thousand cars are sold a year, but the idea that a person would give you a car for free to sell and you don't pay them money up front is a pretty big deal, in my opinion. Once we were proving that we were actually doing that, that's when I think people felt like we had product/market fit. ●

BOOTSTRAPPING

*"Never allow someone to be your priority
while allowing yourself to be their option."*
Mark Twain

Investors rarely consider funding a startup before it achieves
sufficient traction in the marketplace, which is why many founders
will bootstrap their business until it shows promising results.
Yet, not all startups are suited to bootstrapping, and it's important
to consider whether this is the right path for your goals.

In this chapter, we'll explore:

- *How avoiding venture capital in the early stages can lead
  to a greater valuation later on*

- *Why bootstrapping gives you a level of flexibility and control
  that can contribute to your startup's success*

- *Ways to fund your business during its early stages without
  selling shares in the company*

- *Whether your startup is in a position to achieve rapid
  growth without a significant injection of cash*

BOOTSTRAPPING YOUR STARTUP

We'll discuss the key points in fundraising from angels and later-stage VCs in the following chapters, but courting investors isn't the right move for every business. To be sure, most software companies that grow really large end up taking venture capital sooner or later, but they might not actively seek funding early on. There are advantages to bootstrapping your high-growth tech startup without relying on outside equity-based financing (from angels and VCs), at least in the early days.

Bootstrapping isn't an option for every high-growth startup. The nature of your business might simply require too much capital investment before you can begin generating any revenue. If you're aiming to find a new way to manufacture microchips, that could bring real cash into the business, but you will also need quite an infusion of money to build your first fabrication facility. Even if you're developing a SaaS platform (not quite as daunting as microchips), it can be difficult to self-fund if it's going to take months or years to build a product that you can sell to customers.

> *If you can't foresee yourself being able to raise enough revenue in a brief time span or build the product with a very low burn rate, then bootstrapping probably isn't right for your startup.*

A quick rule of thumb for whether you're in a position to bootstrap: software startups need to either generate revenue quickly, raise funding, or have a team with deep technical skills that can build the product with a very low cost of salaries and other expenses (also known as the "burn rate"). If you can't foresee yourself being able to raise enough revenue in a brief time span or build the product with a very low burn rate, then bootstrapping probably isn't right for your startup. O

Benefits of Bootstrapping

If and when your startup raises VC funding from angel investors and venture capital firms, there will be two main incentives for the investor. Obviously, they'll want the economics to be in their favor and to generally exert as much control over the company as possible. By not raising venture capital, you can, if nothing else, be sure to avoid the most nefarious venture capitalists who might steer you astray while you're still finding your feet. Generating your own initial revenue gives you the advantage of raising capital when your company is further along and can command a higher valuation, give up less equity (since raising money is effectively selling part of your company), and raise from better and more selective investors.

Bootstrapping also gives you the luxury to experiment without being accountable to investors who are expecting a huge return on their investment. Your team can make the call and decide when you've reached problem-solution fit and whether it's worth pursuing further as a high-growth venture. This is time very well spent that you wouldn't have if you were chasing down investment dollars.

Sweat equity is the best startup capital.
Mark Cuban

Another good reason not to rush into bed with the VC world is that you simply might not have a startup that has the potential to be a billion-dollar business. That doesn't mean it's not a startup worth building, and it even could still be a million-dollar business. The trouble is that the venture capital model wants to achieve the highest possible outcome on an investment, so trying to build a smaller business with their investment is actually discouraged even though the odds of being successful may be greater. In other words, what you might consider a financially successful enterprise might not fit a venture capitalist's definition of one. Moreover, if you wait until it's clear that your startup has the potential to address the needs of enough people to make it a really huge business, then you can at least raise money while feeling more confident that it's appropriate for the scale of business you're trying to build.

Bootstrapping also lets you build a different kind of company culture. While it's true that any startup employee is going to take less compensation than they would if they worked for a large company, working at a bootstrapped company likely means that they're going to have even more skin in the game because all of their revenue is coming in from customers, not an initial jolt from investors. This can seem like a disadvantage, but it can often ensure that your team has bought into the problem you've identified and your vision for how to solve it, and are committed to helping you make it happen. Lean times can be made easier by working with a committed group. Relying on their dedication and resourcefulness rather than outside funding can lead to a stronger startup in the long haul. ○

Bootstrapping also gives you the luxury to experiment without being accountable to investors who are expecting a huge return on their investment.

How to Bootstrap

If you're bootstrapping your business and you are waiting either for revenue or funding that you plan to pursue later, there are a few well-worn paths to "bridging the gap."

Consulting

Project work or consulting on other projects can be great for bootstrapping for two reasons. The first is the obvious one: it brings in income. But it also does so while allowing you to continue building your skill set and trying new things. Those benefits don't come without trade-offs, however. Doing outside work while you're bootstrapping or building your startup takes you away from your core business and the objective of getting your product on the market as soon as possible. (Whether you join an accelerator or raise venture funding, you'll be expected to go full time on your product if you move past bootstrapping—another choice that you lose.)

Turn a client project into a business

If you're able to do software project work for a client, you might be able to work out an agreement: what you make for them is their property, but what you create is still yours to use in other projects. Essentially, this turns into a bespoke software project, licensing it to the client instead of giving them ownership. Whether you can get the client to approve these terms will entirely depend on them and the project, but you can always try to make the offer more palatable by proposing a discount if they agree to it.

If you are able to build a project that you plan to resell, the upside is that the client is literally paying for you to do product development. The danger, however, is that you will be tasked with optimizing a system that works really well for that particular client's needs but may not match up with those of your startup's target customer base. Throughout the process of building for a client while having the right to spin it out as a standalone product, keep in mind that you need to develop a product that will be useful to your final customer, not just the client.

Microsoft was a bootstrapped company from the beginning, and this is the approach they took. Their first product, MS-DOS, was licensed to IBM for use in personal IBM computers. But Bill Gates negotiated for a non-exclusive license. Keeping ownership of the OS they developed for IBM turned out to be one of the most brilliant and defining deals of the personal computer era because it allowed Microsoft to license MS-DOS to any and all PC makers. This turned PC manufacturing into a commodity business and put their software in a valuable position.

> *Whether you join an accelerator or raise venture funding, you'll be expected to go full time on your product if you move past bootstrapping—another choice that you lose.*

Self-Funding

The last method of bootstrapping gets to the heart of its philosophy for some people. If you put your own money into the company, you're showing the greatest commitment possible. You have "skin in the game," even beyond ignoring other, more stable career opportunities. When you invest your own money into the startup, you're likely to be a lot more careful about how it's spent than you would be if you were handling someone else's money. ○

The Ideal Bootstrapping Scenario

Bootstrapping has a lot of definitions, but it's most useful to think of it as a means of getting your startup to the right place. It's perhaps best captured by Austin entrepreneur and thought leader Bijoy Goswami's mantra: "right action, right time." This stands to serve the startup founder very well. As he explains in greater depth:

> *"At every stage of the startup, there are a set of actions that are 'right' for the startup, in that they maximize return on time, money, and effort. A bootstrapped entrepreneur ignores all else."*

The best kind of bootstrapped business generates revenue quickly without having to invest a lot into the business. This is tough for most software-based startups, but not impossible.

Michael Dell building custom PCs in his dorm room was the birth of a giant global technology company. One reason he was able to delay raising money for as long as he did is that he was simply buying the parts, assembling the machines, and then selling them for cash. It required some capital, but there wasn't a long wait before turning it into revenue. He eventually raised funding, but it wasn't essential at the beginning, and he was able to bootstrap for quite a while. But that was computer hardware, not software.

Jason Fried and David Heinemeier Hansson built Basecamp while they ran a software development firm and developed it alongside their client projects. They launched Basecamp so quickly that when they offered a paid version as an upgrade to the free version, they hadn't even built the software for billing into the system. They got around this by simply giving users a 30-day free trial—just enough time for them to build the billing software! Fried and Hansson are still outspoken critics of taking venture capital. To date, they have only raised a small amount of money from a particularly strategic investor: Jeff Bezos.

It's possible to build a smartphone app and put it on the App Store without having a big database that it needs to connect to or complicated social media login functions. Since you could probably build this quickly, it could possibly be a bootstrap business because it has the potential to generate some modest revenue without having to take a long time building it or even having to maintain it. This is, in part, what led to the app gold rush for developers, and one of the reasons almost no one ever strikes gold anymore is that consumers have just come to expect more. So, it's not impossible, but it takes a lot more time and energy for new software to generate real revenue and users, and it can be difficult to do that for long without funding.

> *But if you feel like you've bootstrapped your way to product-market fit and you can't keep the machine running just on revenue, it's likely time to consider outside funding.*

There are no hard and fast rules on when to bootstrap your startup or for how long. You and your team have to make trade-offs (more power over the company but with fewer funds to fuel its growth, for example). But if you feel like you've bootstrapped your way to product-market fit and you can't keep the machine running just on revenue, it's likely time to consider outside funding.

When (and if) raising money is right for your startup is a question you will eventually have to ask yourself. To answer with any conviction and to avoid (as far as possible) making the wrong choice, it's crucial to understand how funding works. In the following chapters, you'll learn about the different types of external funding available to startups, as well as which stage of your journey is the right time for each. ●

EARLY-STAGE

FUNDING

"Money will buy a pretty good dog,
but it won't buy the wag of his tail."

Josh Billings

This chapter explores the options and ins and outs of
professional early-stage funding sources (compared to the
friends and family option), including some of the trickier
concepts a savvy startup founder will need to understand.

This in-depth chapter on funding will introduce:

• *The pitfalls of friends and family investments and why it's important*
  to choose the right professional investors for your business;

• *The essential funding concept every founder should understand:*
  convertible debt

• *The value of joining a startup accelerator, including funding,*
  support, and valuable learning opportunities

• *How accelerators work and what their business model is*

EARLY-STAGE FUNDING: ANGELS & ACCELERATORS

As you raise money in what's called "equity financing," you are selling part of your company. The process of raising money results in you, the founder, owning less of your company so that you might have additional capital to make the business successful.

The early stages of fundraising involve two different groups of individual investors (as well as the investment that a startup can receive from an accelerator). These groups are easier to access than Venture Capital firms at the early stage, but the norms around investing can vary widely.

Friends and Family

The first are the people you know best: friends and family. These are the people you inherently trust. But investing at this early stage is incredibly high risk, and many of the investors you'll tap into at this point don't actually know what they're doing—proceed with extreme caution.

If you're based in the United States and you're raising money from friends and family, you need to make sure that your investors are accredited by the US Securities and Exchange Commission (SEC). There are minimum requirements for annual income and net worth, and if your investors don't meet them, taking their investment is technically illegal. Violating these rules can cause problems down the track when you start raising funds from professional investors.

There are minimum requirements for annual income and net worth, and if your investors don't meet them, taking their investment is technically illegal.

This early stage is the least formal and really has no set guidelines. The people involved may lend you the money, and they may invest in the company without any official paperwork that outlines what they are entitled to. Worst case scenario: they take an outsized portion of the company. If your uncle is a dentist with some savings kicking around, you may be more than happy to let him invest $50,000 in your company and receive 20 percent of the shares. While these deals are tempting at the outset, they will be a strong disincentive for investors further down the road. ○

Professional Investors

The second group is a lot savvier when it comes to funding startups: professional investors.

By professional investors in these early stages of a startup, we mean independent venture capital investors—angel investors. They are accredited by the SEC, but there are many, many angel investors out there, and their experience and quality runs the gamut. Given that range, don't jump for the first investor who offers you money. Make sure you shop around and ask other entrepreneurs about these investors. You need to get perspective on what you're looking for before you make any decisions.

Don't jump for the first investor who offers you money. Make sure you shop around and ask other entrepreneurs about these investors. You need to get perspective on what you're looking for before you make any decisions.

Angel investors are a critical part of the fundraising lifecycle of a startup because they, in some ways, set the tone for all future investments in the company. If an angel investor introduces a clause or condition in a new term sheet that is non-standard or just plain slimy, this condition could apply to every other subsequent investor, which could jeopardize your chances of getting investment from later stage VCs. Even if they love you and your product, one bad clause could make the investment too risky or promise too little in return. O

Dealing with Professional Investors

Convertible Debt

All of this can seem daunting. The cost and complexity of conducting the initial round of fundraising is a lot to take on, especially for a first-time founder. In response to this, we have seen the rise of so-called convertible debt.

Convertible debt is technically a loan to the company. It collects interest, but unlike a typical venture investment into a high-growth startup, it won't put a price on the company stock at the earliest stages. In fact, that's where it gets its name: the debt converts to stock/equity when the company has a valuation. The valuation could come from an exit event like being bought by a larger tech company, but it usually follows raising a Series A round from venture capitalists after the angel round, which had convertible debt.

In addition to converting funds into shares, convertible debt gives investors further incentive to fund your company by giving them a discount for when the funds invested convert to shares in the next round of fundraising. For example, a group of angels and VCs may fund the Series A round of your startup (which normally follows the early seed rounds that use convertible debt) and pay $1 a share, but the angel who is on the convertible debt note could have their shares convert at a 20 percent discount when participating in that second round. So, their shares are only $0.80 apiece.

There are other complicated and hotly debated aspects to convertible debt, such as valuation caps, and these are seen by some as convertible debt not fully living up to its promise of taking the protracted and time-consuming process of early-stage fundraising to its bare elements. So an alternative to the alternative of traditional fundraising emerged.

SAFE Documents

Using convertible debt to avoid putting a price on the shares or startup early on has great benefits. When you're just beginning to grow and get traction, there's no telling what the trajectory of the company will be. How can you put a price on a fledgling startup that barely has any revenue and is just beginning to understand how to map its expanding user base? Founders are naturally prone to think the value of their startup is higher than the investors do, but neither really have a clue before they can get a real sense of the traction the company can get and how the markets will change. So the price of stock in the startup is taken off the table, and that's a big step toward making this early round of financing more accessible and frictionless. But a term sheet for convertible debt from an angel investor is still going to have small clauses and bits of legalese that your attorney—and the investor's attorney—can go round and round with. And all the while, you're probably being charged by the hour.

Y Combinator saw this friction and unnecessary costs across their hundreds of graduates. To make the process smoother, they created a series of legal documents they call SAFE—short for Simple Agreement for Future Equity. SAFE documents replace convertible debt but offer the same advantages. These are standardized documents that are meant to benefit both the investor and the founder, and they are not up for negotiation. The SAFE documents take into account the reason founders started using debt in this weird way in the first place: as a placeholder for the valuation that occurs in a priced fundraising round when the startup is assigned a value. Angel investors using convertible debt racks are not expecting to get paid back in cash for the loans they issue. They simply want in on the deal in a fair way, and pricing the stock so early in the startup's lifecycle is not a fair way.

> *Money is like gasoline during a road trip. You don't want to run out of gas on your trip, but you're not doing a tour of gas stations.*
>
> **Tim O'Reilly, O'Reilly Media founder and CEO**

Accelerators

Since the mid-2000s, many startups have begun a rite of passage: applying to join other startups for several months in a mentorship and investment program known as an accelerator. According to the Global Accelerator Report 2015, 387 accelerators invested $199 million of early-stage capital in 8,836 startups around the world.

Why choose an accelerator?

They are investors in your startup

Accelerator programs invest money into a startup for a piece of equity in the company. The amount of investment varies from as low as $20k and up to $200k, and the amount of equity is usually between 5-10 percent.

These accelerators have the same investor expectations as venture capitalists do: they are looking for fast, scalable growth. If you are thinking of joining an accelerator, you should keep in mind how this first bit of investment can affect your company by setting you on a course toward eventual death, acquisition, or IPO.

An accelerator expects you to be high-growth, which can give rise to conflicts over how their investment is being put to work. If you're not using it to move your startup toward a big exit that will generate many multiples for the investors, you're potentially putting yourself at odds with the accelerator and the fundamental reason they invested in you in the first place.

You build a network of exceptional founders

As with a typical angel investor or venture capitalist, the top accelerators are more than just a check. There are non-monetary benefits to a good accelerator that can be more valuable than the investment. These intangibles can often help a startup escape its own bubble and thrive in a way that it couldn't on its own.

Once or twice a year, an accelerator will open applications for their program and choose a group of startups to join that upcoming three-month "batch." Everyone starts and finishes (usually with a pitching event, the so-called demo day) the program at the same time.

The quality of the experience depends largely on the quality of the other companies in your batch of the program. You learn together, can collaborate, and generally feed off the energy of the other startups around you for those three months.

How do we assess applicants to Techstars? We don't change our fundamental thesis: team, team, team, market, traction, idea.
Jenny Fielding, Managing Director at Techstars

The founders of Stripe, brothers John and Patrick Collison, joined YC's Summer 2010 batch to develop their developer-friendly payments API. Being part of a cohort of quality startups gave them access to their perfect customer: developers building products with a high chance of success that need to process credit card payments. They didn't just give a sales pitch and explain Stripe to the other founders but literally offered to take a founder's laptop and install Stripe into their application right then and there. This has become known as the "Collision Installation," and it's not an approach they could have used often outside of Y Combinator's high density of promising founders, which illustrates how much the value of being in an accelerator can come from the startups around you.

After your batch ends, the quality of the current and future alumni matter too. They are a part of your network. It's a lot like going to the same college: you've shared the same experiences, worked with the same people, and you've been thought to be worthy enough to join the same accelerator.

The quality of the batch, while in the program and afterward, is one reason that the top programs can have a snowball effect: the best startups want to be in the same network as other great founders. This is one reason that founders work so hard to get into the most selective programs, like Y Combinator, Techstars, and 500 Startups, which all routinely take less than 3 percent of applicants into a given cohort.

The best advisors come to you

There is a saying that startups don't suffer from a lack of advice, they have too much of it.

Anyone can give you advice on your startup (and they will, if you let them), but the quality of advice will vary greatly. The real challenge is to find the best advisors for your startup. Aside from whatever existing connections you may have, finding good mentorship can be very difficult. By virtue of being so qualified and insightful, successful founders have a lot of newer founders hoping to bend their ear.

Accelerators bring these experienced advisors to you. Many who mentor use accelerators as a filter to weed out startups that need more help on the very basics and to find companies that they might want to establish a more formal advisory role with outside of the accelerator relationship. But often, they simply want to help out new founders in the same place with the same types of early-stage problems the mentors went through themselves and lived to tell the tale. (This is an example of the Techstars "give first" philosophy, where they encourage their community to create a virtuous cycle of actions.)

You learn continuously

Being surrounded by exceptional founders and mentors will raise your game—you don't want to be the smartest people in the room, or you might as well stay home. Most programs feature speakers and workshops, but you also pick up small but valuable nuggets of information that improve your efficiency or give you extra traction when you need it most: what code editor is more efficient, how to better manage a sales pipeline, or how to get better ROI on an ad spend.

These are the things you won't pick up in a random co-working space in the same way and not at all if you and your team are holed up in your garage. Being around conversations that you wouldn't normally hear and exposed to tools and methods that are on the cutting-edge is a benefit hard to replicate outside of a quality accelerator.

(example #1) Y Combinator

There are a lot of accelerators across the world, but Y Combinator is most well known for its notable graduates and overall financial returns. Entrepreneur and well-regarded computer programmer Paul Graham and his wife, Jessica Livingston, were living in Cambridge, Massachusetts, and felt that the VC industry was doing things the wrong way: they were putting large amounts of money into a small number of companies and were operating in the old-school way of doing business that doesn't understand hacker culture.

So they founded Y Combinator to spread their bets and play an active role in both investing and actively working with these portfolio companies to help them succeed. After an especially successful first batch of startups that included Reddit and Loopt (the startup of current YC President, Sam Altman, that was acquired for $43m), Graham and Livingston moved the program from Boston to Palo Alto (conveniently close to Stanford) and continued to invest and learn. The startup accelerator was born. YC's notable alumni (Dropbox, Twitch, Airbnb) and Silicon Valley dominance have inspired countless competitors and imitators.

The format of the Y Combinator is relatively spartan, however. They host dinners with extremely notable Silicon Valley figureheads as speakers, and the teams meet with Partners in weekly office hours, but there's not a workspace where all of the teams in a batch work alongside each other.

They tend to keep the programming simple. Paul Graham once addressed a new cohort by simply instructing them:

If you're ever unsure if you should be doing what you're doing during YC, ask yourself this question: 'Am I building our product? Am I talking to users? Am I exercising?' If you're not doing one of these things, you're doing the wrong thing.

With unparalleled returns (the value of the portfolio is estimated to approach $100 billion), incredible scale (over 1,500 startups in twelve years), and current expansion plans that include a formal research arm and work in the life sciences, Y Combinator is, in many ways, now redefining the outer edge of what an accelerator program is.

(example #2) Techstars

Techstars is an accelerator and investment group headquartered in Boulder, Colorado. They are unique for running many accelerator programs in many different cities around the world. (Part of the Techstars investment thesis is that great startups can be built outside of Silicon Valley and that an accelerator supporting them can still do things like have over 100 exits.)

In the first month of their three-month program, they match the startups with several new mentors every day in what's called "Mentor Madness." In this first month, the startups can work with over 50 mentors to find the people who they think can best advise them on their startup. The second month of a Techstars accelerator cohort then asks the startup-mentor pairs to dig deeper on product development and other critical issues before the third month, which is largely focused on demo day presentations to investors.

These mentors also have connections that can really help with a startup's next step after an accelerator: fundraising. You've had the chance to work closely with these people, who have investors in their networks and who may be active investors themselves. It's important for you to choose your investors wisely, and working with them over three months can build a meaningful relationship in a structured process that would be hard to replicate outside of an accelerator.

Some of the Techstars accelerators specialize in a certain industry, or "vertical," like fintech, automotive, internet of things, and media. Part of the appeal is that the mentorship and connections in these industry-focused programs is exceptionally relevant for startups in those industries. Often, these programs are in conjunction with an established partner, such as Barclays or Virgin Media, where the teams can be immersed in the industry.

Techstars embraces its position of operating outside of Silicon Valley to build a unique and global culture of founders. Since startups in their network aren't all clustered in a single dense area, they're vocal about what the Techstars family represents, regardless of where it happens to be located. David Cohen, founder and co-CEO, promotes a code of conduct for the Techstars community:

1. We give first.
2. We act with integrity.
3. We treat others with respect. ●

LATER-STAGE FUNDING

"I swing big, with everything I've got.
I hit big or I miss big"

Babe Ruth

Raising money is seen as a sign of success for many startups, but it's important to remember that VCs have an obligation to get the best deal for their investors and won't automatically give you free rein. To ensure you get the best terms and don't find yourself being pushed in a direction you don't want to go, it's important to do your homework before you agree to a deal.

You should work with an attorney, but to set you in the right direction, this chapter will show you:

• *The two motivating factors for a Venture Capitalist and how this affects their relationship with you*

• *How VCs earn their money, and the lifecycle of a venture capital fund*

• *Key terms and tactics that can make a big difference to the valuation and ownership of your company*

• *How to keep track of ownership with a "cap table," plus when and how to incentivize employees with stock*

LATER-STAGE FUNDING: VENTURE CAPITAL

Venture Capitalists have different priorities than early-stage investors, and the terms of your agreement will likely be different as a result. Brad Feld and Jason Mendelson are startup thought leaders, co-founders of influential seed-stage investment firm Foundry Group, and the authors of Venture Deals, where they point out that there are two things venture capitalists are most concerned with: economics and power. They make the argument that VCs care most about the amount of money they could make and how much power they can have in the management of the company as it grows.

When we're talking about economics in the context of venture capital, we're talking about turning the money that has gone into shares of the startup into a lot more money. Since there are many ways to structure a venture investment, VCs are hyper-obsessed with fine tuning all of the deal's terms to their advantage. And who can blame them? They have a responsibility to maximize returns for the people who invest in their funds.

It's important to remember that funded startups only turn their shares into real money in an exit: they can be acquired by another company or go public on the stock exchange (or, most commonly, die). Being acquired and going public are the two events that turn investors' stock into real money. So investors are looking at every possible little detail of how their shares receive preference or when and how they can resell them.

Power is how VCs ensure that the economics go in their favor after the deal is signed. It could be a clause in the term sheet that protects them when things get tough or that restricts who can be on the board of directors. A startup's board is where the true power can lie: control the board of directors, and you can control the entire company and its fate.

Do founders think that when they raise money, they can take their millions and go off and spend as they see fit? And don't the VCs have faith in them? It's rare that an entrepreneur can negotiate to maintain a large amount of control of their company after several fundraising rounds. Mark Zuckerberg is an exception to the rule. Even after growing Facebook to be one of the largest corporations in the world, Zuckerberg is still in control of the board, an unusual situation for a founder. When investors lined the block to invest in Facebook, he was very meticulous about the details concerning what rights the VCs would have. In other words, he understood that they wanted power and he tried to keep it from them. ○

Get a Specialist Attorney

Saving money by hiring your ex-roommate's law school buddy or asking your uncle to take a break from his maritime law practice to help you out are attractive ideas, but keep in mind that good legal help is worth paying for.

The term sheet for your venture capitalist (or angel investor) isn't a terribly complicated document, so you might think it'll be easy to get it right without a specialist, but there are some traps. Venture capitalists spend all day contemplating structure deals and the contingencies that may arise down the road. But you, as a founder, do not, and you may not be able to see what kinds of consequences will arise from the way a particular sentence is worded. So find a well-respected attorney or firm that works with other startups that you're familiar with. Ideally, ask successful founders in your network who have raised money (and perhaps sold a company) for some personal recommendations.

Obviously, attorneys need to collect fees for their services, but it is possible you could delay your legal expenses until revenue has been raised. Some law firms will work on contingency, which means they will only collect a fee if the deal is closed. Or they may delay payment for a certain amount of time, assuming that you'll reach revenue or raise enough money to pay off your bill in due course. This isn't easy during the early stages, but by the Venture Capital stage, it may be possible to sell yourself and your idea so convincingly that they'll take that chance.

How Venture Capitalists Work

The business of venture capital is complicated and rarely understood by founders. As a result, startups often seek to raise venture capital without understanding the trade-offs. Since raising money is always a negotiation, you need to show up with as much understanding of the venture capitalists as they have of you. With a deeper understanding of a VC firm's investment thesis, the age of their funds, and their past investments, it's easier to see whether it's worth pitching to them at all.

The business of venture capital is complicated and rarely understood by founders. As a result, startups often seek to raise venture capital without understanding the trade-offs.

There's a general myth that venture capitalists are simply rich individuals who invest in companies. This could be a decent working definition of some angel investors, but although a VC can be many different things, they never act alone. Venture capitalists do not fund startups out of their own pockets but draw on a network of investors (known as limited partners) who trust their expertise.

These investors buy into the idea that the venture capital firm can make smart decisions about investing in these highly risky companies. Just like a founder sells themselves to investors, venture capitalists sell themselves to limited partners, such as pension funds, hedge funds, and anyone who might want part of their portfolio invested into high-growth companies (but who don't want to manage it themselves).

Venture Capital Funds

Every VC firm is made up of one or more funds. These funds are the discrete bundles of investors' funds that venture capitalists raise to invest in other companies from each respective fund. Each of these funds has its own thesis or idea, which is an assumption about the kinds of trends and companies to invest in and how to invest in them. Most funds have a length of about 10 years; within that timeframe, the firm must allocate all the money and hopefully have several exit events that will return a profit to the investor.

A VC firm may have six different funds going at once, or they may have a single fund that ended its ten-year life cycle two years ago, but they are still open and seeking to raise another fund. So be sure to do your homework on the firm, and don't pin your hopes on a firm with a single nine-year-old fund—they may be interested in your company, but it's likely they won't be able to invest so late in the fund's life cycle.

What's in a name?

"Venture capitalist" is an industry category, not a job title—like the range of professions that fall under being a "healthcare provider." There is an entire food chain inside venture capital firms that ranges from fresh-faced twenty-somethings analyzing spreadsheets to senior decision-makers who are likely the ones busy raising funds from limited partners. It's important to keep this in mind when you're courting VCs. Just because someone works at a venture capital firm and calls themselves a venture capitalist, it doesn't mean they have any decision-making authority.

Raising money is very time consuming, so you want to make sure you don't waste your time talking to people who can't actually make decisions inside the firm. In most firms, you will only find the decision makers who are authorized to finalize a deal at the top echelon of the company. But don't just dismiss anyone at the lower end of the totem pole. If you and your co-founders get the ear of an eager person who has just been promoted from permit analyst to associate, this could open doors to their bosses. But even in those cases, keep some perspective: don't count on their word carrying any weight when it comes to actually closing a round with them.

Management Fees and Carry: How VCs Profit

There are two ways VCs make money. When a company they've funded gets acquired or goes public, that translates into a big payday for the firm. It's also a big victory for their brand because venture capitalist firms are measured in the media based on their splashy results. Past successes are what allow them to raise more money from limited partners and to be one of the top firms that really hot startups want to raise money from. The portion of the total profit the VC managers earn when a startup is acquired or goes public is "carry"; it's typical for the VC firm to get 20 percent after paying back the management fees listed below.

Unlike angel investors, venture capital firms can also make money by just doing their job. Venture capital firms have historically charged management fees for handling the money that the limited partners have put into a fund. The firm will receive 2 percent of the fund's initial value per year for salaries and operating costs. Two percent doesn't sound like much, but if a VC firm raised a $100m fund with a 2 percent management fee, then they could receive $2m each year to cover the costs of running the fund (although the real goal is to make huge returns on the companies they invest in). O

Venture capital is not even a home run business. It's a grand slam business.
Bill Gurley, General Partner at Benchmark Capital

The Fine Print: What to Watch out For

What does it mean if a VC says they would like to fund your company to the tune of $5 million, but they think your company is worth $15 million?

It can mean that they'd like to buy a third of your company or that they'd like to buy a quarter of it. But that statement alone doesn't actually tell you. Nor does it tell you how much your company would actually be valued at after the fundraising.

Valuation has two different modes: pre-money and post-money. If the VC means that your startup is worth $15m before they invest their $5m, then they're referring to your pre-money valuation. This would mean that your total value after the $5m round is $20m and that their share is a quarter of that. In other words, you just sold 25 percent of your company.

But they might also mean that with the firm's benevolent help in the form of $5m, your company will then be worth $15m. In that case, what they're referring to is the post-money value of your company—what it's worth after they've put in an additional $5m. This means your company has a lower overall valuation if you take the deal (and lower is bad if you want to be worth as much as possible). It also means that the firm effectively owns a third of your company, since that $5m is a much bigger slice when the pie is only $15m, rather than $20m.

It might come as a surprise that one ambiguous phrase could cost you over 10 percent of your own company! Unfortunately, that's not the only confounding part of raising money. Knowing the basics is helpful, but it just won't be enough to guide you when you enter a deal.

Let's consider a few more key pieces of financial detail so that you can at least become familiar with the basics. Let these ideas inform you, but realize that it's only dipping your toe into an ocean of murky change. Be sure to seek out mentors, more detailed information, and a damn good lawyer.

Vesting

One of the cardinal sins inexperienced investors and founders commit is anticipating making a ton of money and getting out quickly. Of course, if your startup idea turns out to be a dud, you'll want to abandon it and move on, but if you've really got something worth pursuing, it's extremely unlikely that you'll go from idea to exit in less than five years.

A startup's success depends on its key employees remaining with the company, and those key employees stand to gain a lot more financially by ushering the company through its first formative years. But vesting schedules aren't just smart; they are written with real legal language and are binding. A startup is a long-term commitment, and you and your co-founders should be in it for the long haul.

Vesting is a safeguard against a founder or employee leaving the company before the startup has been successful or before everyone bails early because the startup doesn't have the potential quick exit they hoped for. Vesting means earning your stock in a company over time, and it rewards the longer-term thinking and commitment that's required to take a high-growth company through to its end game. Early employees (including founders) at startups are often compensated with generous stock offerings instead of extra cash (the employees take a leap of faith that the stock could be worth considerably more in the future), but they don't get all of the stock when they walk through the door on day one.

In a typical vesting schedule, the stock will vest over a period of four years. If you leave the company before that four-year mark, you don't get all of the stock that was earmarked for you. On this schedule, two years' worth of work for the company nets you half the stock.

As an extra incentive to stick around for at least a little while, there's also a minimum amount of time you are required to be there before you can earn any stock at all. This is called "cliff vesting," which means that if you're not at the company for at least one year, you get nothing. In other words, even if the company has a four-year vesting schedule, you can't go in for three months and vest one-sixteenth of your stock. Until you make it over that hurdle, you accumulate nothing, but once you do, you will typically accumulate stock on a monthly basis for the next three years.

This will affect the founders raising venture capital money too. It's typical that you can't raise a fundraising round and walk out the door the next week still holding 20 percent of your company. Founders are commonly required by VCs to vest their ownership stock after a fundraising round.

Life is unpredictable, so no matter how committed everyone is, there's always a possibility that one of your early co-founders might leave or be unable to continue in their role.

One big mistake that founding teams make is not asking the other co-founders to be on a vesting schedule. Life is unpredictable, so no matter how committed everyone is, there's always a possibility that one of your early co-founders might leave or be unable to continue in their role. The last thing you want is to have an absent co-founder who isn't doing any work for the company and yet still gets to hold a third of the stock. And as you can imagine, VCs don't like this either. That company value could be motivating new employees instead of essentially sitting dormant.

"Hit by a Bus" Principle

You can look at vesting as being born from distrust, where founders and employees are locked into staying with the company because they would otherwise try to skirt their company-building obligations. It's also about the uncertainty of life and makes unforeseen events easier to transition through for everyone.

Investors will often ask startups, "What happens to the business if you're hit by a bus?" It's usually a question for later-stage companies, where the investor wants to insure that the status quo will continue, but it applies to the massive uncertainty in startups.

Founders do have health issues, but they also decide to go back to their unfinished PhD program, move across the country with their spouse, or move home to take care of an ailing parent. Vesting sets up a clear and clean guideline for how to deal with the unfortunate situation of a founder leaving the company.

Dilution & the Cap Table

"Dilution" is where new investors inject capital into your business but take a percentage of stock in return, thus reducing the amount of stock owned by founders and existing investors. If 100 percent of company shares are owned by four people, for example, they will each have to reduce their percentage to make space for a new investor buying 20 percent.

As you grow, you have to make room for new investors, and those new investors dilute the share percentages of all the others (there is such a thing as "anti-dilution," which we won't go into here, but you should read up on it). The amount of your company that you own will decrease as you continue to raise money, and your early investors will likely see a reduction in the total percentage of the company that they own.

Capitalization Table for NewCo, Inc.

	Before			After	
	Shares	Undiluted	Fully Diluted	Shares	Undiluted
George	250,000	25%	17%	250,000	21%
Harry	250,000	25%	17%	250,000	21%
Sally	500,000	50%	33%	500,000	42%
Total Common	1,000,000	100%	67%	1,000,000	83%

This can quickly get complicated. Perhaps a new venture capitalist funder put in a few million and is getting 25 percent of your company. Your angel's investment converted to 20 percent of the company. You and your co-founders are equally vesting 45 percent of the company, and you're leaving 10 percent of the stock available for future employees as an incentive. Furthermore, this could all change with a future investment round. Now, how the hell will you keep track of all that?

A "cap table" is your startup's most important Excel document. It is a living document detailing the capitalization of your company, which is just a fancy way of saying that it shows who owns what.

When you're building your company's first cap table, you will make up a number to represent the number of shares in the company. The actual number doesn't really mean anything; what matters is who owns what percentage of that number. You can say there are 10 million shares in your company, and you and your three co-founders need to start with 2.5 million apiece. The VC firm that is buying 20 percent of your company would join the cap table and have two million shares (each founder would have their share of the startup's stock diluted from 2.5m to 2m shares each). Again, only the percentages matter, not the actual numbers—those two million shares could represent anything from 60 bucks to $60m.

Incentivizing Employees with Stock

You can't compete with Google or Facebook on salaries and perks. You can't even compete with startups who have raised a big Series D round and are on track for a big acquisition in a couple of years. You simply don't have the cash to write competitive paychecks. And if you do get some cash from your venture capitalist investors, they would strongly prefer that you not spend it on lavish employee salaries (including your own, by the way—a painful rookie mistake is proposing that, as a founder, you deserve a big salary). To convince the most qualified and promising people to join you, you have to give away the most valuable thing you have: stock in your company. But even though it's the most valuable thing you can offer, it could end up being entirely worthless. Every dead startup is full of vested stock options that never amounted to anything. So you have to sell talented people on the idea that the numbers in your cap table not only represent who has what stock but also that those stocks are actually going to translate into real money.

> *You can't compete with Google or Facebook on salaries and perks. You simply don't have the cash to write competitive paychecks.*

How much should you offer to new employees? Sam Altman, President of Y Combinator, has a great founder- and employee-centric answer to this question: "Whatever your venture capitalist says, double it." But in the end, it's less about the actual amount. Whether you're offering 2 percent to your dream VP of engineering or 0.1 percent to a very qualified salesperson who will also work on commission, what matters is that you get these early hires to buy into the dream and actually give them a piece of the reward if that dream comes true. O

Why Do VCs Invest?

Vesting and dilution are important concepts to explore, but what you're really interested in is knowing how to raise money. And that means knowing why venture capitalists make the investments they do—and what will make them invest in you.

Unfortunately, there is no simple answer here. Since venture capital is one of the riskiest forms of investment, there is no playbook. There are, however, some patterns that VCs use to evaluate the companies that pitch to them.

There are some outspoken VCs who have clear, ordered criteria that they claim guides all of their investment decisions. But there is only one thing that legally binds all venture capitalists: making decisions that will make the most money for their investors and limited partners. In fact, not only do they have a fiduciary responsibility as investors to make money as best they can, but they also have to follow the investment thesis they built the fund on when soliciting money from the limited partner.

If a VC firm invests in software and you are a fast-growing software startup that looks like it could have explosive growth if it was fueled by VC funding, how does a venture capitalist make the decision to invest in you? Assuming that your startup falls within their investment thesis, it's a lot like deciding who to marry—it's basically gut instinct. Private equity firms who are in the business of wringing efficiencies out of companies can spend all day crunching numbers: looking in depth at operational costs, considering the effects of laying off a number of employees, and so on. Venture capitalists don't have that luxury. VCs invest in new, often unproven markets. They're looking for companies that demonstrate traction, but that's not easy to quantify, and forecasting from it is a lot less like accounting and a lot more like meteorologists trying to predict next week's temperature. Venture capital, in other words, is highly speculative, and spreadsheets can only take you so far—at some point, investors just have to take a leap of faith.

So funders are looking for something that will make the unpredictable investment feel like a sure thing. Many VCs and angels say that this something is the founding team. The growth trajectory of their business definitely matters, but all startups encounter unforeseen problems—potentially very big problems that could change the entire business model—and whether it can withstand those problems depends on the resourcefulness and ingenuity of the founding team. A CEO can't succeed by staying on autopilot; they need to be engaged in constant iterative considerations about how to grow their business to hyperscale.

VCs don't just want someone who came up with a good idea that started growing on its own momentum; they want founders who they believe can keep growing the company no matter how much it changes. They want people who can deal with constant adversity and uncertainty. They want, in other words, someone who is fit to lead the startup in all scenarios, not just when things are going well

VCs are also looking for things that have nothing to do with you. Startups, by their nature, have to grow, which means they need a market that is large enough for them to grow into. Judging the size of the market for a radically new and disruptive business model is an art, not a science.

For every investor who had a feeling that Uber and Airbnb were going to be the biggest startup successes of their time, there is a long trail of unsuccessful VCs who funded innovative startups that just couldn't return any money for their limited partners. Often, those failures resulted from a miscalculation about how big of a market the startup could grow into.

All of this uncertainty about the future causes venture capitalists to do strange things. The last thing they want to do is miss out on a big opportunity, like investing early into an incredibly successful startup. No one wants to miss out on an innovative business model that turns out to be the first ripple of a wave that starts to dominate the market. It could be the fear of missing out on investing in one single startup that seems to be extremely popular, like getting in on one of Uber's funding rounds. The fear can also come from seeing Uber and Lyft and Sidecar all growing in the ride-sharing space, and the investor is concerned that they aren't invested in at least one of these types of companies.

Both of these impulses, driven by FOMO ("fear of missing out"), lead to bad decisions. When a startup is hot and everyone seems to want to put money in it, this can trigger a deep feeling of anxiety that can push some VCs to invest where they wouldn't otherwise. An emerging popular market, like ridesharing, might be so enticing to an investor that they invest in a company predominantly because of the sector that company operates in—putting aside how they feel about the team, for example. One semi-rational strategy for investing in a sub-par startup in a hot market is even if that startup isn't doing too well, there can be reasons for its competitors to acquire it in order to gain market share.

Remember, angels and VCs are invested in your startup's success but also in running a business and negotiating for the best deal that they can get.

If you're fortunate enough to have strong growth and the interest of investors, celebrate your progress but move with mindfulness as you consider fundraising. Remember, angels and VCs are investing in your startup's success but also in running a business and negotiating for the best deal that they can get.

In the ideal scenario, you'll take your startup to the next level of growth with the help of investors who are as dedicated to your success as they are to their potential payout. ●

INTELLECTUAL

PROPERTY

CONSIDERATIONS

"Originality is nothing but judicious imitation."
Voltaire

Although less often a consideration for product-based startups, when and how to protect your intellectual property becomes important when a unique process forms the basis of your startup's success. In this chapter, we'll explore the different types of intellectual property protections in the US, their relevance to a tech startup, and how to secure protection if you need it.

Just like raising funding, IP deserves the advice of a good lawyer, but use this chapter to become familiar with:

- *The difference between trademark, copyright, and patent protections and how you might use them*

- *The level of protection that is automatically afforded by law*

- *How patents can impede creativity, instead of driving innovation*

INTELLECTUAL PROPERTY CONSIDERATIONS

Fundraising and intellectual property have something in common: before making any decisions about either, you will definitely need an attorney.

Founding a startup means creating new stuff: code, design, marketing emails, etc. So, it's easy to get tangled up in pressing legal questions. If you are in the United States and plan to raise money, the accepted standard is to register as a C corporation in the state of Delaware. This is also the case if you are a startup based overseas and plan to raise money in the US. If you are in the fundraising process for a priced round (not a SAFE document), there are intricacies related to preferred stock and vesting schedules that will vary according to the situation.

This book can't begin to address all of these and related issues, but let's take time to focus on intellectual property because it's not just something you need to understand, it's something you need to avoid spending too much time on, so you can dedicate the maximum amount of time to building and growing your startup.

Intellectual property rights are a confusing topic for founders, partially because the nature of VC-backed startups has changed. Traditionally, funded startups have relied on new technology they've developed themselves, which forms the basis of the business (e.g. a microchip, a server deployment system, etc.). The VC game was more focused on funding companies on the basis of these specific proprietary technologies and their growth potential (since the companies usually won't have an actual product until they secure funding). This is still true in some cases, but it's increasingly rare in comparison to software and web-enabled startups who are funded because of their traction in the market, network effects, and simple ability to acquire customers cheaply and monetize relatively heavily. Many software startups

> **Intellectual property rights are a confusing topic for founders, partially because the nature of VC-backed startups has changed.**

now compete on the basis of their product design differentiation and how effective their growth strategy is. Much of their intellectual property protections can—and we should stress can, there are always exceptions—become less important.

There are three primary types of intellectual property. To make these abstract concepts more concrete, imagine your startup has written some code and consider how each category would apply to your software and how you might benefit from each type of protection.

Trademark

Trademarks protect your company's visual icon (like the familiar red-and-white Coca-Cola script or the Nike Swoosh). Registering a trademark has almost no business being at the top of an early-stage startup's to-do list. If your startup becomes wildly successful, your attorney will send you a stack of documents to sign, which will likely include an application for trademarking your logo. There's little reason to worry about protecting your logo before you have users and your product's showing traction. ○

Copyright

Copyright is more applicable to software startups than trademark, but they're not usually proactive about securing it. Legally, they don't need to be— US intellectual property laws automatically award creators (musicians, programmers, writers) copyright protection for their work once it's been written down. That's all it takes. Once you actually write your code, anyone who uses it, sells it, or modifies it without your permission is infringing on your copyright. (However, you can formally register your copyright with the USPTO, and media companies routinely do this for a more concrete documentation of when the work was created and what it is comprised of.)

A lot of creative work involves rearranging, remixing, and paying homage to found sources, which makes intellectual property issues tricky, but there are some clear-cut cases. A hip-hop artist who makes an album and samples loads of 1960s Motown records without first asking Motown's permission is, sooner or later, going to have a problem on their hands. Finding a similar real-world hypothetical for software is tougher. There's no reason you'd display your code online (unless you're contributing to an open source project, for example), so if someone got their hands on it, chances are that there was theft or carelessness involved. If, however, you want to demonstrate how your product works by putting it in a repository like GitHub, you might as well open source the code. Even if you wanted to protect your copyright when publicly sharing some of your code, once you make it available like that, there is no real way of knowing whether another startup has taken the code and used it for commercial purposes. You'd have to be able to identify the code running on their server, and there's no way to find this out on your own.

> *A hip-hop artist who makes an album and samples loads of 1960s Motown records without first asking Motown's permission is, sooner or later, going to have a problem on their hands. Finding a similar real-world hypothetical for software is tougher.*

If you find yourself in a highly competitive market and battling other startups (or established players in the industry), your code may be considered valuable if it was really fast or created an extraordinarily smooth user experience. But that's not likely. Besides, even if it were, the ideas and principles behind its smoothness matter more than the particular engineering itself. In most b2b and b2c customer experiences, it's the way users are incentivized to take action in the product that is revolutionary, not the behind-the-scenes stuff. And while the technical aspects of building startup software do take serious time, the actual code isn't so complicated or revolutionary that the process can't be copied and rewritten from scratch.

Rocket Internet: The Startup Copy Machine

Berlin's largest internet company houses dozens of young startups that go into over 100 countries outside the US. Their websites are well-designed and describe innovative business models and disruptive, customer-first product offerings.

And almost none of them are original. The business model is to copy well-known startup success stories like eBay and Zappos, launch them in new markets, and then sell them to the company that they copied in the first place or run them as independent companies that have a big advantage against the original entering that new market.

To date, Rocket Internet has faced plenty of criticism from Silicon Valley and beyond, but no serious legal trouble based on infringing on the intellectual property of the startups that it clones.

Despite all this, establishing and protecting your copyright does have some value and relevance for your startup. Since copyright is automatically granted, every blog post and explainer video you churn out can't be "sampled" without your permission. This is rarely an issue that will make or break a startup, but it's nice to have the peace of mind. And you worked to build that material, so it's fair that someone can't use it unless you give them permission.

Copyright does have certain limits. It can't, for one thing, protect your right to the underlying idea or way of doing something. Having a copyright on your software won't prevent another company from copying your process, which they can do even if they don't exactly know how you've done it. For that kind of protection, you need a patent. O

Patents

Patents are the most common kind of intellectual property protection sought by startups. Patents protect a process, a way of doing something—not the outcome of the process, the product itself. A notorious example is Amazon filing for a patent on their "one-click" checkout in 1997 that was granted two years later. They weren't looking to protect the unique look and feel of their button; they wanted to own a patent that would cover any and all e-commerce systems that used a one-click interface to allow shoppers to easily complete their online purchases.

Patents on software in general are very controversial because they tend to favor large companies with enough money to go to court and defend them. Startups that get entangled in patent cases, even if they're in the right, are often outgunned into bankruptcy.

Patents are important to the success of software startups who build value based on highly-specialized technology. But that doesn't mean they're irrelevant outside this hyper-specific set of companies. If your startup is raising tons of money and growing like crazy, you might be advised to put in a few patent applications under the advice of your attorney (or VC). This is a good step to take, but again, it's not what will make or break your social networking startup (unless you're building revolutionary tech with computer science PhDs).

The process (that a piece of software accomplishes) isn't always complicated enough to warrant applying for a patent, yet many companies still try (Amazon is the most well-known case but they are far from alone), which has made the patent system very controversial in Silicon Valley. Of course, not every patent application is granted, but some are, even for very simple processes. Because these patents effectively take some basic tools off the table for other companies, they are considered damaging to innovation and to startups in particular.

But aren't patents meant to promote innovation? Don't they protect creators and incentivize them to work on original ideas they know they'll be able to capitalize on?

> **Because these patents effectively take some basic tools off the table for other companies, they are considered damaging to innovation and to startups in particular.**

Let's consider a hypothetical startup. Say you're working to build a service that delivers the ingredients your customers need to make a full meal. While it's a web-based service on the user's end, it's really a mix of functions, many of which have to exist in the real world.

Now, say you write some code that takes the order from your site, and you want to protect your claim to it; you can get a copyright on those exact lines of Python or node.js code. But if you want to go even further, you can apply for a patent that will protect the process your startup makes happen.

You're not likely to see the order-taking process or the surveys as unique, but you might decide to patent the algorithm that matches meals to customers. After all, that process is your differentiating factor—it's what makes you a truly new service and not just a copy of an existing model.

You could describe the process as "a system to determine taste preferences for future meals based on expressed interest in food attributes." That doesn't exactly roll off the tongue, but the legalese of patent applications is always clunky. It's also not exactly clear what's really being described, and so there can be volumes of backup exhibits to make the claim that the feature meets the standard of being a "non-obvious" innovation—what Amazon's one-click was routinely criticized for not being, as it was, in fact, obvious to many.

IT WOULD BE MORE THAN ONE PROCESS AND COULD INCLUDE:

- The order-taking process

- The survey that gathers information from the customer about their food preferences

- The algorithm that takes this survey data and processes it to determine what types of meals each user is likely to enjoy

Now, let's say you've released your first MVP and you're getting a positive response. You give your first customers a short survey about the kinds of foods they like, and it seems to improve their satisfaction with the meal kits you send them. Everything seems to be working really well. All you need to do now is wait for the patent to protect your right to the algorithm.

Then, you run into a snag. You find out that another startup built an engine for recommending grocery items for stores based on past purchases. They secured a patent for their process, which they describe as "a system to determine food preferences for future meals based on past interest in certain food items." This product is very different than your personal ingredient delivery service, but the wording in their application is pretty close to yours. You or your attorney approach the company, but they express interest in retaining rights to their patent; however, they are willing to license it to you. Yikes!

The end result is a driving up of costs and a slowing down of innovation.

This and similar cases show how patents can be an impediment to bringing ideas and solutions to life. Rather than protecting the creator's rights to the precise products they invent, they often make it difficult or impossible for other companies to develop products that are roughly adjacent to patented products. The end result is a driving up of costs and a slowing down of innovation. ○

Do you need to do anything now?

Whether you think you might need a trademark, a copyright, or a patent, there are two things you need to ask yourself before you make a move to try to secure intellectual property rights. The first is, "What does my attorney advise me to do?" Intellectual property is a complicated and sometimes murky realm, full of legal technicalities and complex consequences. Make sure you get an experienced professional's opinion before trying to acquire these kinds of protection (or before deciding you don't need them).

The second question you need to ask yourself is, "What are the opportunity costs of securing these rights?" It's easy for a large, established corporation to spread itself far and wide, but an early-stage startup needs to make sure its limited resources are being spent wisely. Any time you and your team spend trying to trademark logos, copyright products, and patent processes is time not spent focusing on developing your product or growing your userbase. ●

THE PITCH DECK

"Very simple ideas lie within the reach only of complex minds."

Remy de Gourmont

A pitch deck introduces investors to your startup—the problem, solution, and its potential for growth—and what can make or break your investment pitch. This final chapter dives into how to structure your pitch deck, create compelling slides, and present the content in different situations.

We'll explore how to:

- *Structure your deck into three clear sections that present exactly the information investors expect*

- *Demonstrate your product's ability to meet a pressing need*

- *Convey the right amount of information in each slide for presentations or for a "leave-behind deck"*

THE PITCH DECK

The pitch deck is the atomic unit of a startup. It is the representative document that lays out everything a startup does and the key document for fundraising, partnership deals, recruitment of key employees, and any other time you need to convince someone of your progress and credibility.

The pitch deck's primary use is to promote your startup by telling its story in a compelling and concise way. Most people inherently understand the need to sell, but many startup founders don't understand why they should also tell a story. And yet, if we look back to even our earliest human ancestors, we can clearly see that storytelling is our most important and effective tool for capturing an audience and ensuring that they retain your message. (Although some people do think PowerPoint is only incrementally more effective than cave painting.) ○

Structuring Your Pitch Deck

There are three basic sections of a pitch deck. First, tell your story. German philosopher Georg Wilhelm Friedrich Hegel created a framework for understanding historical and cultural change that has become known as the Hegelian dialectic. The dialectic has three movements: thesis, antithesis, and synthesis. The thesis represents the status quo, the antithesis is some new challenge or problem that the status quo faces, and the conflict is resolved in synthesis—a resulting combination of the two.

The story of your startup should have the same structure. Something or someone (thesis) meets an obstacle (antithesis), but the result of confronting and dealing with it leads to something different (synthesis)—and in the case of your problem-solving startup, better than it was before.

We are not yet focusing on the exact problem your startup aims to solve. In this initial telling of your company story, you are relying on the narrative of conflict, an essential ingredient for compelling storytelling. What matters is that you show there is a struggle in need of a positive resolution.

Every detail perfect, limit the number of details.
Jack Dorsey, co-founder of Twitter and Square

Once your conflict narrative has hooked your audience, you move to the second part of the pitch deck: framing this conflict as a problem-solution set. Let's say your narrative is about Ethel. She's a homeowner in Chicago, and even though she has a college degree, she has trouble understanding the complex paperwork involved in selling a house on her own. In the end, Ethel has to pay more fees than she should have to a real estate attorney. Once your audience is invested in Ethel's situation, it's time to put a specific frame around this problem-solution. Here is where you will outline the general problem: homeowners who don't want to sell their homes through an agent face bureaucratic complexity and potential government fines, which dissuades them from saving money by handling the sale themselves.

The value that you can offer Ethel is a combination of online document management and a remote adviser who can walk her through any issues she might face via video call—and the cost to her would be far less than what she'd pay to have an agent.

You've laid down the fundamental principles of the pitch, created a narrative that sticks in the audience's mind like a scene from a cinematic masterpiece, and put a razor-sharp point on the exact problem and solution that your startup addresses. From a storytelling angle, you've made a good case for yourself, but an investor will still have a lot of questions: How big is this market? Is this the right team? Do they really understand who the customer is and the exact problem they face? So, now it's time to do the hard work and provide answers to these questions and the proof to back them up.

From a storytelling angle, you've made a good case for yourself, but an investor will still have a lot of questions

This is your opportunity to demonstrate the growth potential of your startup idea. Investors will particularly want to understand the size of the market you're moving into and additional business opportunities that could stem from your original concept. ○

Market Sizing

To pitch investors for capital, the market that you're pursuing has to be big. And I mean big: beyond-a-shadow-of-a-doubt big and with lots of room to spare. Venture investors make their money by having relatively few but very big hits. If you're in a small market, even a complete success is not a big hit. You need to have a market (or grow an undeveloped market) big enough to accommodate ten or twenty times the initial investment.

Market sizing is an imperfect science, but you need to make plausible estimations. There are three components: Total Addressable Market, Serviceable Available Market, and Target Market (also called a Serviceable Obtainable Market, or a "beachhead" market). And for any startup, there can be intense debate as to how to define and bucket potential customers.

TOTAL ADDRESSABLE MARKET

TARGET MARKET

SERVICEABLE AVAILABLE MARKET

It's easiest to illustrate these concepts through an example, so let's look at how we might start sizing up the market for people like our protagonist Ethel, who potentially need help with the legalese of selling their home without an agent:

Total Addressable Market

You would probably define this as all homeowners, since that's the population you could eventually serve. But that isn't very helpful, since the interval of how often these people might sell is so irregular, and your value is to help a customer once they're in the process of selling. Many are not yet in the house-selling market, they're in the house-owning market.

For calculating a grand "this market is worth X" figure, you could then take that number and multiply it by what you think the total value of each customer could bring in. (As you can see, it's easy to get gargantuan numbers here.)

Serviceable Available Market

This group is directly in your sight line and within geographic reach. This could be all of the people who are planning to sell their home. You could scope it in different ways: those who are selling and are dedicated to selling without an agent, or also including those who just haven't formally committed to using an agent (so that the fresh value proposition of your startup could change their decision).

Target Market

This is a group that you plan to pursue immediately and hopefully have a strong method (or at least a realistic hypothesis) for how to acquire them cheaply, and have a theory on why they'd be especially good early users (might they be prone to referring others, for example?).

Your Target Market could be older homeowners who live in dense cities, since they regularly seek assistance with similarly complex tasks and they're perhaps likely to know other aging homeowners in close vicinity who might be considering selling their home to downsize and are looking for the most affordable way.

A mistake that founders often make is calculating a huge TAM for their startup, which they think gives them a cushion where only taking a small piece of that market would still be a robust business.

A mistake that founders often make is calculating a huge TAM for their startup, which they think gives them a cushion where only taking a small piece of that market would still be a robust business. But this is an apples-to-oranges comparison: a wide-ranging TAM is endlessly heterogeneous. For credibility, focus on a well-thought-out SAM and a realistic Target Market. O

Adjacent Markets

The most compelling pitches will also look beyond the market you're immediately targeting. Investors will want to see your proven case but will be interested in what kind of adjacent opportunities will be available further down the road. In other words, you will want to demonstrate how your business can grow both vertically and horizontally.

First, let's consider horizontal growth. This is growth you achieve by broadening the scope beyond your initial target market. In the case of the real estate home-seller platform, this could involve moving into new geographies or having some basic information about why certain other markets also face the same bureaucratic hurdles that your customers would have and that your solution could address. In other words, the bureaucracy is complex enough for it to create a problem but not so complex that it can't be tackled with your solution. You might also be able to tantalize your audience with a second product. For example, you might tell them about the high fees charged by commercial real estate brokers and how commercial property owners may face the same problems as someone who wishes they could save money by selling their own house.

Expanding the business vertically is to own and control more components up and down the value chain. In addition to just helping real estate sellers fill out complicated paperwork, you could also offer an enhanced marketing platform for their home, something superior to what third-party sites offer. You could even get as detailed as having a stable of public notaries who attend the signing ceremony, rather than having the seller outsource this, and have it included in the overall cost.

Whatever your vision for expanding the business down the road, what you're essentially offering are more opportunities for revenue and therefore, a bigger overall profit potential for the investor.

You also need to show some amount of traction, whether your product is live and onboarding users or whether you are relying on customer interviews and early demand indicators like a landing page and Google AdWords. Since the bar of beginning a startup and pitching ideas is really low, you have to show that you can provide a service and that what you've been doing has been successful. Your success at this stage can be measured in any number of ways: prototype development, user metrics, or revenue. Whatever metric you use, the point is that you need to show progress before you can receive the money or accept a business deal with a strategic partner. ○

Make Your Slides Work for You

Designing a bad slide deck can torpedo your chances of success, but the good news is that there are simple principles you can follow that will help you avoid some of the common pitfalls.

There are two kinds of pitch decks: the presentation deck and the "leave behind" deck. Each has its uses, so we will take the time to focus on both.

Many startups only think of a pitch deck solely in terms of the presentation deck: standing up and speaking in front of a group of people with a presentation on an overhead projector. And it's no surprise: because of its theatricality, it has made its way into popular culture, with television programs like Shark Tank. Essentially, you're in front of a group of people, offering commentary to walk them through the main points of the deck.

Since you have limited time in front of your audience, it's vitally important to adhere to some visual rules. Guy Kawasaki, an early Apple employee, created the 10/20/30 Rule of PowerPoint. The rule is simple: a PowerPoint presentation should have 10 slides, last no more than 20 minutes, and contain no font smaller than 30 points. In practice, the number of slides will vary, but the basic principles still hold: limited information presented quickly and in very large type.

Venture capitalist Vinod Khosla used a simple test for whether someone had crammed too much information on a presentation slide. His Five-Second Rule basically gives the viewer five seconds to take in all the information on any given slide. If the slides are clear, the people in the room should be able to recall everything on the slide after it's taken away. The basic principle here is that when a slide is too dense, the audience has to stop paying attention to the presenter so they can process the information on it. If a slide fails the Five-Second Rule, it fails to serve the basic function of any visual: to aid the presentation (not do the work for you or repeat what you say). You never want to make the audience choose between listening to you and looking at your slides. The information you present should be simple, graphically represented, and not require any calculations or inferential leaps. Even if you need to use quantitative data points, just give the audience the most important numbers—less is more.

You never want to make the audience choose between listening to you and looking at your slides. The information you present should be simple, graphically represented, and not require any calculations or inferential leaps.

A very common tactic for achieving a lot with minimal information is using an "X for Y" comparison. Tell your audience to think of your startup as Uber for dog walking, Airbnb for hot tubs, or Facebook for record collectors (which basically describes discogs.com, an amazing site for vinyl nerds). This makes a little information go a long way by using the audience's existing knowledge. In other words, you don't have to put all of the information about the Uber-, Airbnb-, or Facebook-like things your startup does on the slide, because it's already in the viewer's head.

Take our running example of the real estate app. You can convey a lot of information by just telling the audience that it's "Gusto for Homeselling." If they know that Gusto's payroll service takes care of the government paperwork for its users, they will immediately see how the real estate app will provide a similar solution to anyone who wants to sell their home.

NDAs

An easy way to damage your credibility is asking investors to sign a non-disclosure agreement. Don't do this. Non-disclosure agreements can be very useful in business for limiting the amount of information that a partner can share, but they invite too much potential legal liability for an investor. Any experienced investor will refuse to sign. Conversely, an investor who does sign is likely not very experienced and probably not the best person to be talking to about your earliest stage funding, which can fuel your execution of the solution (and is more valuable than the idea that you might have the impulse to protect).

The other approach to a deck is the "leave-behind" deck. This is a document that is meant to be emailed, printed out, and circulated among people in an office. It's less common—and a lot less flashy—than a presentation deck, but it has the advantage of being more comprehensive. You wouldn't want to put detailed calculations or lots of narrative text in a deck that you're presenting on stage, but it's important to ensure your potential funders see the whole picture in the supplementary leave-behind deck.

This brings us to the one major landmine when it comes to the leave-behind deck: it needs to speak for itself. The startup founders aren't present to answer questions in real time, so the deck has to not only provide lots of information but also answer key questions any potential investor will have. If it fails to do so, it may reflect negatively on you and your team. O

Adapt Your Speaking Style

Public speaking is a difficult skill to master. But even when you have mastered the aspects universal to all public speaking, you may still find yourself tripped up by some factors that are specific to pitch deck presentations.

There are two scenarios in which startup founders usually pitch. The first is the celebrated public pitch. These may happen as part of an accelerator's demo day or a conference such as the LAUNCH Festival. The public pitch is where traditional public speakers will feel most at home: the founders speak in front of hundreds of people and hold the floor for up to ten minutes, often followed by a Q&A.

Things are markedly different when pitching to a couple of investors or an angel. In these private pitches, you have to stay authoritative while also relinquishing control of the presentation. If you're visiting the office of the venture capital firm or meeting an angel investor for coffee to show your deck on your laptop, you can expect to be interrupted and questioned along the way. You need to be ready to go off-script. In fact, one of the biggest mistakes you can make when you're preparing for these small-scale pitches is to memorize a script. Instead, go in having done your homework and let the minimal information you included in your slides serve as cues for the key points of your pitch. That way, if you're interrupted or lose your train of thought, all you need is a single bullet point to bring you right back to where you need to be.

You need to be ready to go off-script. In fact, one of the biggest mistakes you can make when you're preparing for these small-scale pitches is to memorize a script.

The pitch deck is a living, breathing document that will change as your startup evolves and you respond to the ever-changing market and customer needs. This is true for everything that you'll work on as a founder: your value proposition and customers will evolve, your product will go in new directions, and you'll keep charging toward new ways to innovate and stay ahead of the game. This is the essence of evidence-based entrepreneurship: being flexible and open to change. Keep that in mind on your journey, and it will serve you well. ●

BILL REICHERT

Managing Director
Garage Technology Ventures

With a long and distinguished career in Silicon Valley as an entrepreneur and venture capitalist, Bill Reichert has both given a lot of pitches and seen a lot of pitches. His "Getting to Wow" framework provides clear rules to founders on how to sell their message effectively.

ELLIOTT ADAMS I remembered your "Getting to Wow" talk that you did for us a couple of years ago at Startup Next. If you wouldn't mind, would you share the key parts?

BILL REICHERT Sure, sure. There are two key parts to it. The context is that there's a ton of stuff written and videoed and blogged about perfecting your pitch, right? There are all sorts of templates out there for entrepreneurs to develop their pitch and all sorts of tips about your elevator pitch and your investor pitch, etcetera, etcetera. A few years ago, I was struggling to try to understand why entrepreneurs consistently get it wrong—despite all of this coaching for pitches—and

> **"I had no idea, first of all, that investors had a heart, and second of all, I had no idea that they weren't using some powerful analytic tool that had an algorithmic calculation of investable projects."**

I realized that a big part of it is actually our fault. What most people call "pitch coaching" is actually presentation coaching. If you think about it, all the people who come and do pitch coaching, what they're really doing is presentation coaching. That raises the

question, well, what's the difference between a pitch and a presentation? A presentation assumes you've got a fixed chunk of time and an audience that is committed to sitting there and listening to you for that fixed chunk of time. But the reality is, in 99 percent of your communications as an entrepreneur, that's not the case, right?

EA Very true.

BR I realized that with all this work we put into helping entrepreneurs with their elevator pitch, everybody has a different definition of an elevator pitch. Usually it's sixty seconds, ninety seconds, two minutes, even four minutes. The idea is that it's a pitch that's much shorter than what you would do if you got into the conference room at a VC firm. But, the only place you can ever use an elevator pitch is at an elevator pitch competition, right? I mean, you can't

really use your elevator pitch in any normal situation in life. Would you get somebody on the phone and give them your elevator pitch? Or at the shrimp bar at a trade show?

EA Do you mean because it's unnatural in conversation to talk continuously for ninety seconds?

BR Exactly. And a lot of people include slides with their elevator pitch, right? But even if it's a non-slide, sixty-second elevator pitch, they're not natural. It's not the way any human being would speak to another human being.

I mean, it's really designed to try to cover all thirteen critical points of your business model in sixty seconds. So, that was my epiphany, and in all of this behavioral economics and psychology stuff, I learned that the human attention span is essentially twenty seconds maximum. That's what all the psychologists have told us. So, my first point is that we're coaching entrepreneurs to make presentations, not pitches. My second base point is that you really only have twenty seconds to be compelling, or you may as well go home. You've got to figure out a way to get people excited, or at least intrigued, in twenty seconds. And it's not by asking them some clever question or giving them a riddle, as a lot of pitch coaches advise to start with in order to hook your audience.

EA I've seen that end pretty badly.

BR There are two classes of people who have no patience for clever presentations. One class is customers. Every customer has heard hundreds, if not thousands, of sales guys come into their office and pitch something to them. They've heard it all. They just want you to cut to the chase. The second class is investors. Any investor who's been in the game for any amount of time has heard it all.

They both just want you to cut to the chase. And those are the two most important kinds of people for an entrepreneur, right?

EA It seems like a lot of what these people are learning is effective only in less critical situations, like a pitch night.

BR Yes, exactly. We have constructed in this ecosystem these things called pitch nights or pitch competitions.

Every VC on the planet will tell you that a tiny, tiny fraction of the companies they've ever invested in came from seeing them at a pitch competition.

EA They seem to be a strange cottage industry that doesn't actually relate to the larger VC industry.

BR Exactly. Now, I'm not saying that entrepreneurs should not participate in pitch nights. I think there's some virtue in trying things out and getting reactions and stuff like that, but it's not really the way you get investors. And it's certainly not the way you get customers, right?

So, that's sort of the key point on "Getting to Wow" and the difference between having a good pitch and developing an authentic presentation. The three themes I say are clear, compelling, and then credible—the three C's.

The way I try to get this across to entrepreneurs these days is I talk about the fact that almost all pitch coaching, including the entire approach that I was given for developing my pitch when I was an entrepreneur, is based upon creating a logical argument full of data, evidence, facts, and analytics. That was the way I was trained to pitch to investors. For those of us who survived and went on, we thought: "Oh, well it worked for us, so that's what we should teach everybody, right?"

But being heavily influenced now in recent decades by the combination of behavioral economics and neuro-linguistic programming, we realized that humans don't make decisions with their brains, they make decisions with their hearts. So, I talk about how we spend all our time focused on the head, but what you really have to do is figure out how to get to their heart. You've got to get them to fall in love with you. This was my other epiphany when I became a VC. I had no idea, first of all, that investors had a heart, and second of all, I had no idea that they weren't using some powerful analytic tool that had an algorithmic calculation of investable projects.

EA Many founders seem to have this idea of venture capitalists having a lot more objective insight than some actually do.

BR I watched our team and I watched my new comrades in the venture capital industry go through the investment decision-making process, and I realized that the key to being successful was getting

> **"Part of the instinctive reaction that investors and customers develop is getting to a fast no because with the vast majority of pitches, you're going to have to say no at some point, and you don't want to waste time on something you're eventually going to say no to. Therefore, you want to say no as fast as you can."**

the investor to fall in love with you, and then having enough data to be able to make a compelling, brain-oriented case that it was a good investment to make.

But the key is always differentiating yourself from the unwashed masses of entrepreneurs that are constantly hitting on investors. I thought when I was an unwashed entrepreneur that each of my companies were so brilliantly unique and compelling and exciting, that of course I would knock their socks off if only they heard about what I was up to. What I missed was that the reason they invested in my companies was that somehow my co-founders and I triggered something that got them emotionally excited about the investment rather than concluding it was a good investment by rational means. They became emotionally excited that it was a good investment. So, the key is, you have to get them emotionally excited, and I say that means you have to get them to fall in love with something about your company.

The other body part that you have to communicate with is the gut. We have a whole bunch of psychology research on this that says that humans react instantaneously in one direction or the other. I will tell you that in any given professional or sales situation, you have an immediate instinctive reaction to each person that you come across, and usually it's directional, one way or the other. Rarely is it purely neutral, right? That's because neutrality doesn't have any sort of socio-biological advantage.

EA If you're investing, you wouldn't have a neutral reaction. If you're hunting and evaluating, it's almost impossible.

BR Exactly, you're constant. Part of the instinctive reaction that investors and customers develop is getting to a fast no because with the vast majority of pitches, you're going to have to say no at some point, and you don't want to waste time on something you're eventually going to say no to. Therefore, you want to say no as fast as you can.

Sometimes I think it's baked in, and I will be the first to admit that that's dangerous. We absolutely know it's dangerous to have an instinctive negative reaction just because somebody doesn't profile quite the way you ideally want them, right?

Regardless, that's your challenge as an entrepreneur. You don't know what they're thinking in terms of their gut instincts, so your challenge as an entrepreneur is to make sure you don't trigger that negative reaction. Most of our negative reactions are the guys coming on too strong and making it seem like he's just blowing smoke, which leads to feelings of mistrust and deceit. So, the head, heart and gut correspond to the three C's. For the head, you've got to be clear; for the heart, you've got to be compelling and get the heart racing; and for the gut, you've got to be credible, and you've got to pass the gut check and get over the instinctive reaction.

EA Could you elaborate on that?

BR Well, they're all difficult. The thing that's amazingly difficult for entrepreneurs is to be clear with what they do. Unfortunately, what happens is there are pitch coaches out there that say the secret to your elevator pitch is to be able to say what you do in twelve words or eight words or seven. That's in every pitch-coach training exercise I've ever seen. They force these poor entrepreneurs to distill their essence into twelve words or something crazy like that, right?

Every entrepreneur then thinks they've only got twelve words, so they go super high level. So then you have, "we empower enterprise customers to maximize their profitability with mobile services."

EA They take all the meaning out of it.

BR Exactly. So, you go super high level and there's nothing there. There's certainly no clarity when you go super high. The other end of the spectrum is that a lot of entrepreneurs are so deep into their core technology. They assume that everyone understands which tech stack they've combined with which deep-learning convolutional neural network and that everyone's going to appreciate why it is that there's only 150 milliseconds of latency compared to everyone else. So, you get both sides of the spectrum. It's stunning how difficult it is for an entrepreneur who's deeply embedded or enmeshed in what they're doing to create a simple sentence that most intelligent people can understand and that explains what they're doing. They usually go way too high or way too technospeak, so what I encourage entrepreneurs to do is imagine a good TechCrunch journalist writing a story on their company. What sentence would they use to describe their company? They're not going to use "empowering global enterprises to whatever," right?

EA They take the hyperbole out.

BR What can you say to six strangers at a cocktail party and have at least five of them repeat it back to you accurately? And that's your test. Can you do that? You can't craft compound, multiple subordinate clauses into an eighty-five-word sentence, you know? Which is why all these pitch coaches ask you to do it in twelve words, but that's kind of going to the wrong extreme, right?

It's just a normal sentence. A normal sentence spoken in ten seconds contains twenty-two words for most people. That's plenty of words to be clear with what you're doing. So, number one is being clear. Number two is being compelling. What causes the heart to race? You've got to give them some compelling benefit that separates you from the rest of the pack. Something that

makes them go, "Wow, you can do that?" Normally, entrepreneurs spend the first thirty seconds describing their product. You can't talk about your product for thirty seconds because everybody's eyes are going to glaze over. They're either going to think they've heard about products like this before, or they're thinking to themselves, "Well, so what? What's in it for me?" So, what I'm telling them is to be compelling. You've got to offer a customer benefit. It's value proposition 101. You've got to offer them a value proposition that is significantly better than the alternatives that are out there. For example, you're five times faster, or you're one-tenth the cost, or you're half the weight, or whatever a customer would consider a benefit.

Everybody on the planet who speaks English knows the difference between a benefit and a feature. You hear it so much in the world of business, at least, that you know you have to talk about the benefit, not about the feature.

And yet, so few entrepreneurs ever translate that into a compelling value proposition. I ask every entrepreneur to complete the following sentence: "The big idea behind our product/service is . . . " That sentence has got to be a compelling value proposition for your customers. The whole idea is getting them out of the habit of describing the product, which, in essence, is its features, and get them focused on what value the customer will appreciate.

No matter what, every company needs a compelling value proposition. I mean, you don't have a company if you don't have a compelling value proposition. The unfortunate thing is there are a lot of companies that have been widely successful without a clear, compelling value proposition.

And that, unfortunately, is a false positive for a lot of entrepreneurs.

EA Are we thinking Twitter here?

BR Right. Twitter and Facebook. If you think about it, how would you articulate the value proposition of the original Facebook? I mean, it's kind of entertaining, you know, as personal existential validation, but no investor would invest in that. You have this problem that a lot of things that are highly successful. It would have been very hard for the entrepreneur to originally articulate a compelling value proposition for it. I mean, Zuckerberg had the benefit of momentum. It was the same with Google. Nobody could tell the difference between Google's search and anybody else's search, but Google developed a cool factor and that gave it an exclusivity aspect. You had to be invited to get a Gmail account. Anybody could get a Hotmail account, anybody could get a Yahoo account, but you had to be invited to get a Gmail account. It's the same with Facebook. If your company's success is dependent upon you being totally cool, then frankly, I can't help you, you know? Either you are or you aren't, and that's where my partner in Garage Ventures, Guy Kawasaki, says, "If your 'wow' is that you're totally cool, then the only way you get that across is if you can demo the product in the first thirty seconds." That's hard to do, but that's what's going to get people interested. You could not describe Facebook in words at a cocktail party and get people to go "wow," right?

EA It's the experience.

BR You couldn't describe Twitter. For companies that are dependent upon being cool, you have to communicate in a different way. I would say 99 percent of real businesses are more objective in terms of what their value proposition is. I think probably 50 percent of entrepreneurs think that their advantage is their coolness, but I think that's a really risky strategy. But it's compelling, right?

EA It certainly can be.

BR And then the third C is being credible—the gut check. There are two big components to credibility that are tightly interwoven. As soon as you start talking to a potential buyer or customer, or as soon as you start talking to an investor, their reaction as soon as you open your mouth is, "Oh yeah, I've heard this before." Because, overwhelmingly, most entrepreneurs are pitching something that is some flavor of something that we've seen before. The challenge is, you've got to get out of that rut as fast as you can, so you can't wait

until slide six—the template says you don't have to talk about competition until slide six. You can't wait until slide six to pre-empt that skepticism. To get over the negative gut reaction, you've got to say something like, "You might have heard of other companies doing something similar, but unlike those companies, what we can do is . . . "

EA It can really undermine a pitch's credibility, as you say. If you're sitting there for ten minutes until they show you that they understand the competition, by that point, you've largely written them off.

BR Exactly. So, the key to the third C, credibility, is pre-empting the competitive noise problem. Then the other piece of that is, do you have evidence that what you're saying is, in fact, true? Meaning, what do you have other than your pathologically high confidence and optimism that this is going to work?

I encourage entrepreneurs to give us some reason to believe them. I mean, the fact that Unilever is piloting

your product in South Asia, for example, means that you've got some credible third party who's already decided you guys are the best thing they could find on the planet. So, give us whatever level of traction you've got. Maybe the best you've got is that your professor happens to be one of the world's experts in this domain, and he signed on and lent his reputation to your advisor report that you're two guys in grad school who've got a clever idea. But today, most people are smart enough that

> *"Every entrepreneur then thinks they've only got twelve words, so they go super high level. So then you have, 'we empower enterprise customers to maximize their profitability with mobile services.'"*

they've talked to some customers, they've got some sort of traction in terms of, for example, "we over-subscribed our Kickstarter campaign by 250 percent."

EA Ha! I can agree with that.

BR Add some credibility. So those are the three Cs: clear, compelling, credible.

JENNY FIELDING

Managing Director
Techstars

Jenny Fielding left her career in finance to do what at the time was the unthinkable: start a startup. After selling Switch Mobile, she later became a managing director at Techstars, where she runs accelerator programs across verticals such as FinTech and Internet of Things.

ELLIOTT ADAMS You've been a Managing Director for different Techstars accelerator programs, is that right?

JENNY FIELDING Yes, I'm focused on IoT (Internet of Things) right now, but I'm more generally focused on creating ecosystems. The truth is, I'll probably be running a different program next year because I just like doing different things.

EA IoT and hardware products have such a different timeline of developing and testing than software products. When someone is working on an IoT product, what's the right sequence of events where you say they're ready to come into Techstars?

JF I think it's one of the reasons that we restarted the program this year with a number of corporate partners who could fill in the gaps. Our program is associated with six corporate partners—people like GE and Siemens, Bosch, and Verizon—all these corporates who have deep expertise in the various components around IoT. It isn't just software, though; it's hard for two people in their garage to start a hardware company. You usually need more people and capital, and you need more industry expertise. So, that's why we've partnered with the corporates. I think in terms of what we look for, it's even more fundamental that the team is technical. You can kind of get away with a CEO who isn't technical for a software company because you can get a good CTO, but that doesn't work for a hardware company.

EA Say you've got something more ideal: three or four people, and they've got an idea. They've been building some kind of prototype. With software, you're measured by traction. For IoT, how far along should they be for your program?

> "So, if you've done this before, if you've been working on hardware products for the last five years and now you're telling me that you're going to build something, I have greater confidence that that's going to happen."

JF No product, no traction, no problem.

I mean, I really do revert to great teams. My last class had a mix. We had a few companies that had products in market and were working on a second version, but we also had a few companies that were pretty far from it. I do like to take a mix because I think the dynamic of the cohort is that the ones who are further along can help the ones that are earlier. There's a nice interaction there. We don't change our fundamental thesis, which is the team, team, team, market, traction, idea.

That said, if you have never built a prototype in hardware and you don't have a prototype to show

us, then I think that starts to get hard. So, if you've done this before, if you've been working on hardware products for the last five years and now you're telling me that you're going to build something, I have greater confidence that that's going to happen.

EA With IoT and hardware, it's obviously tough because it's the infrastructure of a supply chain. How do you empower startups to not only design something, prototype it, and start to fabricate some early models but also really scale? Is that what the corporate partners are about?

JF I think for some of them, it's expertise around the development. But if you take Verizon or SAP, it's around distribution. One of our corporate partners is PWC. With all their corporate clients and all their know-how around going to market, they worked some joint white papers with some of our companies, and that gave them a lot of validity when they went to market. That's where the corporate partners come in quite a bit.

EA That's obviously easier for a company that's been doing it for twenty years than a team of four founders who are just getting going, right?

JF I think there are a few things that contribute. One is that we've now invested in about sixty to seventy hardware companies at Techstars, so we have the legacy of alumni helping the younger startups by giving them access to facilities, best practices, and kind of holding their hands through the process. Now that Techstars has been around for ten years, there's a lot of knowledge transfer, which is pretty awesome.

The second thing is, we have mentors who have built hardware and who are literally in the office every day working with the companies. Even if you don't have that person with certain particular skills on your team, having a mentor who's going to be in twice a week and who's going to guide you is helpful. We had a 3D-printing company, and we had half the executive team at MakerBot helping those guys.

EA That's a huge advantage.

JF Yeah, and then there are companies out there, whether it's PCH or others, that are willing to work with startups on very favorable terms. So, everyone now—whether it's supply chain organizations or whatnot—realizes that if they want a long-term relationship with this company, they need to start earlier. They need to roll up their sleeves, help the companies, and not milk them for all their cash. So, we're seeing far more favorable arrangements, and that extends to the manufacturing as well. If you look at the Foxconns and Flextronics of the world, they're also involved with startup-friendly programs.

EA You mentioned companies working with PWC and other corporates. Are those startups selling into enterprise? Is that the reason for that?

JF Our first program around IoT was mostly consumer. The second one was half consumer b2b, and this last one and the one that's coming up are all b2b industrial and enterprise. With that focus on selling into businesses, it's exactly why we've partnered with consulting companies, as well as large industry players.

EA There seems to be a danger of commoditization with hardware products. I'm wondering how focused a startup is on a given industry coming into your program and how big does that have to be? Do they need adjacent, follow-on opportunities that you want to see as well?

JF What I've learned after investing in all these hardware companies is that the hardware is much less important. It really is the software that is scalable and that can go into all these adjacent areas. So, I think that's exactly right. The hardware is becoming commoditized for the most part. I mean, there are still some really amazing bespoke hardware products that are coming out, but they're definitely on the b2b side. If you're measuring the environment in a construction site, that device you create can probably measure a lot of things in different industrial settings. Maybe construction is the first area you go into, but then you're able to go into lots of others. We're less focused now on what the hardware does and more focused on the software and what the network effect of that software can be.

EA How long have you been in New York with the program?

JF Well, I live between New York and San Francisco. I'm born and raised a New Yorker, so I've always lived here, but about ten years ago, I bought a place out in San Francisco because I was doing more venture investing and I just really liked the lifestyle out there.

EA How have you seen things change in New York? I know New York's a pretty well-developed market relative to some places, but what are some of the things you've seen—like accelerator programs, more investors, and other things—that have been a positive force in developing that New York startup community?

JF I started a startup here in 2006, and you can imagine the landscape was pretty bleak, right? There was just nothing here, and I founded my startup in my apartment. There were no co-working spaces. It was a different world. One of the reasons that I run my programs in New York is because it's near and dear to me. When I see all the resources and when I see the ecosystem that's come together, it's just so awesome.

So yeah, we've seen an incredible change. People thought I was crazy when I left my finance job in 2006 to found a startup. And now, no one bats an eye, right? So, there's just been a general attitude shift. I think a lot of it has been fostered in by a few groups, one being the universities. When I went to Columbia, there was nothing that even approached entrepreneurship. Now, if you look at just Columbia and NYU with the number of entrepreneurs they're pumping out, the investment that they're putting into it, and the classes that are supporting entrepreneurs, it's just incredible.

Coming from that, because New York's such an academic-type city with so many universities and whatnot, I think that's really changed things, as well as the ups and downs in the economy. Around 2008 or 2009, in the sudden crisis, all those bankers and other workers were laid off. Even all the engineers were laid off at places like Lehman Brothers, and so they had to get creative—hence this shift in mentality that came from necessity. All of a sudden, they didn't have a job. Some of them had money and they could wait it out, but a lot of them got into the startup world, so a lot of money and talent flowed into it

just from that. I think that's an interesting inflection point from New York.

EA It's interesting to think about those knock-on effects of the financial crisis. Is there anything else that's been a catalyst for New York?

JF We're definitely behind Silicon Valley, but just having some companies that have been relatively successful and having those people invest in startups has made a huge difference. My company was really small, but when I exited, I made a little bit of money

and I started angel investing. If you were a bigger company, like Tumblr or any of the success stories of New York, way more money was flowing in. That happened a good generation after it happened in Silicon Valley, so that definitely took until the 2000s for us to see. But I think it was those three things coming together that really changed New York.

EA What were the effects of the Tumblr acquisition?

Did people spin out, leave, and start new companies and start investing?

JF There were definitely a lot of people that were let go who started other companies and could bootstrap. The ZocDoc guys are another example. They're big investors that started a fund and are really an example of somewhere you've more recently seen the overflow.

Also, FourSquare hasn't necessarily

made a lot of money, but you have a lot of successful people who've come out of FourSquare and started other things, right? They're not doing very well now, but there was a heyday when they had raised a lot of money and there was a lot of excitement around it. People spent a lot of time there and started other companies. It's all been really helpful for helping New York evolve. ●

> "People thought I was crazy when I left my finance job in 2006 to found a startup. And now, no one bats an eye, right? So, there's just been a general attitude shift."

QASAR YOUNIS

Partner & COO
Y Combinator

Qasar Younis came into the role of Chief Operating Officer at Y Combinator via an extraordinarily unique path. He did a stint at Google after his startup, TalkBin, was acquired by Google, but he's also had the uniquely non-Silicon Valley vantage point of seeing an industry in decline and transformation from his time in Michigan's automotive giant, General Motors.

ELLIOTT ADAMS How do you see the role of what Y Combinator does?

QASAR YOUNIS When we're investing in startups, there's some concept or belief that's an inflection point we can help the company get to. It's to propel the company. The infrastructure to build a company is now even more free than it was even five or ten years ago. And just like there's all this free stuff as a consumer, free stuff exists on the developer side or on the company-building side. I mean, you can get credits for Amazon Web Services, there are a lot of open-source products out there, and you can distribute freely through app stores.

EA I was hoping to touch on this with you: distribution channels—primarily Google, Apple, Facebook—in terms of big ad networks and app stores. How much of an existential threat are the big tech companies to startups in general?

QY I've heard some people say these companies are different because they're more sophisticated than the old companies, like the General Motors of the day. I think if you look at General Motors, though, in their heyday—in the 1940s, '50s, '60s, '70s—they're just as aggressive at acquiring. I mean, General Motors literally is a conglomerate of all these individual coach shops which were making cars together. And that's what Google is. Google is buying up software shops. There will one day exist

a General Software, just like General Motors exists, and then in maybe thirty or forty years in the future, people will say "Oh, look at how stagnant this business is."

EA "Dinosaurs."

QY Yeah. Then biology modification—or whatever the next big wave is—is actually the more interesting business. So, I agree that there is a handful of companies that have a dominant position, and they'll buy companies like WhatsApp rather than letting them stay independent. But, for the WhatsApp founders, twenty billion dollars is—

EA Well, they're happy, but what if instead you're the guy who creates a WhatsApp that Google clones, with a billion people on their distribution channel?

QY I think that happens a lot less than one thinks it happens. And the main reason is that the genius is not in the pixel, the genius is what got to that idea.

It's like what they say, "Money can buy fashion but not style." There's something similar here. They can buy the product, but they don't buy the underlying genius behind it.

> "Nobody would think that—that "we're into the Microsoft century." I think people would even maybe doubt that it's going to be the Google century, you know?"

EA Right.

QY Now when they acquire, that's one of the main reasons to acquire. Google has done a very smart job in acquiring companies—I would say myself and my startup, Talkbin, included, YouTube, all these. When I say myself, it's not as in "we're geniuses," but in the sense that we're founders who then lead within the company and inject a lot of that entrepreneurial, founder mentality within the company. My personal culture and the culture that our team brought within Google Maps was unique, and I think we brought that in and that was a huge value for the company. If you look at Google itself, Google really built search and a couple of other smaller apps but acquires the vast majority of the assets that it seizes. YouTube is an acquisition, Android is an acquisition, a bunch of

Maps are acquisitions, a bunch of things in Chrome are acquisitions, a bunch of things in social space are acquisitions, so, you name it. There's more—it would be an interesting study to see how much of Google is in-house and how much is outside. When you think about it, big, big silos like YouTube and Android are completely separate companies.

So, you have this Big Five. Does that mean if you're a startup, you're kind of boxed out? They

you know what? The Kmarts and the Sears and the emerging Walmarts—if you don't get stocked by them, you're never going to be a big jam maker." But the truth is, you can look at Snapple as a great case study on this. Snapple emerges from selling to lots of small mom-and-pop shops and then ultimately breaks in. Analogously in software, what'll ultimately dislodge these players is probably a new distribution channel in itself—that can happen. Also, it's in those big firms' interest to distribute

QY Exactly. So, it's important to know that nothing is permanent. I mean, I was watching this Charlie Rose interview with Bill Gates from 1996 on YouTube, and Charlie Rose asked him, "So, it's going to be the Microsoft century, and how are you preparing?" And that's literally a laughable statement today. Nobody would think that—that "we're into the Microsoft century." I think people would even maybe doubt that it's going to be the Google century, you know?

EA Sure.

> ## "It's absolutely absurd, and so I do believe there's room for growth—endless growth. Certainly in our lifetimes. I think, maybe, beyond our lifetimes."

either copy, or they acquire you, or they hold the distribution channel. History is the best teacher because we're basically re-living the same thing with different metaphors, and I think you could have made that argument with television a few years back. Or retail—if you go to 1985 and you have a CPG [consumer packaged goods] product—let's say you have a new jam. People then were like, "Oh,

whatever's successful. They might hate what's happening. They might hate Instagram, and let's say they decided not to sell. Instagram, WhatsApp, and all those companies would still keep those products in their stores because they provide so much value.

EA Right, there are definite benefits.

QY But now, people will start saying, for the next ten years maybe, it's the Elon Musk, the Telsa, the SpaceX century. It's a lack of understanding about how these business cycles work. It's a lack of sophistication. And so, if you're a founder, and you feel this overwhelming, impenetrable force of the Big Five or whoever, wondering how you are going to get around it, it's just not true.

EA So, you're absolutely bullish on software?

QY Oh, 200 percent.

EA In addition to looking at all the new things you're looking at for YC?

QY Yeah, absolutely. It's like the automotive industry in the 1920s and the 1930s. The cars in the 1930s were dramatically better than in the 1870s and 1880s when Mr. Benz and Mr. Mercedes and Daimler were actually starting their own individual motorcycle shops, basically. And it would be hard, I think—and imagine when you look at the original motorcycles in the 1880s—to even comprehend that in the 1950s, you're nowhere near the peak of automotive. They could not imagine what a Ferrari today is or Tesla today is because they could only see, "Look how far we have come: this car can go in any weather and it can run for five, ten years, and anyone can afford it."

EA Interchangeable parts, to start.

QY Interchangeable parts. How could it get better than this? Well, guess what? It can get a lot better, and I think software will look back the same way. Let me give you some concept of the ridiculousness of software today. We come into this place, we sit down, open up a computer, and make sure the battery's there. Now, okay, let's find a power outlet. Okay, now turn it on. Wait for it to start up. Okay, now let's look for Wi-Fi. Oh shit! Who has Wi-Fi? What's the Wi-Fi address? Well, is this secure? Okay, we need a secure one. Okay, let me go find somebody who has a password for the secure thing. Okay, we finally got the password. Now

we're fifteen minutes into this thing. Then you're going to fire up a browser. Oh, it needs to update. Okay, let's update that. Then it's going to fire up the—oh, the OS needs updating. Ah, it's forcing me to update. Okay, let's hold on. Let's wait. Okay, it's updated. Now, let's, let's . . . what was that website again? Let me go to another website to locate the website I was trying to find. Ah, there it is. Okay. Damn! I forgot my username. Let me open up this document. Ah, I don't have the password for my docs.

It's absolutely absurd, and so I do believe there's room for growth—endless growth. Certainly in our lifetimes. I think, maybe, beyond our lifetimes. If you're in your twenties or thirties right now, in the next thirty years, you can safely put your chips into software and it will be productive.

EA Let's talk about leadership. YC is just doing things that no one else is doing.

QY YC was doing this for a few years before other companies started in similarly, and I think there's always been that distance. I think it's just not been apparent numerically or through press releases. I think YC, post-Paul-Graham era, is better at press.

EA You were pretty low key back in the day.

QY Relatively speaking, we're low key. But from 2005 to about 2012 or '13, YC did virtually zero press, and it was very insular. And so, part of that is just us coming out and having more partners. And look, we never went to conferences. That was a normal thing, so now we'll go out here to make sure we can evangelize a little bit of the message because there's some image of us being elitist or some version of that.

EA One of things that I was referring to a moment ago is that you're talking publicly about how technology can make human labor less necessary.

Do you feel like you guys have good company around that conversation in Silicon Valley, or are you just kind of out there on your own with it?

QY So, when we talk about basic income, we're never looking at it as, "Okay, what's the cohort doing, and let's see how we can move ahead of it." I think we've always, from the early days, looked at carving our own path, and so it's not a response or reactiveness to the market.

Now specifically, are there other people in Silicon Valley who emotionally understand basic income and things like that? One of the reasons research exists, one of the reasons the Gates Foundation and a bunch of other things exist is—I mean, Gates Foundation is the one that says, "We want to invest where capital markets are ignoring," and I think we feel similarly in that degree. It's like, "Let's do research where the others aren't." There's certainly a market fundamentalism that exists, probably more in America than anywhere else, and maybe more in Silicon Valley than anywhere else in America.

That's not speaking for YC, because on a personal level, I just don't agree with that view of the world. Capital markets are not this end-all, be-all solution for everything. It's like saying that socialism would be the end all, be all of everything. It isn't. Within all these different ideas and different concepts, there are powerful points, and that's where the difficulty and the nuance arise, in picking the best.

And so, specifically: basic income, and is there an issue? You know, early in my career, I worked in Detroit, in manufacturing. I went to the General Motors Institute in undergrad. I worked at General Motors for five years. I worked at Bosch for two years. I lived in Flint, Michigan, for five years. I mean, I've been in it, you know? I've probably worked in five different factories for long periods of time, here and in Japan. So, this is my bread and butter. I really know it—my life is split between that, and then I do software and come to the Valley. So, I know that world maybe better than anybody, you know, certainly better than any of my venture capitalist peers in the Valley. And so, I think it's a real problem. I think it's absolutely a real problem. I mean, ten years ago when I managed robots, I managed robots on the line with humans. Humans were definitely considerably better. That will tilt one day. Will it tilt in the next five to ten years? Maybe not, but it will definitely tilt. And I think we have to have real answers for that.

I mean, when I was finishing my MBA at Harvard, we had this last conversation as a section, and I made this point at the time: I grew up in a farming village in Pakistan, so before I came to Detroit, and all the way until we sold that company, I was not in the elite, let's just say. We were always poor. I paid my undergrad and my grad school, and I was finishing Harvard—it was my first exposure to the elite class of society. The business school has some great people. And it's strange, actually, that very few of them are very, very rich. Most of them are actually middle class, but for the first time, you interact with people who own private jets, and you're like, "Oh, I've never flown first class, let alone . . ."

And so, my closing argument—this is in 2008, the closing point that I made to my section—it was a very controversial point. I said, "You know, it's our responsibility, the people in this room. I think wealth inequality will be the dominant conversation of the next fifty years." And what you see with the election or what you see with automation is just the manifestation of those things. It was almost like you saw from far away what the picture is and now we're getting closer. We're seeing, "Oh, this is the tactical way it's going to get to this picture of automation forking wealth inequality to a huge degree." I mean, you have that movie Elysium, where you have this separate class of people who live outside of Earth. They live in this, like, satellite station above Earth.

EA Or Palo Alto, perhaps.

QY Yeah, exactly. And so, I think those are real forces. And are people in Silicon Valley looking at them? Probably not, only because it's not what the market cares about. And that conversation—I think we're all responsible for it. But I think that conversation happens as it happened last night on the national stage [Note: This interview was conducted the day after the election of Donald Trump]. It's like saying the automotive industry is responsible for solving wealth inequality. And it just sounds kind of crazy to say that. Or the shoe manufacturers of Old

Boston, should they be? And the main reason I think that conversation comes up right now is we have, in all of our hands, software technology, and so you can't avoid the subject, even if you wanted to. And there's incredible wealth being created in this business, and they become the poster children.

EA They embody it.

QY They embody it more than anywhere else. I don't think people necessarily look at the Valley as a scapegoat, like, "Oh, you are responsible for my manufacturing job." But they do look at it as, "Why do you have all this stuff and I don't?"

EA "You're part of this new world that I'm not a part of."

QY I mean, the single biggest decision I made in my life in 2000, and roughly 2004, 2005, was to leave automotive for Silicon Valley. I had this conversation—I had this guy, Joe Lantini, who was another GMI (General Motors Institute) and Harvard Business School grad. And Joe said to me, "You know the automotive industry in the future is not what it is in the past. As your manager, I want you to stay at General Motors. But as a friend, I say you should really consider making

a pretty dramatic move." And that's a very hard conversation to have. Imagine if you grew up in Palo Alto and you did software, and then you went to Stanford, and you're working at Google, and then your engineering manager comes in to say, "Hey listen, hey buddy, I know you're kind of all-in on this software stuff, but software is kind of fucked, and you should go move to Detroit and Flint and learn a new business because . . . " And my own personal economic

So, what I did was I first made the transition out of General Motors into Bosch, and I thought, "Well, maybe I can sort of get into consumer goods and maybe just leave automotive altogether." And then I got into business school, and that was, like, my hardship. That was '06 to '08, and I was like, "Okay, now I can really make this change." And that's when I started my first software company. ●

> **"I don't think people necessarily look at the Valley as a scapegoat, like, 'Oh, you are responsible for my manufacturing job.' But, they do look at it as 'Why do you have all this stuff and I don't?'"**

success has been indicative that I made the right decision because I think if I hadn't, I would still be an engineer, maybe toiling away in some factory. So, it was a real significant inflection point, and I knew that even then. I didn't fall into that decision; I had to sell my stuff and move to the Valley.

MARVIN LIAO

Partner
500 Startups

After spending many years on the corporate side of Silicon Valley at Yahoo!, Marvin Liao now runs the San Francisco accelerator program of 500 Startups. He's selected hundreds of startups from around the world to join the accelerator, many of which are from outside California—a key tenet of the 500 Startups investment thesis.

ELLIOTT ADAMS It seems like the 500 Startups thesis has a big international focus, is that correct?

MARVIN LIAO I would say for 500 in general, Dave (McClure) and Christine (Tsai) had the insight that the whole world's changing, right? Nobody's going to argue that fact twenty years from now. When you look at population growth, middle class growth, urban growth, and technology and mobile, you see all these things coming together. The US is not the center of the world. You're going to see huge opportunities, and the reality is that VCs in Silicon Valley have widely ignored, with a small exception, all of these trends that are happening everywhere else. So, I think Dave was always very interested in this area, but the fact that probably 30-plus percent of our portfolio is actually outside the US means that we're putting money where our mouth is. Having said that, it's still really early, and we do think that it's going to happen. And so, we are making very, very long-term bets here.

EA What are you looking for when you're taking applications and looking at teams?

ML We're an early stage VC, right? The only difference is we're doing the investment through a mechanism of an accelerator. The reality is that we look at companies the exact same way traditional VCs do—the only difference is, we're just doing it very, very early. We're doing it as a sort of larger portfolio, so the reality is that, numbers-wise, we're probably getting 2,500 applications and companies that we've looked at. We end up interviewing and talking to about 250 of them, and we end up taking forty-three companies. So, it's a very large funnel, so to speak, but we're looking for all the same things. Are these awesome founders? Is this a balanced team? Is this an interesting problem and a big market? Is this fundable? Are they at the right stage where we can be helpful when the forté of our program is really more on the customer acquisition side? It's like all these things that a VC would be looking at, just a little bit early, along with more of a hands-on process when we invest in them afterwards.

EA They need to have, I assume, at least an early product and some sort of traction. What's your preference there?

ML I think a lot of it depends on space. For example, if you're a FinTech or digital health company, where there are a lot more regulatory things to deal with, then your stage is probably okay. But say you're a SaaS business. I want to see some level of MRR (monthly recurring revenue) growth, right? Or if you're enterprise software, I want to see a couple of very good customers, right? So, it just depends, but generally speaking, we're looking for some initial proof that something's working.

EA Is there a single thing that definitely takes someone out of the funnel or something that keeps them in? The quality of the founders, for example?

ML For sure. I think the key things are these founders, and is this a really interesting market, right? Is this a fundable market?

EA What do you guys do differently that you think is the secret sauce?

ML I think it's a couple of things. Number one, it's the fact that almost everybody on our team has done twenty batches just in the Bay Area alone. Most accelerator programs do not even get past number two or number three. So, the knowledge and the large sample sets that we have of companies is very, very helpful.

I think the other part is our customer acquisition. We have about fifteen full-time and part-time online-marketing b2b sales experts that help our companies figure out how to get customers in a scalable way. The fact that we have so many ex-entrepreneurs, all founders, working for us is critical. Except for my project manager and one of my venture partners who just handles the community, everybody on my team has founded companies. They've all done this before. I think half of them have been successful, half of them haven't, but the fact that they've all done this is actually helpful. I think the fact that we recruit everywhere, across the US and internationally, is a plus as well. My batches probably always turn out to be about one-third Silicon Valley, one-third from the rest of the US, and one-third international. It's just a very unique group of highly qualified founders in general. But also, the fact that this is personally my seventh batch—you just learn. I know so much more now than I did when I first started. I've had 271 companies go through my program. You're an idiot if you don't learn anything after all that.

EA What have you learned in the last few years?

ML Basic things are what I look for in companies. Who on my team is really good at picking companies? But also, who on my team is not so good at picking companies but is much better at helping the companies and coaching, for example? I look at all the different skill sets: how to run the program itself and also the programming of the types of things we're focusing on that will help the

companies. I look at how much bigger our network is now or how much bigger my network personally is right now compared to when I first started, the types of speakers that we bring—all these kinds of things are very helpful.

EA You sound pretty bullish on software as an opportunity right now. Like, you still feel there's plenty to go around.

EA The larger ones can't get in early and do what has to be done to make something proven or prove the concept, if I'm understanding you.

ML Yeah, but the nature of big scale and processes works against fast innovation like early-stage growth. So, the idea of [Clay Christensen's] the innovator's dilemma is still from the late '90s. It's still very relevant.

> "You're going to see huge opportunities, and the reality is that VCs in Silicon Valley have widely ignored, with a small exception, all of these trends that are happening everywhere else."

ML Yeah. There's this idea that there's no more innovation happening out of the Valley, which I think is just ridiculous. The stuff that I see—there are just so many new things, and it's not even just the companies I invest in, but in biotech and in voice. And mobile, we're not even close to where mobile needs to be, like with messenger products. There's just so much in the payment space, and if you think about it, software really is eating the world. It's true.

Let's just look at SaaS. SaaS is a fraction of total enterprise software out there or even software in general. There are so many opportunities, and I'm just not concerned with this idea that there's no more innovation happening. Like I said, as you see companies getting bigger and bigger, they get slow and they get dumber.

EA So, you bring in companies from all over the world. What are your thoughts on companies staying in Silicon Valley? Once they come and participate in a program like 500 Startups, do they need to stay?

ML To be honest, it depends. If your core market is, say, the developer market, you should probably stay. But if your core market is Fortune 500, a lot of them are on the East Coast, you should probably go back home. Let's say you are a company where your customers are in Germany or the UK. You should go back home.

EA Be close to the customer. Okay.

ML Yeah. And go where your customers are. That's what I think makes the most sense. ●

GREG GOTTESMAN

Managing Director
Pioneer Square Labs

Greg Gottesman has been an integral part of the Seattle startup ecosystem as it's blossomed over the last two decades. He's been a partner at the premier venture capital firm Madrona, founder of several highly successful startups, and is running Pioneer Square Labs, a unique spin on the accelerator model that incubates ideas with an internal team before finding founders to run the business.

ELLIOTT ADAMS You've been in Seattle for a while now, right?

GREG GOTTESMAN Yes, I've been here twenty years. I saw it from the beginning days as one of the founding managing directors of Madrona Venture Group, which has been the leading venture capital firm in Seattle. I've watched the tech scene really grow into something much more meaningful and significant over the last twenty years.

EA What are some of the key things that have happened in the Seattle startup community over the last twenty years?

GG Well, there's the whole Amazon thing, which has also been really helpful. I mean, for a lot of these ecosystems, you need elements to come together, mixed with a little bit of luck. The fact that Bill Gates was born here, and then Jeff Bezos decided to move here—those have played no small part and have been critical to how meaningful this ecosystem has become. So, there's always a little dash of good fortune in addition to all the other things. One of the great things about Seattle is, we've got a great research university with a very strong computer science department. It's been very strong for a long time, and that certainly has helped create sort of a hub for some really smart folks. Even when I had moved back here twenty years

ago, it had Microsoft, and Amazon was just starting up, but it had an example at least. Having someone like a Bill Gates or a Jeff Bezos that people can look to as a role model is really important.

> "The difference is that we actually create the companies from scratch. A lot of times, the ideas are from the people on our team, sometimes they're ideas from entrepreneurs that come and join us, and sometimes they're ideas from people in the community."

EA What else has contributed?

GG I think a lot of it has to do with there being so many success stories. As the University of Washington or any other computer science department starts to have success stories, people start to think, "I'm doing this great research, and that guy over there started a company and made a bunch of money. My husband/wife is telling me I'm just as smart as that person. How can I take this research and commercialize it?" I think we underestimate how important role models are for success.

We just have incredible engineering talent, and I believe people with that engineering talent are at the heart of great startups. One of the reasons why this ecosystem has developed is because we have an unusual abundance of very strong engineers. They come from the University of Washington, they come from Microsoft and Amazon and all these other great startups that have flourished here. Lately, there's a number of larger companies that are opening up engineering offices, and startups can come from there as well. So that's a really key point.

EA Seattle doesn't have as much VC as Silicon Valley; does that give companies a tougher time who are staying in Seattle, or does that really not matter?

GG There's definitely capital here. What happens is some companies will go on a short flight and find capital in the Valley. I think that what Seattle has that's better than the Valley is it tends to have more loyal employees. In the Valley, people are always looking for that next shiny penny.

EA Let's talk about Pioneer Square Labs, which has a unique model. Can you explain how it works?

GG As opposed to an accelerator, where companies come and pitch you and then come and spend a couple of months with you, like Y Combinator or Techstars, or a venture capital firm, which is looking to invest, we are a startup studio. The difference is that we actually create the companies from scratch. A lot of times, the ideas are from the people on our team, sometimes they're ideas from entrepreneurs that come and join us, and sometimes they're ideas from people in the community. We're basically starting from scratch. Since the beginning, Pioneer Square Labs has owned all the company, or it may have owned all the company with an entrepreneur that we start with. The traditional model for us is that we would start a company. Last year, for example, we started thirty-five different projects and we killed thirty-two of those.

EA How do you decide which move forward?

GG Typically, there are three hurdles for a studio like ours. The first one is, we'll build a product and go out and talk to customers. The question is, can we validate that there's a real customer need? We can do that by talking to customers, by putting out a product, and seeing what happens. Most companies, even ones that we think are going to work, fail that test. They can fail it because the unit economics don't make sense. In other words, it costs too much to acquire a customer.

The second test is whether once we have that customer attraction, if we can somehow recruit a team of founders to work with us to spin off that company. We call them founders because they're really the ones that are ultimately going to take this company and make it successful. So, the first hurdle is whether we can get customer validation, and the second is whether we can find world-class talent to work with us to take this idea to the next level.

The third test is whether we can get funding from third parties. We actually have a lot of capital, but we really want to have third-party, sophisticated capital tell us, "This is a great idea, and we're willing to put our objective money behind what it is that you're doing." If we can't overcome all three of those hurdles, then the idea is killed. Of the 35 that we tried in 2016, thirty-two failed the first stage.

So, our hit rate will change, but we expect it to be in that 10 to 20 percent of ideas that we try. When they work, we find really incredible entrepreneurs that take us to a meaningful portion of the equity, along with us, and off it goes.

EA I'm curious about how you recruit the leadership team to move these ideas forward.

GG There's this myth that the person who comes up with the idea is always the best person to run the idea. For example, I've started this company called Rover.com, which is the world's largest online pet services company. It was my idea, but I'm not the right person to run that company. In fact, if I were running that company, it would have died many years ago. Aaron Easterly is the perfect person to run that company and scale it.

The reality is that he's much better at running that company than I ever would have been. It's not even close. What this studio model says is, "Hey, we can work on our ideas. People much better than ourselves go and run them." And that's what we're trying to do. We're trying to find people that would be, literally, the best in the world at running something. We give them a huge part of the company and try to make them as successful as possible, and hopefully, they're the right folks to take it to the promised land.

EA And when do you try to bring those people in?

GG I like it to happen as early as possible. But it doesn't always work out that way. It just depends. Sometimes it happens early in the process. You start talking to folks who want to jump in, but you want to have it so that the person jumping in really takes ownership and believes. We're giving them the founder title because we believe that they are the founder. The earlier you can get them involved, the better.

EA When you recruit a CEO, you're going to provide them development, design, and resources from Pioneer Square Labs for the company for a while?

GG Yeah, that's the model.

EA So, you're not starting a whole team from scratch?

GG We are building new products in-house, so for many months after that, we're the whole team. We're taking you to market, and we're helping you to recruit a team to replace us over time. Part of the value proposition is that our people on engineering and design and everything else are really good. But we have to have the right leadership.

EA Is that the thing that's toughest to solve, or is it the initial ideas?

GG People wonder how it is that we have enough exciting ideas. For whatever reason, that hasn't been our issue. We have too many ideas that we want to start and spend time on. We just don't have enough resources. The hard thing about this model is the people.

EA How does that play out?

GG If we are the world's best at coming up with ideas and validating them, but we're mediocre at finding talent, we're going to lose all our money. If we are mediocre at coming up with ideas but world-class at finding talent, we're going to do fine. If we're great at both, that's what you want to be, but the key is really that second step of going out and finding truly great entrepreneurs to work with. That's our customer. When we're starting these companies, we're really thinking, "Can we show enough here to go find someone world class to work with us on this?"

We're privileged to be able to work with incredible founders, and hopefully we're adding enough value to them that they feel like it was a great trade-off. The trade-off is you're getting our idea, our developers, our designers, our machine-learning folks, our digital marketing, our investor contacts. You're getting a lot of things, but you're giving up a lot of equity too. So is that trade-off worth it?

> **"It was my idea, but I'm not the right person to run that company. In fact, if I were running that company, it would have died many years ago."**

Some people are going to say that's not going to make sense for them, and others are going to say it makes a lot of sense. ●

CATHRYN POSEY

Founder
Tech By Superwomen

Cathryn Posey has worked in Silicon Valley and in 2015, made the move to Washington, DC to join the United States Digital Service, essentially a tech startup at the White House. Before any of that, she founded what's become an international movement, Tech by Superwomen.

ELLIOTT ADAMS So, tell me about how Tech by Superwomen came into being?

CATHRYN POSEY Tech Superwomen has really evolved. It honestly started off as a hashtag.

EA Really?

CP I was living in Alaska at the time, which is where I'm from. I had left for school, went back, started my career. I had an unusual career because for the longest time, living in Alaska, we didn't have jobs titled "product managers," but that's what I was doing. I was actually working with a development team developing products that we could use to market the city of Anchorage to tourists. I found social media as a powerful way for me to stay connected and build a community of people who were into my space because I didn't have that locally, right?

I was heading to SXSW for the second time in 2011, and it was a month out, and Alicia Keys's song "Super Woman" had been released. I just love it because what's she's saying is what makes us super is not being invincible. It's resiliency, it's the ability to keep going, it's the ability to get back up after being knocked down. That's a message I could identify with, and so this hashtag popped into my head of calling all tech superwomen.

So, I did an informal meetup with SXSW in 2011. What happened there was, listening to all these women talk about what they're going through, I believed we needed more leadership in this space to produce a talk for them in 2012 or 2013, and it just took off. It turned into this platform. I started traveling, writing, blogging, profiling different women in tech, and for me, I wanted to have a platform that was inclusive. Often when you talk about women in tech, the stories that were told were from the same top tech women who'd already arrived, and that's not very accessible, right?

EA Sure, I can see that.

CP It was also often not very intersectional. It would be women in tech, but it wasn't showcasing the women of color as a part of the narrative, so it's tech superwomen. It's diverse and wonderful. It wasn't that we're going to "do diversity." We just integrate the voices. It's just a big difference. It started growing and taking on a life of its own. I moved to Silicon Valley, and then people started saying, "You need to produce your own platform." And at that time, I didn't even know where to begin, right? But 2014, I found the right partners and produced the first ever Tech Superwomen Summit in 2015.

What we were focusing on was, for me, when I think about women in tech, oftentimes the conversation takes one of two metanarratives, right? Either this is a gender war or it's a scarcity message. There's not a lot of opportunity, and we need to push women through. It's women versus men, and someone's losing.

That's a very dangerous narrative if you're trying to actually make progress, but it's also just false. The goal of feminism is not that. It's about equality. It's about creating more. And then the other side of it is we're "fixable." So, this looks like, "Ladies, if you would just be a little more confident in your negotiations, you'd have a different outcome." Or, "Girls don't like math and science, so we need to help them understand math and science to be cool." That's all around, that there's something broken in women that needs to be fixed, and then the problem's solved. And that's completely false.

For me, this is an opportunity. In the tech entrepreneurship space, in the startup space, we want the mantle of entrepreneurship, and we also want the mantle of disruption. We're really proud that we can have breakthroughs that people swear could never be done or would take years and years and years. We want to get there faster. We need to take that same mentality and energy and apply it in the context of our culture. How do we hack the bias in our culture, conscious and unconscious, so that we create environments where women and people of color can bring their whole selves to work and thrive? So, that's the platform that I've been building for it.

EA That's great. So, in the summit, what does it look like, and what's come out of some of this?

CP What I was really proud of has actually resulted in where I am now, but what I was really proud of

was that we got really powerful content. We had a sponsor that also sponsored students, we had students in the room, we had young professional sponsorships with young professionals in the room. It was this great mix of women who've arrived in leadership roles and people who were emerging. Sara Millstein gave a

> "What happened there was, listening to all these women talk about what they're going through, I believed we needed more leadership in this space to produce a talk for them in 2012 or 2013, and it just took off."

phenomenal talk about eleven ways companies can hack bias, and it was very practical with concrete steps people can take.

Harper Reed and Dylan Pritchard actually did a talk on how they failed the first two times to build diverse teams. It was a very humorous talk. One of the favorite lines for some of us: "We just would go to the white dude store and take a couple of those" and build their company. But they value diversity and what they were learning in building their third business together around building a diverse team. We had Raina Kumra talk about, as a mom, how building a startup was just like having a baby if she did it with a pitch deck. So,

just celebrating the power that motherhood actually has, relevant to entrepreneurship..

It was just this really beautiful community space. And then from there, the White House were asking for some advice and counsel, and then asked me to join the United States Digital Service. So, I've put the summit on hold, and once my tour of duty is over, I'll be able to re-energize that piece. But in terms of advocating for women in tech, that work continues. ●

PETER ARVAI

Co-founder & CEO
Prezi

As the co-founder and CEO of Prezi, Peter Arvai is a thought leader not just in the startup world but also as a figurehead of the nascent startup scene in his native Hungary. He's a partner in initiatives that promote entrepreneurial motivation in Hungary, as well as promoting diversity as both the right and financially-wise choice for companies.

ELLIOTT ADAMS Hungary, one of your two home countries, probably needs a little more support than the other, Sweden. Let's start with how you've been involved with the entrepreneurial community in Budapest.

PETER ARVAI Well, when I arrived in Budapest in 2008, I got the feeling that the whole idea of startups wasn't a very big thing at the time, and we started Prezi. As we grew up, so did three other global successes. LogMeIn—that's on NASDAQ—Ustream, and NNG. Actually, NNG is a very successful company, but they are not a consumer-facing company, so you wouldn't know about them. But a lot of the cars that you drive and their navigation systems are actually made by this Hungarian NNG company. And so actually, as we were growing up and reaching increased numbers of users and successes around the world, I sat down with the people of these companies, and we also created an NGO.

EA What's the goal?

PA We feel like one of the things that holds Hungary back today is not a lack of knowledge, talent, or abilities, but it's actually the challenge of there being very, very few role models of entrepreneurship in the country. So, think about it. It was only twenty-five years ago that the country transitioned from a socialist system to an entrepreneurial, or at least market-driven, economy.

We have these initial successes, and other than that, a lot of the economy in Hungary is really a lot of people who you'd think about outsourcing—how Americans think about outsourcing, that happens to Hungary as well. You have car manufacturing, for example, or support centers,

and that kind of stuff. But now, there's a whole new generation of young people—and Prezi is a great example of this—who are kind of building their own companies and starting to establish a new way of thinking: "Okay, we can actually be global leaders." Right now, the thing that we believe keeps Hungary back in that process is, while we have this handful of examples, still very few people understand how that works and what is required to make those stories happen. So, we have built an NGO where, essentially, the only goal is to contribute to a self-image for Hungarians. Optimism is not just sufficient but actually a necessary first step to take, and you can take that for granted, I guess, where you're from.

great results from that work. In the last four years that we've been doing this, we've measured annually the awareness of it being possible to build global success out of Hungary. We've taken that number from about 7 percent awareness to about 47 percent of Hungarians who have, in about four years, learned about the possibility of this. We're also working with leaders and educating them in how to grow businesses. So, this is a very, very conscious thing that we've taken on.

EA There are initiatives that are typical—for example, putting up a co-working space or an accelerator. Is that part of what you're working on as well?

> **"Optimism is not just sufficient but actually a necessary first step to take, and you can take that for granted, I guess, where you're from."**

EA We do take it for granted. I mean, it's a cultural issue that I think many in the US don't understand is different.

PA Even in the US, it's very different, depending in where in the US. I mean, I think this is one of the big challenges for the US right now. A lot people are starting to not believe in the American dream anymore, and so we have all of these political shifts happening, but I don't think we can take it for granted, even in the US. The point being that there's a lot of work, actually, in helping people to understand how they do have opportunities in their countries and in their world. We actually have

PA Actually, it's not. Everyone is involved with startups now, and we didn't feel like the money was important. That comes in time. People are taking that initiative, but actually working on the internal narratives that we have around entrepreneurship, that is something that very few people are tackling, even in the US.

In my view, why it's so important is because without the understanding and the belief that this is possible for people, we immediately end up in a non-functioning society.

EA Yeah, it happens in these geographic locations around demographic issues, but the issue is also going outside of different regions and classes.

PA Entrepreneurial inclusiveness. Maybe that's a concept we should be talking about.

EA It sounds like this is, if it's not too dramatic to say, a consciousness-raising effort.

PA Oh yeah, totally. I mean, our main goal is to spread inspiration. We do that with the NGO. If we're focusing on that, through television shows, books, meet-ups, it's never as practical as incubating companies, but we do think that the conversation itself is extremely important.

EA As you said before we sat down, there's no shortage of intelligence or talent. It seems like you're in the same situation as many countries in the region, having a strong engineering talent, being a hub for outsourcing at times, and transitioning to being owners. Is that generally correct?

PA I think so. One of the things we need to create more awareness around is that a lot of places like Hungary actually have a very rich tradition of assets that we can tap into. For example, a lot of people don't know this, but the movie Casablanca was directed by a Hungarian. The oldest studio alive right now in Hollywood, guess what? Founded by a Hungarian. All the four companies that I've mentioned do some form of visual communications.

Hungary is actually extremely strong, and Hungarians are also quite proud of the strengths we have in

mathematics and engineering. But again, those stories sometimes get lost in the noise. A lot of the time, even Hungarians aren't aware of their fantastic competitive advantage in the world.

"One of the things we're doing with these companies that are now going global is we are actually creating a whole new generation of people who don't just study engineering, they also think about how to build businesses."

When we talk about entrepreneurship, it's very helpful framing to ask, "Okay, what is the problem that we're solving for users?" And sometimes, when we don't recognize and appreciate the skills, how can we help those users? We can actually miss the biggest assets that we have to bring something valuable to the world. That is not a relevant question in Silicon Valley because everyone there already thinks that they have something very valuable to bring to people. But if you look in many other places around the world, that is a very key question. Gaining appreciation for the special insights and perspectives that you have is so important because without that, you won't ever take the first step.

One of the things we're doing with these companies that are now going global is we are actually creating a whole new generation of people who don't just study engineering, they also think about how to build businesses. Going back to this idea that twenty-five years

ago, Hungary had a centrally-planned economy, the idea of building sustainable businesses that would go global was probably a pretty foreign concept. So, I think that is an area where we can see there's a lot of momentum.

I mean, in many, many ways, it creates a tremendous opportunity for people who are willing to take that step. If we compare Budapest to London, where London is already a bit overcrowded, everything is super expensive. In Hungary, right now there is already a critical mass on global success that you can actually be in a community where people have that mindset. It's also still a place where you don't have to sacrifice quality of life and you can live a really good life.

EA I also wanted to talk about the diversity initiative you've started. Can you talk about the impetus behind We Are Open?

PA I think it's important to recognize that a lot of people believe that diversity is not just the right thing but the good and beneficial thing, in terms of business. In my view, creating a work environment where people can bring their whole selves to work and they don't have to waste energy on being nervous about being accepted with their unique background is very important. That is a really great way of actually creating not just a diversity of backgrounds but diversity of thought, which is what you really need. In that creative economy that we talked about, diversity of thought is really important. I have personal experiences with this. The Financial Times put me as number eleven of the most influential openly gay business executives. What I meant to say with that is, even in my lifetime, I have seen a huge change on this topic. Sweden is seen as one of the most liberal places on earth, and yet when I was growing up there, I didn't know of one openly gay business person. I mean, I knew about a comedian, I knew about a TV host that was dying of AIDS, and I knew about a cross-dressing makeup artist. They were my role models as a child growing up in Sweden. I was like, "Okay, can I identify with any of these people? Does this mean I have to be like them? Can I go into business and build products, which I would like to do, and be gay at the same time?" There were no signals that that was actually possible.

Similar to Bridge Budapest, what we're doing in Hungary is we're gathering people who know that diversity helps businesses to grow and do well. We help them share the best practices, and in a similar way as with entrepreneurship, we share inspiring stories of people who are leading a business. For example, being a woman in the workforce, and sometimes it may sound trivial, but the truth is that there are lot of barriers.

EA I'm not familiar with the zeitgeist around diversity in Hungarian society. I would not necessarily guess it would be the most accepting, to put it mildly. It seems like it's a bold move.

PA It's an authentic move.

EA I think what's really interesting is that the typical story is, "I'm from this company, and I am going to fund an accelerator back home." But you're pushing against the societal norms to make things better in a broader way.

PA I think that is the best form of entrepreneurship. I mean, if you go back in history, there have been a lot of examples of entrepreneurs taking a lot of responsibility. For example, the city where I grew up in Sweden pretty much exists thanks to Alfred Nobel.

Many people don't know that he was an entrepreneur and made all his money on business, which he then donated to these prizes. But even before that, he was building outhouses for the factory workers, and he had a very, I would say—I'm certain there are parts that we'd think of his thinking that would be outdated today, but there were parts that were very enlightened. He was all about, "Okay, how do I help people to have better lives?" That was a natural thing to be thinking of as a part of your business. I think of similar stories with Ford and, you know, these were entrepreneurs who were thinking very deeply about how to not just create better lives for customers, but also the employees and in general, society. How do we contribute?

EA It's not always the narrative that's been in capitalism from the beginning, and so we're in a place that's relatively new to capitalism with these issues.

PA Yes, and the other aspect that I feel very strongly about is this narrative among entrepreneurs that the first year is supposed to make all this money and join the dark side, or whatever—

EA Be a Rockefeller or a magnate?

PA Yeah, and then, once you've made all your money, it's almost like then you're going to race to do some good in the world and redeem yourself before you die.

EA Put your name on buildings.

PA Yeah. Because you've, perhaps, screwed so many people over. That's such a sad—like, why aren't we thinking more about how to integrate those things throughout your life journey? That, I think, is really important.

I wish that we would talk more about that, even just to educate other entrepreneurs, again, back to this question of, "What is the narrative that we create around entrepreneurship?" ●

MATT MULLENWEG

Founder & CEO
Automattic

Matt Mullenweg's open-source blog and content management platform, WordPress, has grown into one of the most dominant and powerful tools on the web. In addition to leading development of the project, he's the CEO and founder of Automattic, which makes products that add value on top of the WordPress ecosystem and reach over one billion people per month.

ELLIOTT ADAMS Can we start by you sharing some quick background on WordPress and Automattic?

MATT MULLENWEG WordPress was, and still is, an open-source project. Years after WordPress started, I founded Automattic. Automattic was bootstrapped for probably the first six or seven months. Then, we raised an initial round of about $1 million. That was in 2006, and I brought in Tony Shatter to be the CEO. Then, in 2008, we raised a larger round of $28 million, and then in 2014, we did $160 million into the company.

EA Are your acquisitions and products complementary in terms of how they function or the ethos of how the software's built? What's the driving thesis for you guys?

MM We've done a few things over the years, but right now, we're focused in three main areas: WordPress, Jetpack, and WooCommerce. WordPress.com allows us to host WordPresses from all over the world and give people a really easy place to start. Jetpack is basically that, but it's for all of the people who host someplace else, like GoDaddy, BlueHost, Amazon Web Services … wherever they might be. Then finally, WooCommerce is an e-commerce platform on top of WordPress. Even though it's very young, it has been extremely successful. That was our biggest acquisition thus far, with fifty-five people joining the company.

EA Wow, that's huge. How do those products fit into the WordPress family?

MM It's all WordPress and stuff that makes WordPress better. If it's WordPress related, I either invest or acquire it or whatever through Automattic. Then through my seed fund, Audrey, it's all things that I may want to be working on if I wasn't doing WordPress.

EA Why did you choose those things that you are working on?

MM I really love publishing and this idea of democratizing publishing and giving people a voice online. I believe that humans are fundamentally good, and that the more communication we have and the more you allow people to share their thoughts, of course some bad stuff happens, but it ultimately makes the world a better place and brings us closer together. I was into that when I was nineteen, fourteen years ago, and I think it is even more important now, as I round my thirties.

EA There are always these big, crazy stats that about 20 or 40 percent, or some crazy number, of the web runs on WordPress. It's a great success for you guys. What do you see as the outlook for the so-called open web?

MM I think that the open web is really more important than ever, because as people come online, they might have their training-wheel platforms that are somewhat closed, but ultimately, people express themselves in very unique ways. Once you have a taste of freedom, it's hard to return to the previous state of mind. I feel like the inevitable march on the web is not a straight line. Progress is not always a straight line, but it's towards more freedom, towards more openness, towards more inter-connected systems, because these are the things that the web is really good at. There are companies which have created incredible centralized systems—Facebook, Google, etc.—but when you look at them, what do they have to do to make that work? The countless billions in infrastructure and data centers and running fiber under oceans and everything. It's valuable, because they're able to centralize things, but that's not how the web is natively. Over time, I think things that are more the approach of Bitcoin or WordPress or IPFS—the Interplanetary File System—or email are more the things that thrive, again, over several decades.

EA The mobile experience for a lot of consumers that have come online in the last five to ten years is that it's the containerized app experience. How does the open web thrive in that kind of environment?

MM Well, if you look at actual time spent, even when people are inside, say, the Twitter app or the Facebook app, a lot of that time is actually spent on web views. They're looking at websites. The content on the newsfeed side, I mean, that's really web driven through and through. Messaging, I think, is perfect for apps. Games are also pretty good for apps, but I think that's okay. We don't need the open web stuff there.

EA Some people look at what's going on over the web and say, "It's the Wild West." They mean that in the pejorative sense. And there's what people consider fake news, so people say that maybe it's better to have a moderated platform. How do you feel about that?

MM I think if you provide distribution, you do have a responsibility … not to moderate, per se, but to give your customer, the people you're serving this information to, as much relevant information as possible. A good example is that Amazon will sell anything, but they have a really great review system.

So, you can find the electric broom that accidentally catches on fire, but you're going to probably figure that out before you buy it, and you'll be able to make a smart decision to buy a Dyson or something like that. We optimize for growth in kind of these first

complex problem. Personally, with WordPress and with our own services, we fall pretty far towards free speech and libertarianism.

EA Sure.

> "I believe that humans are fundamentally good, and that the more communication we have and the more you allow people to share their thoughts, of course some bad stuff happens, but it ultimately makes the world a better place and brings us closer together."

iterations of newsfeeds, and so we're just trying to get as many clicks and people reading things. Of course, that's not new. A hundred years ago, people bemoaned the "yellow journalism" and this idea that truth was lost because these printers had to move so fast and the newsies were distributing it. If it bleeds, it leaves. We've known that for a century. But Paul Graham has this great essay on the acceleration of addictiveness and how society develops antibodies to this. It's interesting, and the commercial and moral imperative that Facebook is now taking is a great example. I saw something at the top of my feed the other day that said, "Here's How to Tell Fake News." And they're starting to bring things in line next to article links. It's hard to say if that works or not, but I think it's awesome that they're taking the initiative and trying to solve what is a very hairy,

MM But we're not really as involved in distribution. We're really about publishing, so we give you a space, and we don't necessarily help you distribute that message out.

EA Since you're with WordPress, what are some of the advantages of being able to offer to people open publishing that's not moderated in any way?

MM Oh, I think that people use it and expand it in ways you'd never expect, and being known as an open platform also helps you attract the best authors. You give people the control and the autonomy and the agency over their own content and their own site and how they'll interact, and that's what's openly going to attract the best people. ●

SURVEYED
STARTUPS

ARGENTINA

DIEGO BOLETTIERI — *BE BETTER HOTELS*

AUSTRALIA

QUIRIN SCHWAIGHOFER — *HIKEY RESOURCES*

CANADA

BEN SYNE — *DOGSYNC*
MARION VOLLMER — *IQBIOMEDICAL*
VLAD KHOMUTOV — *GOFAST*
NICK KUHNE — *SMALLROOMS*
LEE HABER — *COTUTO*
RUSSELL WARD — *MASSIVELY*
STEVE DOSWELL — *SOUNDPAYS*
WILLIAM MASIH — *WELLIN5*
MIKE CHATZIGRIGORIOU — *IGEN TECHNOLOGIES*
EDMUNDO RODRIGUES — *AUTOWALLET*
SEAN POWER — *REPABLE*
FRED REGO — *VANHACK TECHNOLOGIES*
TYLER HANDLEY — *INKBOX TATTOOS*
JAMES SUKOSD — *NOTEORIETY*
MICHEL ALLEGUE — *AERIAL.AI*
ONOME IGHARORO — *ROBOT PLAYTIME*
MARCEL BRADEA — *HAPP SOCIAL*
JOSEPH WEINBERG — *PAYCASE*
MARK VECCHIARELLI — *KRUVE INC.*
CHRISTIAN COTICHINI — *HEROX*

CHILE

VICENTE ALVAREZ — *MAKER*
CAMILA MANNS — *CASA TRUNK*
FELIPE VALDÉS-VALENZUELA — *IRIS ELECTROMAGNETICS*
RITA ALEJANDRA SEVILLA MACIP — *WOOPIE*
VICENTE HERRERA — *DAEKI SALIVA TECH*
GONZALO ENEI ROSAS — *EL VASO MEDIO LLENO*

RODRIGO FARCAS — *POSTEDIN*
PABLO CAVIEDES — *NNODES*
AAKASH BAROT — *EN ALEPHANTS*
MATIAS — *GRUPO AG PROPIEDADES*
RODRIGO RIVERA — *CASE SURFER*
SEBASTIÁN CAMPOS TOLOZA — *MY BOOK MAP*

CHINA

LUIS CANCELA — *FROSTIMO*
DIEGO ROJAS — *BITHIVE TECH LTD.*
CHI SHING TSUI — *BRIGHTER OIL GROUP*
PAK TING — *VOTEE*
ANDREW CHUNG — *FIFTEEN PROSPECTS LIMITED*
DR. MILES WEN — *ACCOSYS LIMITED*
RACHEL CHEUNG — *RENT-A-SUITCASE*
STANLEY PANG — *KIMMO*
JAMES HUI — *INNOSPACE*
ABHINAV DAGA — *SELASFORA*
TAK LO — *ZEROTH*
PERRY STEEGEN — *WHALECLUB*
RYAN — *PARNANA*
FLORIAN GARIVIER — *SMARTALPHA*
FRANCESCO GRILLO — *STEEL AVAILABLE*
CASSIE MAK — *HAPPY OWL*
ROEE LAHAV — *OUT OF X*
DMITRY FEDOTOV — *RESUME GAMES*
OLIVER MAULE — *TAYBL*
MICHELLE YUAN — *ASIA WEDDING NETWORK*
KELVIN LEE — *BONI - DRY CLEANING AND LAUNDRY DELIVERY SERVICE*
EDDIE CHEUNG — *ZERAPH*
AARON LEE — *DASH SERVICED SUITES*

COLOMBIA

HARVEY BOTERO — *MAGICVILLE*
CHRISTIAN GONZALEZ — *TIATA*

MILAGROS — *TODOC*
FRANCISCO OCHOA — *RUMIS*
ANDRES SUAREZ — *COMIDA EN LA U*
JULIAN BUILES — *DAYSPRING*
SANTIAGO RODRIGUEZ — *VLIPCO*
ERNESTO LLANOS — *DOGJUAN*
LEONARDO MARCHANT — *BHIVE MANAGEMENT CONSULTING*
DIEGO CHAPARRO — *TRYTRACKS*
SERGIO ANDRÉS TRUJILLO — *LOOPA*
SIMON SORIANO — *TOPTAL*
CAROLINA GIRALDO — *DRESSINGLAB*
JAIME CORREDOR — *TUIMPUESTO*
RICARDO JIMÉNEZ — *FÚTBOL FIT CLUB*
EDWIN PARDO — *DATAWIFI*

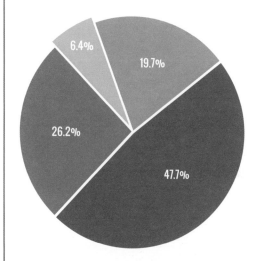

HOW DO YOU MEASURE TRACTION FOR YOUR STARTUP?

47.7% REVENUE   26.2% SIGN-UPS
19.7% OTHER   6.4% TIME IN THE APPLICATION

DENMARK
MARIA FLYVBJERG BO	*HUFSY*

ECUADOR
RAFAEL VASCONEZ	*ENMOVIMIENTO*
CHRISTIAN VORBECK	*FREELOS*
PABLO PAZMIÑO	*IDUKAY*
AHMED BOLICA	*PIMULA*

EGYPT
MAHMOUD GHOZ	*RAWY*
RANA SAID	*EDUKITTEN*
AHMED FAWZY	*AN GAMES STUDIO*
MOHAMED EZZAT	*BOSTA*
ABDALLAH ZIDAN	*CODLY*
MOHAMED FERGANY	*YOUTTA FREE INTERNET*

FINLAND
RILEY RAMONE	*BOMVIA*
MARCUS RADER	*HOSTAWAY*
LARS CARLSSON	*MUUVIN*
TUOMAS RYHANEN	*KERROS SOLUTIONS*
JUSSI MÄÄTTÄ	*BUDDY HEALTHCARE*
JONAS FORTH	*MOOMIN*
JUHA WIKSTRÖM	*BUSINESS ROOSTER*
TUOMAS ILOLA	*NIMBLE DEVICES*
IDA MANTY	*CUCKOO WORKOUT*
JENNY LAURONEN	*YOGAME*
TUOMO VIRKKUNEN	*BOARDIO*
TOMAS WESTERHOLM	*SESSIO SOFTWARE*
KRISTIAN LAIHO	*DIMCOS*
OTTO SARVAMAA	*SCOTCH & CO*
PETTERI HIRVONEN	*KLINIK*
SAMI KUUSELA	*UNDERHOOD*
OLLI SINERMA	*FINNISH VIRTUAL REALITY ASSOCIATION*

TOMMI OJALA	*RUNTEQ*
SAMPO HIETANEN	*MAAS GLOBAL*
VARUN SINGH	*CALLSTATS.IO*
ARTO MARTONEN	*MOTLEY AGENCY*
SERGEY ANDRYUKHIN	*VIDEOLY*
SAKU EVERI	*HELSINKI VENTURES*
MARKUS MERNE	*EVERON*
ANTTI KANANEN	*KOUKOI GAMES*
JUKKA HILVONEN	*SEEPIA GAMES*
ANTTI SIHLMAN	*NEONTO*
HENRI NYSTRÖM	*JEVELO*
MAX PECHERSKYI	*PROMOREPUBLIC*
RAKHIM DAVLETKALIYEV	*HEXLET.IO*

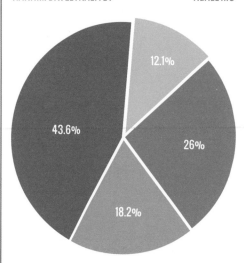

WHY DID YOU START YOUR STARTUP?
43.6% SAW A PROBLEM THAT NEEDED TO BE FIXED
26% HAD AN IDEA THAT I WANTED TO BUILD
18.2% I WANT TO CHANGE THE WORLD
12.1% OTHER

DAVID BROWN	*TEICOS PHARMA*
DONNA KIVIRAUMA	*TEAMUP*
SAMI PIPPURI	*MAAS GLOBAL*
JUHO KOPONEN	*MEEDOC*
DANIEL BYALSKY	*SPEEDHIRE*
DANIEL HOLMSTRÖM	*LIVERING*

FRANCE
GRÉGOIRE LINDER	*RAIZERS*
MARTIN SAINT-MACARY	*VYTE*
LUCIE ALLAVENA	*EDUPAD*
JOHAN PAGES	*NILAND*
MICHEL VERMEULEN	*YOULOOP*
DORIAN DAWANCE	*CLOTHERAPP*
NANS THOMAS	*WINO*
ZOUHEIR GUEDRI	*DATA AND DATA*
DAMIEN TAMPE	*LABACAR*
SAMY BERRABAH	*TRIPFRIENDIZER*
ARNAUD AUGER	*STARTUPBRICS*

GERMANY
ADRIAN BORSOI	*BLACKWALL*
ELDAR GIZZATOV	*FAIRFLEET*
MARTIN HOFFMANN	*RESIAPP*
MATTHEW BUXTON	*MXDN*
NIKITA GORSHKOV	*CAESIUM*
THOMAS WITT	*SCRIVITO*
WILHELM USCHTRIN	*AUTORENWELT*
STEFAN SULISTYO	*ALYNE*
NICOLE SIMM	*PERSONIC*
KLAUS RAUTENBERG	*SAAS CRM & FAKTURIERUNG*
ANDRE HORNUNG	*POKOKO STUDIO*
JONATHAN HARCLERODE	*BOTTLEBOOKS*
GUY GALONSKA	*INFARM*
DENNIS KIRPENSTEIJN	*TAISTY*
JANINA MÜTZE	*CIVEY*

STEFAN SULISTYO	ALYNE
LIN KAYSER	HYPERGANIC
DANIEL MCGLASHAN	GLOBAL DESIGN COLLECTIVE
MARTIN STAUDACHER	WOHNUNGSHELDEN
CONSTANTIN VON SALMUTH	HALLO JAMES
MOHSEN FAZELINIAKI	BOHÈME
MATHIS BUECHI	TAXFIX
JAN DZULKO	EVERPHONE
FABIAN HADIJI	GOEDLE.IO
JOHANNES SRÉTER	SHOPEUR
FELIX HAFFNER	NAVIGATOR2LAW
OLIVER STOLLMANN	ACTYX
ANNA LUKASSON	EVERYBAG
DANIEL HEITZ	URBAN CHALLENGER
MARK SCHLEICHER	BRIGHT INTUITION
LELE CANFORA	DECKARD A.I.
XAVER LEHMANN	E-BOT7
KARIME MIMOUN	SMAP!
PHILIP MOHR	SHAREPOP
IONUT CIOBOTARU	PUBNATIVE

GUATEMALA
DAVID BARAC	BACKEND MED

INDONESIA
CHANDRA TJAN	ALPHA JWC

IRELAND
MICHAEL FLANAGAN	KABZY
ANDREW RHATIGAN	CARYARD
ROD SMYTH	TEMPBUDDY
BRUCE BALE	SPORTDEC
MARK CUMMINS	POINTY
SHANE BRETT	GECKO GOVERNANCE
ALAN BENNETT	HEADSTUFF

SHANE LYNN	EDGETIER
TENA GLASER	ABIGAIL
LOUISE MURPHY	CYC-LOK
KEVIN MCCAFFREY	TR3DENT
EVAN GRAY	LAUNDRIE
JAMES O CONNOR	VABBLE
MICHAEL O'DWYER	SWIFTCOMPLY
OMAR MEAS	THE MEDIA TRADER
CONOR CURRAN	COURSIQA LTD.
CHARLIE BYRNE	ENGAGER
TIM BYRNE	JUGGLE
DR SAMEH ABDALLA	INTOUCH
ENDA LEAHY	COURTSDESK
DANIEL TOWNSEND	VR RETAIL
OISIN RYAN	LEAPCHAT
DEIRDRE LEE	DERILINX LTD
MARK MCLAUGHLIN	CORAS
KYLE HYUNSUNG KIM	LINGOSPY LIMITED
SHANE CURRAN	LIBRAMATIC
JOHN KENNEDY	4PM PROPERTY
DANIEL LOFTUS	URBANFOX
ALIN CHIRCULESCU	ART HISTORY LAB
EAMON LEONARD	EAMONN MCCRYSTAL
VLADISLAV BOROVSKY	PLUGINFUTURE
TIM ARITS	INTOUCH
LOUIS GRENIER	SLICES CONSULTING

ISRAEL
DUDI PELES	MAKEREE
URI SCHNEIDER	TVIBESAPP
ASSAF LUXEMBOURG	CROWDMII
ERAN ARYE	WE-TEST
CHEDVA KLEINHANDLER	LEAN ON
DOTAN BAR NOY	RESEC
URI P. HADELSBERG	VOL TRAVEL
GAD MAOR	STOREMAVEN
YARIV SADE	KIMONEX

WHAT'S THE BIGGEST CHALLENGE THAT YOUR STARTUP IS FACING?

32.9% LACK OF FUNDING
24.4% LACK OF TIME
18.2% OTHER
14.1% LACK OF REVENUE
10.2% LACK OF USERS
0.2% NEED TO HIRE MORE TEAM MEMBERS

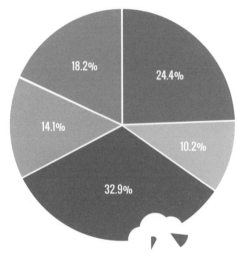

SHAUL AVIDOV	MUSKETEER
BENTZI TREGE	TIKTALK
LITAN YAHAV	SEGOMA TECHNOLOGIES
ISRAEL EREZ	YAPQ
TAL BROCKMANN	FINNOVEST
ALEXANDER SEIDES	HOMEPPL
DROR AHARON	DAYSTAGE
RONEL MOR	DROPREVIEW
DR. ILYA FINE	ELFI-TECH
DEDDI ZUCKER	BOOKSONMAP
AMIR ISENBERG	WAKEAPP

TOMER LIMOEY	ASKOURT	BOAZ LANTSMAN	ROUTEPERFECT	DANNY TUTTNAUER	SIMPLY VISION
ANDREW GELLER	VALUE YOUR STARTUP	ROI SHTERNIN	HELP - LIFE SAVING APP	YONA CYMERMAN	WATER.IO
RONNY DAHAN	GOTIMENOTE	HAMUTAL WEISZ	JOYA	DANNY LAHAV	KARZ
ANI TERADA	ANIWO	ANAT SHPERLING	TOYA	GILAD MADAR	TRAFFIQA
OREN ATTAR	SEEBLINGS GREETINGS LTD	NOAM GRESSEL	ECOOS	DEAN IFRACH	HOOP
OREN JACKMAN	EXAMPAL	YARON RECHER	BANDMANAGE	NIMROD COHEN	ONLINEPIANIST
GUY ALTAGAR	JOVO	ANTON GOLDSHTEIN	ZIPY	LEON VAIDMAN	HOTELSBI
AVISHAY FRIEDLER	TO-BE-EDUCATION	AMIT PALOMO	BLOBIX	YOTAM GUTMAN	CYBERDB
EREZ YERUSHALMI	SLING	ASAF NISENBAUM	TAILORTAB	YANIV MORGENSTERN	SCENSEIT
BEN NOVAK	WEDIVITE	ALEX POVERENY	M-RECRUIT	RON LEVINSON	IAGO CHAT
ARIEL ASSARAF	CORALOGIX	YOSI DAHAN	CONFIGO	URI ISHON	GEM ALLIANCE
OR RIGLER	WEAVE	MORAN ZUR	SAFEBEYOND	LEON HULLI	CHECK-ER
AVI PRICE	PEAKARDO			YAU BEN-OR	SOLARCHANGE
SAPIR SHPIGEL	MERKSPACE			SHLOMI ZADOK	KOZO
SHAUN WAKSMAN	COUPONROLLER			AMIR KONIGSBERG	TWIGGLE
EREZ TAL	TIPIT			SARA KLABEN	SCENA
ELAD SHMILOVICH	JOONKO			ANDREA K KRELL	MICROFY
DVIR BAR	AYDRATE			YOUVAL ROUACH	BITS OF GOLD
JAN KÖSTER	JOINVR			ALEX BOUAZIZ	LIFESLICE
AMIT GUR	BANDPAD			RACHEL BRENDER	PITAYA
ORI GREENBERG	ALGOPIX			YAIR PREISS	TOUR DE SHOPS

JORDAN

WASEEM ABUDAWOD	TOP STEERING
BISHER ABU TALEB	IZIF
NASSER SALEH	MADFOOAT
MOHAMMAD ISSA	AUMET
FOUAD JERYES	CASHBASHA
FADI ALSABBAGH	SOSIO
AHMAD ALMASRI	PROGRESSIVE GENERATION STUDIOS
OMAR KOUDSI	JEERAN
YAHYA AQEL	AUMET
KHALED ELAHMAD	DIGIARABS
HASSAN ATMEH	REPZO
MOHAMMED HUJEIJ	PLANET TOULAN
EMAN HYLOOZ	ABJJAD LTD
NIDAL KHALIFEH	EDAURA

NATHAN RESNICK	SOURCIFY
ODED FARKASH	NULOOX
ITAMAR WEIZMAN	COOL COUSIN
IRIT BARZILY	GIRAFFE LIST
AMNON LAHAV	ADNGIN
JONATHAN SCHOR	CODEMONKEY
YARON SAGHIV	FUNZING
YOAV MAOR	SIGMENTO
GIDEON MEIRY	CMESAFE
ADI SHEMESH	TRENCH
MICHAL MEIRI	LEMMENO
BORIS (BARUCH) KOGAN	SWARMBUILD
ALON GAMZU	ROUNDFOREST
GAL BAREKET	ROUTIER
AVI SNIR	ELEVATION ACADEMY

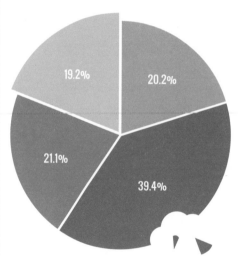

HOW HAVE YOU FUNDED YOUR STARTUP?

39.4% BOOTSTRAPPING THROUGH REVENUE
21.1% RAISING VENTURE CAPITAL
20.2% OTHER
19.2% MOONLIGHTING & SIDE PROJECTS

LEBANON

ANTIUN TOUBIA — *UNIVERSAL CROWD-FUNDING INVESTMENTS*

LIECHTENSTEIN

JULIAN FREESE — *REACHBIRD*

MEXICO

ALAN IRAZOQUI — *SWAPWINK*
JOSÉ MAURICIO TAMAYO MELÉNDEZ — *DPRISA*
ALBERTO VILLA — *SPARTAN GEEK*
ALDO LEÓN — *MEXICAN LIGA MX*
EFRAIN OROZCO — *FLETEASY*
RUBEN SANCHEZ — *BUNKER GRAPH*
JOS LABARTHE — *WISHUS*
JAVIER IBARROLA DÍAZ TORRE — *CODEACAMP*
LUIS MUNOZ — *GOGUAYA*
JUAN CARLOS ORTEGA — *IDECORE*
ALEXIS FUNES — *ANVAU*
RICARDO GARCÍA — *TERAPPI*
ALEJANDRO ROJAS — *BLUMON PAY*
LUIS EDUARDO LÓPEZ — *MOSTRADOR*
PABLO RENA — *MAYOREOTOTAL*
ERIC HULBURD — *ARBOL*
PHIL PRICE — *SLICE*

NETHERLANDS

SITESH SHRIVASTAVA — *POW WOW*
DANIEL PAAIJ — *BYLDER*
MOHAMED ELRAHAWAN — *G2M WORLDWIDE*
VICTOR SWAAB — *TEAMLEAGUE*
CORSTIAAN HESSELINK — *FLUXMATRIX*
ALISSA BOLT — *DEVMOB*
EVA GOUDSWAARD — *FIT PAARD*
ALWIN VAN DER VELDEN — *SUPERSCANNER*

MARC JELLEMA — *TOM KABINET*
CARMEN DE OUDE — *PEPER & CO*
ALEXANDER KET — *ZILVERLINE*
LEONARDO CARACAS — *GOCASE*
MARTINE ROOTH — *EHEALTH EXPERT*
IMRE TIJSSE KLASEN — *DANAE*
MASSIMILIANO SILENZI — *KOOMALOOMA*
LOUAIE EL ROWIDI — *CABTURE*
DETLEF LA GRAND — *VRMASTER*
JOOST SCHOUTEN — *NESTR*
HUBERT NIJMEIJER — *HI,HI GUIDE*
DANIQUE WILTINK — *NIMBLES*
SILJA THOR — *RESTORANTO*
ROGGER LACERDA — *NEWATT*
JIM VAN OOSTEN — *WATT-NOW*
KRISTIAN RONN — *NORMATIVE*
ALESSIO DELMONTI — *WITHOUT INTERNET TECHNOLOGY*

PIETER ORANJE — *BIRDS.AI*
DAAN GRASVELD — *POPPED MUSIC*
SANDIP PANDEY — *SORIOLE*
JUNIOR MEIJERING — *ZEROCOPTER*
ERIK VAN LUXZENBURG — *LUXZEN - LEAN & AGILE COACHING*

TOMAS MOSKA — *TURING SOCIETY*
JASPER MIDDENDORP — *REFLOW FILAMENT*
KEES BLOK — *BIDDY*
FLORIS TER HAAR, STEFAN VAN DER FLUIT — *INTELLIGENCEPAY*
RORY DEEN — *NUKLIUS*
JO ANN — *IMSYSTEMS*
ONNO SPEK — *NOEL'S TRAVEL*
FLOR ROJAS — *SHOOTLR*
ROY VAN VEEN — *WELOCAL*
LEONARDO VIDA — *TOTHEM*
— *YOUNICO*

NORWAY

ESPEN GRIMSTAD — *PAYR*
DANIEL DÖDERLEIN — *AUKA*
KLAUS VOGSTAD — *WINDFARMDESIGNS*
GEIR BÆKHOLT — *CRYPHO*
THOMAS LUZIO — *WILDSCOOP MOBILE MARKETING*
THOMAS JEPSEN — *ACT COOPERATIVE CORPORATION*
BIRGER LIE — *SHAREACTOR.IO*
MARK NIJHOF — *NEON SOLUTIONS*
OLE JØRGEN SEELAND — *STAAKER*
JONAS RYEN — *LEARNLINK*
DAVID ALEXANDRE SALVAIL — *ZEIPT*
OLE GOETHE — *WESTERDALS HØYSKOLE*
KATE MURPHY — *PLAY MAGNUS*
DANIEL WESNER — *VIVIL*
PAAL KRISTIAN LEVANG — *NORNIR*
KEVIN BELLINGER — *GLIDER.IO*
STIG ZERENER — *DOPLR*
KRISTIAN HAANES — *WEBINARA*
INGEBORG KVAME — *ARTPEAS*
AGNES DYVIK — *VIO MEDIA*
STIG OLA JOHANSEN — *TRYBE AS*
OLAV NEDRELID — *DOMOS*
SVEIN WILLASSEN — *APPEAR.IN*
LAUGA OSKARSDOTTIR — *UNITED INFLUENCERS*

PAKISTAN

UMAIR SHEIKH — *ARAZI*

POLAND

ŁUKASZ PODGAJNY — *SCANYE*

PORTUGAL

CHRISTINA LOCK — *YOOCHAI*

RUSSIA

ALEXANDER BRITKIN	NFWARE
IGOR KHMEL	BANKEX VENTURES
ALEX KHODORKOVSKY	WHIZZMATE
IGOR LUKYANOV	ADGUARD
HAYK GABRIELYAN	LLC OTAL GROUP
TARAS ZAGIBALOV	SMALLSTEP
MAX TOLSTOKOROV	NANO

RWANDA

BARRETT NASH	SAFEMOTOS

SAUDI ARABIA

JAMAL SUBOH	JOBZELLA

SCOTLAND

RUSSELL BARNARD	WEBFOLIO

SINGAPORE

MARNIX ZWART	GOBEAR
LIM KIEN LEONG	TRANSWAP

SLOVAKIA

VLADISLAV BOROVSKY	PLUGINFUTURE

SOUTH KOREA

KANGHAK KIM	FLUENTY INC.
JAMES NOH	THE GOOD COMPANY
KANGMO KIM	SCALECHAIN
JASON BAE	DINALOG
JASON KIM	ACTNERLAB
CIREN JANG	STYLEWIKI
MIA S. CHOI	HAMMIE HAMSTER LABS, INC.
HYOJUN WOO	FRASEN INC.
JOONCHEOLYANG	ONOFFMIX
JUN YOUNG JUNG	N.CODE

SPAIN

ROGER FERNANDEZ GURI	ASSIST
NIR HINDI	THE ARTIAN

SWEDEN

DOUGLAS HEIDERGREN	CIRQS
ANDREW NEHAUL	DELUXE VACATIONS
DIDDE BROCKMAN	DREAMS
AXEL ERIKSSON	STAM.IO
HOUSIN AZIZ	VINTRO
JOHANNES SCHILDT	KRY
EUGENE SHELKAPLIASAU	BILANDIA.SE
HERALDAS	LOLITA STÄD CLEANING
JOAKIM JOHANSSON	STORY WARS
KRISTOFFER FÜRST	LIMINA FINANCIAL SYSTEMS
ARIAN BAHRAMI	KILIARO
ANDREAS AHRENS	DEVV
EMIL BERGDAHL	FILMYR
JOHAN MARKUS	POCKETBEAT
SEBASTIAN PLENGIER EHRNFELT	WDC MEDIA GROUP
ALBIN STÖÖP	ZALSTER
RICKARD EBERSJÖ	ADSSETS
MATTEO MONARI	MIND MUSIC LABS
RICH TELLA	BITJOIN
ADALSTEINN JOHANSSON	BERINGER FINANCE
DAVID KINNBERG	GETSPACE
PHILIP SKOGSBERG	CHALLENGER MODE
JACOB RUDBACK	YEPSTR
ALI AMIN	UBI GLOBAL
SEBASTIAN STIERNBORG	TOOLSPACE
MICAEL GUSTAFSSON	LEARNING TO SLEEP
HANNA LINDQUIST	TRINE
TOMMY PALM	RESOLUTION GAMES

DAN WILLSTRAND	STROSSLE
ANTON SKYBA	MOGGIE
ONDREJ PAPANEK	CLEBAG
EMELIE ZETTERBERG	HAPPYTAIL
CAROLINE FJELLNER	&FRANKLY
GUSTAV EK	MOANK
ERIK JOHANSSON	RAFT CALENDAR
ANDREAS NORDGREN	MODCAM
KRISTOFER COOK	CARBIOTIX
MICHAEL HOY	GLANCE
JOAKIM BOTHA	ELIQ
LUDVIG EMGARD	SPOTSCALE
DENNIS DEMIRTOK	IMPERIOO SPORTS
DANIEL GROSSFELD	KLOKIE
DANIEL ZAND	PHOODSTER
JOHAN NORDSTRÖM	MEETIO
MARTIN ZACHRISON	STRAWPAY
MARCUS ZETHRAEUS	CLOUDCOM
EMIL KARLSSON	TUVA
THOMAS BACKLUND	BLOCKIE
ASIAD MAJEED	YAMZU
OLOF SJÖSTEDT	PINS COLLECTIVE
DANIEL GROSSFELD	ODALISQUE MAGAZINE
VINAY NARAYAN	ANIMATED MATHEMATICS

SWITZERLAND

FLAVIO TROLESE	4QUANT
DAVID DELMI	HARDAH
ALEXANDRE POCCARD	BLURRED
CHRISTIAN KEHR	FLYNT
MARKUS KOCH	YAWAVE
THOMAS HARLANDER	DECOAGENTUR HARLANDER
RALPH SCHONENBACH	ENVOY WORLD
FABRIZIO BALLABENI	BRIAN FIOX COMMS. AGENCY
RAGHAV BELAVADI	ANDIAST TECH
ANDREAS BESTLER	POSHBERRY
PHILIPP RINGLI	PEAKHUNTER

THAILAND

ANTHONY CALABRESE — *IMAGINME*

TURKEY

CANER ULUER — *HAIRMOD*

UNITED KINGDOM

PAOLO BARTOLO — *ROOFORA*
JASON FUTERS — *HUUPE*
DR JOHN L COLLINS — *SYNBICITE*
JEROME RUSH — *PASSIVE EYE*
KARIN KALLMAN — *VILLOID*
LIZ RICE — *MICROSCALING SYSTEMS*
PAE NATWILAI — *GETTRIK*
RICHARD MASON — *WISODATA*
ERIC MUSHEL — *FEAST HAPPY*
JAMES PRINGLE — *SUGGESTV*
TINO MILLAR — *R&D SQUARE*
JEROME RIGAUD — *DESIGNMARKETO*
NIGEL WALLEY — *CHIMNI*
MAVIA SIDDIQUI — *GAMBAN*
JULIE ALLEN — *FINE ART CLUB*
ELEN STORM — *INQ.SOCIAL*
SEBASTIAN COCHINESCU — *LISTPLORER LTD*
IAN THOMPSON — *BEAVER BRAINS*
EYTAN LERBA — *WIZITAPP*

UNITED STATES

ELLIOT ROTH — *SPIRA INC*
MASOUD ALHELOU — *BAYT*
CONNOR GROOMS — *BASELANG*
MEERI KLAUSEN — *INZMO*
PETER HUNN — *CLAUSE*

JANAE BUSHMAN — *ALIIM SMARTPHONE SCHOOLS PROGRAM*
ANNE KAVANAGH — *HELLO ZERA*
MANUEL PINEYRO — *SQWAD SPORTS INC*
THOMAS WALLE — *UNACAST*
WALLY HARIZ — *HARITEL*
JACK LANGWORTHY — *NINAYO*
LUDOVIC HURAUX — *SHAPR*
RICARDO HERNANDEZ — *VIVARENA*
OSCAR ROJAS — *BROADWAND*
MICHAEL SHEA — *ECOTECH VISIONS INC.*

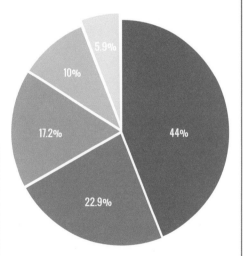

WHAT PERCENTAGE OF YOUR STARTUP IS FEMALE?

44% 0 TO 20 PERCENT
22.9% 20 TO 40 PERCENT
17.2% 40 TO 60 PERCENT
10% 60 TO 80 PERCENT
5.9% 80 TO 100 PERCENT

ALBERTO MAZATAN — *WINWINMS*
FABIO SEIXAS — *LEADGRID*
ALBIZU GARCIA — *GAIN*
ALEJANDRO SANCHEZ — *4GEEKS ACADEMY*
CARMINA SANTAMARIA — *KWEMA*
CHARLES WALTER — *HELLO FOROS*
MICAELA JOHNSTON — *GRATES*
JONATHAN RAMIREZ — *DWELL*
JOY SCOPA — *JOYSCOPA*
CANDY WASHINGTON — *THE BILLIONAIRE BLOGGER SOCIETY*

RAZ YALOV — *ZCAST*
KARIN KLOOSTERMAN — *FLUX IOT*
OMER KLEIN — *MEDFLYT*
LIN DAI — *HOOCH*
MAAYAN LEVY — *EVERTHERE*
TOMMY BARTH — *CYBEREASON*
MARK MONTGOMERY — *FLO CO*
MICHAEL BRILL — *CRUZU*
ANDREW BACKS — *PILOT44*
NIR PELEG — *REDUXIO*
DANIEL ART — *DIFRACTIVE TECHNOLOGIES, LLC*
PREET ANAND — *PATRONUS*
MIKE LIN — *T-SHIRTS MATTER*
ZACHARY WACH — *FARADY FINDER*
TATE H.C. COUSINS — *ASSEMBL XYZ*
R.J. ROMEO — *VIBE ROOM*
ALAIN EAV — *ROVITRACKER*
NELSON CHU — *TRITAN COLLECTIVE*
LUC BERLIN — *MIIGLE INC.*

ACKNOWLEDGEMENTS

This project happened because of so many people. First and foremost, I have to thank the 341 backers on Kickstarter who pledged their hard-earned money to support this book months before it would ever be in their hands. Their leap of faith in me and the concept of The Startup Mixtape gave me an unending reserve of motivation to make this book everything I envisioned it might be.

I also can't express enough gratitude to the founders and companies who were willing to be a part of the book. They donated precious time from their schedules to talk with me about the project and, more importantly, to share with me their candid experiences in building and launching startups—the good, the bad, and the ugly.

There are over 1,400 startups I owe thanks for taking the time to fill out the survey for the book. Every founder has many competing demands on their time. It's beyond gracious that they each took a moment to not just take the survey at the request of one of the interns who helped me out during the summer of 2016 but also to reply and engage with the intern team. This means more to them than you might realize.

So of course, I should thank the interns too. I had the great pleasure of working with my finest and most promising undergraduate students from Hult International Business School. I cannot offer enough thanks to Alex Nam, Hernan Lopez Montemayor, Monserrat Irazoqui, Leila Iranmanesh, Omar Shawky, Anderson Klein, Bernardo Calderon, or Naya Akel. Each of them has an extremely bright future, and I was lucky to have had their talent and ideas influence the book.

If I'm due any recognition for the idea of the book, I owe the praise for its final form to a group of extraordinarily talented individuals who truly worked tirelessly to produce the book you now hold in your hands.

With only a few rough ideas of how I thought the book's layout might support the content, Russ Atkinson came to the rescue and worked tirelessly to make it into the beautiful and cohesive volume you now hold in your hands. Thanks a million, Russ. The first ideas of what the book might look like were translated into its exceptional logo and graphic identity by Jude Goergen and Luiz Aro, respectively.

My words have any gravity or clarity because of a group of amazing editors. I owe a great debt to Meg Ward, Mathieu Roy, and Nathalie Arbel for guiding (and at times, wrestling) my puzzling paragraphs into cleaner, more crisp language. Hayley Cruz and Chloe Sklavounos were both invaluable with their well-trained and meticulous proofreading.

The execution of the Kickstarter campaign that supported this book was a Herculean task. It would not have taken flight without the amazing video editing work of Glenn Allyn (because "it takes some getting used to"), the pitch-perfect footage shot by Jude Goergen, the always dependable and industrious Sunil Sodegaonkar, and the steadfast glue of the campaign, wonder woman Amelia Shroyer.

Everyone I have mentioned above is someone I consider a friend. And there are, of course, many more friends whom I have endless gratitude and thanks for, as you supported me through this journey that felt Sisyphean at times. Thanks for reminding me that I just needed to trudge on. I'm also lucky to have had the communities of Outsite (globally) and Doorhaus (in San Francisco) around me to inspire me and motivate me with all the amazing work you're doing.

This book would not have been possible without the support of my parents, Ken and Lindy, and my sister, Elizabeth.

If you've read this far, I hope that you have found this book to be useful or intriguing, or at least it made you think. It's more than axiomatic to say that we're in times of change unlike any before. That goes for business, technology, and the way in which we communicate with one another. I wish the best of luck to anyone, no matter your field or circle of influence, working to enrich the world and counteract the forces that would seek to do anything less than support equality and freedom. ●

Elliott Adams has worked in tech, government, and academia. He was the CTO of CD Baby leading up to its acquisition for $22m in 2008 and then served in the State of Louisiana's Department of Economic Development after Hurricane Katrina, where he focused on legislative and outreach efforts to strengthen the state's tech and startup ecosystem. Formerly an Assistant Professor of Entrepreneurship at Loyola University New Orleans, Adams is now a faculty member at Hult International Business School's San Francisco campus. He is a proud member of the South by Southwest Interactive advisory board and is currently an author-in-residence at the Nasdaq Entrepreneurial Center in San Francisco, as well as an entrepreneur-in-residence at Techstars.

Russ Atkinson is a freelance graphic designer based in Jersey, Channel Islands, with a fixation for almost anything with wheels. After graduating from the Arts Institute at Bournemouth in 2007 he returned to his island home and spent a few years working as an airport fire-fighter before returning to the creative industry full time. When he isn't staying up late designing books and magazines or creating corporate identities you'll probably find him in the garage late into the night wielding a set of spanners, restoring and modifying classic cars and motorbikes.